Contents at a Glance

Introduction

Table of Contents

About the Author

Clayton Walnum started programming computers in 1982, when he traded in an IBM Selectric typewriter to buy an Atari 400 computer (16K of RAM!). Bit hard by the programming bug, he mastered Atari BASIC in a few months before moving on to assembly language. Clay soon learned to combine his interest in writing with his newly acquired programming skills, and started selling programs and articles to computer magazines. In 1985, *ANALOG Computing*, a nationally distributed computer magazine, hired him as a technical Dedicationeditor and, before leaving the magazine business in 1989 to become a freelance writer, Clay had worked his way up to Executive Editor. Clay has since acquired a degree in Computer Science, as well as written over 30 books (translated into many languages) covering everything from computer gaming to 3D graphics programming. He's also written hundreds of magazine articles and software reviews, as well as countless programs. His books include Que's *Special Edition Using MFC and ATL*, *Java By Example*, and the award-winning *Building Windows 95 Applications with Visual Basic*. Clay's biggest disappointment in life is that he wasn't one of the Beatles. To compensate, he writes and records rock music in his home studio. You can reach Clay at his home page, which is located at `http://www.connix.com/~cwalnum`.

Dedication

To Lynn.

Acknowledgments

I would like to thank the following people for their contribution to this book: Sharon Cox for her patience and encouragement, Chris Denny for combing a few snarls out of the manuscript, and Jesse Reisman for making sure the facts were correct. As always, a special thank you goes out to my family, who puts up with Dad's weird working hours.

Tell Us What You Think!

As the reader of this book, you are our most important critic and commentator. We value your opinion and want to know what we're doing right, what we could do better, what areas you'd like to see us publish in, and any other words of wisdom you're willing to pass our way.

We welcome your comments. You can email or write me directly to let me know what you did or didn't like about this book—as well as what we can do to make our books stronger.

Please note that I cannot help you with technical problems related to the topic of this book, and that due to the high volume of mail I receive, I might not be able to reply to every message.

When you write, please be sure to include this book's title and author as well as your name and phone or fax number. I will carefully review your comments and share them with the author and editors who worked on the book.

Email: cigfeedback@pearsoned.com

Mail: Alpha Books
            201 West 103rd Street
            Indianapolis, IN 46290 USA

Introduction

Have you ever wondered what goes on inside a computer program? Did you ever want to sit down at your keyboard and conjure digital magic on your computer's screen? If so, there might be a computer programmer somewhere inside you, clawing to get out.

Unfortunately, you might have found computer programming not only intimidating but downright scary. Heck, you get new gray hairs every time you try to write a simple batch file, right? If you feel this way, *The Complete Idiot's Guide to Microsoft Visual Basic 6* is here to prove that programming your computer is rewarding, fun, and, most important, easy.

Who This Book Is For

This book is for anyone who wants to learn to program his or her computer with Visual Basic. More importantly, this book is for anyone who's flipped through other programming texts only to be discouraged by obtuse language, jargon-ridden prose, and stuffed-shirt attitudes. *The Complete Idiot's Guide to Microsoft Visual Basic 6*'s conversational style incorporates plain-English explanations along with short programming examples to lead the novice programmer by the hand through the techno jungle of computer programming.

Because it focuses on beginning programmers, *The Complete Idiot's Guide to Microsoft Visual Basic 6* is not a full Visual Basic reference, nor is it a comprehensive tutorial in the techniques of professional programming. It is meant to give you a quick taste of Visual Basic programming so you can decide whether programming is as interesting as you thought it would be. By the end of the book, you will know all you need to know to write many useful and rewarding programs.

Software and Hardware Requirements

In order to run Visual Basic and create the programs in this book, your system and software must meet a set of minimum requirements. Those minimum requirements are listed below:

- ➤ Visual Basic 6
- ➤ IBM-compatible with a 66 MHz 486DX processor (Pentium processor recommended)
- ➤ 16MB RAM (24MB recommended)
- ➤ Microsoft Windows 95 or later
- ➤ Hard disk
- ➤ CD-ROM drive

➤ VGA or better graphics (Super VGA recommended)

➤ Mouse

Visual Basic for Free!

This book comes with a CD-ROM that contains the Visual Basic Working Model, a free version of Visual Basic (courtesy of Microsoft) that'll do everything you need to do to complete the lessons in this book. How can you beat that?

However, programs written with the Visual Basic Working Model cannot run as stand-alone programs. If you don't understand what that means, just know that the Working Model gives you a chance—without spending any extra cash—to decide whether you want to continue with Visual Basic after completing this book. However, if you decide to continue with Visual Basic, you'll almost certainly want to upgrade to at least the Visual Basic Learning Edition.

An Overview of the Book

The Complete Idiot's Guide to Microsoft Visual Basic 6 comprises 26 short chapters, each of which concentrates on specific topics of importance to novice programmers. The chapters are organized into four general parts, as follows:

➤ Part I, "First Steps," is a brief introduction to the art of programming and is your first chance to start using the Visual Basic programming environment.

➤ Part II, "Writing Basic Program Code," teaches you the Visual Basic programming language, as well as introduces you to many programming concepts such as input/output, looping, computer decision-making, file handling, and more.

➤ Part III, "The Elements of Visual Basic Windows Programs," introduces you to the general controls and objects you need to create a user interface for your programs. Here, you're also introduced to the important topics of properties, methods, and events.

➤ Part IV, "Writing Windows Applications," gets into the nitty-gritty details of using Visual Basic's objects and controls to create Windows applications with professional user interfaces.

How We Do Things in This Part of the Country

To get the most out of this book, you should know how it is designed. We've tried to put things together in such a way as to make reading the book both rewarding and fun. The following list gives you the lowdown of the book elements you'll run across:

➤ New terms are presented in *italicized text*; pay close attention to these terms.

➤ Visual keywords, commands, variable names, and the like are set in monospace type; for example, `Form1.Print "Hello!"`.

➤ Text you need to type appears in **bold**.

➤ Multiple-key keystrokes are indicated using a plus sign between the keys to press. For example, Ctrl+T means to press the Ctrl and T keys simultaneously.

Other visual pointers found in this book include:

Step into the Strange and Wonderful World of Visual Basic

Still with us? Just around the corner is your first Visual Basic programming lesson. We could stay here and chat all day, or you could turn the page and start your fun-filled vacation in VisualBasicLand. See you there.

Check This Out

These boxes contain warnings, notes, and other information about Microsoft Visual Basic 6. Be sure to read each of these boxes. Failure to do so might result in missing out on some important points.

Techno Talk

These boxes contain high-tech info that provides more in-depth information about a topic related to the chapter. If you don't want to dig deeper into Visual Basic, you can skip over these boxes. If you want to impress your friends and loved ones with your technical knowledge, though, this is the place to look.

3

Part 1
First Steps

Before you can start learning Visual Basic programming, you have to know what programming is. Moreover, you must know how to use Visual Basic's programming environment, including the menu bar, the toolbar, the toolbox, and the various Visual Basic windows. In this part of the book, you'll not only get an introduction to programming in general, you'll also discover how to use Visual Basic's tools to create simple programs.

Chapter 1

An Introduction to Programming: A Walk on the Wild Side

In This Chapter

➤ Discover reasons to program

➤ Find out what a program is

➤ Learn about different computer languages

➤ Explore how to write a computer program

Before you get started with computer programming, it might help to have a basic understanding of what it's all about. You undoubtedly have some ideas about what a program is and how it works, or you wouldn't have bought this book to begin with. Some of these ideas might be right on the money; others might be as crazy as a whale in a tutu.

Whatever your ideas about programming, this chapter gives you the skinny. After reading this chapter, you may find that your perceptions about programming are pretty solid; or you might find that you know as much about programming a computer as you do about building a submarine. In either case, you'll be a better person for having spent time here.

The Surprising Secret

The computer-programming world has a well-kept secret. You won't hear programmers talking about it (which is, of course, why it's a secret). If you've been using a computer for any time at all, you'll probably find this secret hard to believe. Nevertheless, it's as true as the sky is blue. So brace yourself. You're about to learn a shocking fact.

Computers are stupid.

Fact is, a computer can do absolutely nothing on its own. Without programmers, computers are as useless as rubber razors. Computers can do only what they're told to do. If you think for a minute, you'll realize this means computers can only perform tasks that humans already know how to do. So why do we bother with computers? The great thing about computers is not that they're smart, but that they can perform endless calculations in the blink of an eye.

Programmers, of course, are the people who tell computers what to do. That's not to say when you use your computer you're programming it. For example, when you plop yourself down in front of a word processor and hack out a letter to your congressperson, you're not giving commands to the computer. You're only using the commands contained in the program. It's the computer program—which was written by a programmer—that actually tells the computer what to do.

The following figure shows the relationship between a computer user, a program, and a computer. That's you, the computer user, way up at the top of the hierarchy. You probably use your computer for many activities besides word processing, such as organizing data in a spreadsheet, keeping track of information in a database, and maybe even for playing games. In all those cases, you run a program, which in turn provides instructions to the computer.

As a computer user, you're at the top of the heap.

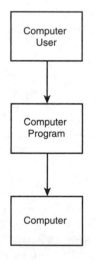

The bottom line is that if you want to give commands directly to your computer, you must learn to write programs.

Why Learn to Program?

There are as many reasons for learning to program as there are raisins in California. Only you know what it is about computer programming that makes you want to learn it. But some common reasons are

➤ You're looking for a fun and rewarding hobby.

➤ You want to be able to write the programs you really need—the ones you can't always find at the software store.

➤ You want to learn more about how computers work.

➤ You have to learn programming for school or work.

➤ You want to impress your friends.

➤ Some misguided person gave you this book as a gift, and you don't want to hurt his or her feelings.

These all are legitimate reasons. You might have a better one, but whatever your reason, after you get started with programming, you'll find it can be both fascinating and addictive. Your significant other, however, might ban computers from your home and burn this book after he or she realizes just how addictive computer programming can be. Consider yourself warned.

What's a Computer Program?

A computer program is nothing more than a list of instructions that tells a computer what to do. The computer follows these instructions, one by one, until it reaches the end of the program.

Each line in a computer program is usually a single command that the computer must obey. Each command does only a very small task, such as printing a name on the screen or adding two numbers. When you put hundreds, thousands, or even hundreds of thousands of these commands together, your computer can do wonderful things: balance a checkbook, print a document, draw pictures, or blast invading aliens from the skies.

As you see in the next section, computer programs can be written in one of many different languages.

Programming Languages

Computers don't understand English. They can't even understand BASIC, the computer language upon which Visual Basic is based. Computers understand only one thing, machine language, which is entirely composed of numbers. Programming languages like BASIC allow people to write programs in an English-like language, which a BASIC interpreter then changes into machine language so the computer can understand it.

Visual Basic programs are a dialect of the BASIC computer language, which was developed not to help computers, but to help people make sense out of the numerical nonsense machines delight in. Visual Basic replaces many of the numbers used by machine language with words and symbols we lowly humans can more easily understand and remember. Moreover, Visual Basic enables a programmer to visually assemble a program's window from parts in a toolbox.

Lowercase or Uppercase?

Often, you see the name of the BASIC language spelled with lowercase letters like this: Basic. Even Visual Basic uses this spelling. However, BASIC actually started out as an acronym, which is why you also see the name spelled in all capital letters. The BASIC acronym stands for Beginner's All-purpose Symbolic Instruction Code.

A BASIC program uses words and symbols (and a few numbers) that people can understand. How, then, can the computer understand and run BASIC? The truth is, when you load Visual Basic, you are also loading a compiler, which is a special program that takes the words and symbols from a Visual Basic program and converts them into machine language the computer can understand. Without the compiler's interpretation of your programs, your computer wouldn't have the slightest idea what to do with the program.

By the way, there are all kinds of computer languages, including Pascal, C++, FORTRAN, COBOL, Modula-2, and BASIC. All computer languages have one thing in common: They can be read by humans and, therefore, must be converted to machine language before the computer can understand them.

All Kinds of BASIC

There are many versions of the BASIC language, of which Visual Basic is only one. Older versions of DOS (pre-5.0) came with a version of BASIC called GW-BASIC. Newer versions of DOS come with QBasic. You can also go down to your local software store and buy QuickBASIC. All these software packages allow you to create computer programs with BASIC, but they all implement the BASIC language slightly differently. However, of the versions of BASIC mentioned here, only Visual Basic enables you to write Windows applications.

Compilers and Interpreters

Some computer languages, such as some types of BASIC, convert a program to machine language one line at a time as the program runs. Other languages, such as Pascal and Visual Basic, use a compiler to convert the entire program all at once before any of the program runs. In any case, all programming languages must be converted to machine language in order for the computer to understand the program.

A compiler changes your program into an executable file (for example, WORD.EXE or SIMCITY.EXE) that can be run directly, without a compiler or interpreter. An executable program is actually a machine language program that's ready for your computer to read and understand. With few exceptions, most computer programming languages come with a compiler.

The Programming Process

Now that you know something about computer programs, how do you go about creating one? Writing a computer program, though not particularly difficult, can be a long and tedious process. It's much like writing a term paper for school or a financial report for your boss. You start out with a basic idea of what you want to do and write a first draft. After reading over the draft and resisting the urge to throw the pages into the fireplace, you go back to writing—polishing your prose until it glows like a gem in the sun. Over the course of the writing process, you might write many drafts before you're satisfied with the document you've produced.

Writing a Visual Basic program requires development steps similar to those you use when writing a paper or report. The following list outlines these steps:

1. Come up with a program concept and sketch out on paper how it might look on the screen.
2. Create the program using Visual Basic's toolbox and editor.
3. Save the program to disk.
4. Run the program and see how it works.
5. Fix programming errors.
6. Go back to step 2.

As you can see, most of the steps in the programming process are repeated over and over again as errors are discovered and corrected. Even experienced programmers can't write error-free programs (unless the program is extremely short). Programmers spend more time fine-tuning their programs than they do writing them initially.

This fine-tuning is important because we humans are not as logical as we like to think. Moreover, our minds are incapable of remembering every detail required to make a program run perfectly. Most of us are lucky if we can remember our telephone numbers. Only when a program crashes or does something else unexpected can we hope to find those sneaky errors that hide in programs. Computer experts say there's no such thing as a bug-free program. After you start writing full-length programs, you'll see how truethis statement is.

Invasion of the Digital Insects

Bugs are programming errors that stop your program from running correctly. (Bugs are also nasty creatures with spindly legs and crunchy shells that make you scream when they leap out of shadows. But this book doesn't deal with that type of bug.) Before a programmer can release her program to the unwary public, she must be certain she has squashed as many bugs as possible.

Is Programming Easy?

After reading all that's involved in writing and running a computer program, you might be a little nervous. After all, you bought this book because it promised to teach you computer programming. No one warned you about such mysterious topics as machine language, interpreters, compilers, and program bugs. So, is programming easy or not?

Yes and no.

It's easy to learn to write simple programs with Visual Basic. The Visual Basic language is logical, English-like, and easy to understand. With only minimal practice, you can write many useful and fun programs. All you need is the time to read this book and the ambition to write a few programs of your own. In fact, what you'll learn in this book is enough programming for just about anyone who's not planning to be a professional programmer.

However, if you want to make programming a career, you have much to learn that's not covered in this introductory book. For example, consider a word-processing program such as Microsoft Word, which took dozens of programmers many years to write. To write such complex software, you must have intimate knowledge of how your computer works. Additionally, you must have spent many years learning the intricacies of professional computer programming.

Still, there's a lot you can do with Visual Basic, whether you're interested in writing utilities, simple applications, or even games. And, after you get the hang of it, you'll discover programming in Visual Basic is not as difficult as you might have thought.

The Least You Need to Know

Before you dig into writing your own programs with Visual Basic, it's important to know what computer programs are and how they work. Such background knowledge will help you to understand why Visual Basic does some of the things it does, as well as make it easier to locate errors in your programs. From this chapter, you should remember the following points:

➤ A computer can do only what a human instructs it to do.

➤ A computer program is a list of commands that the computer follows from beginning to end.

➤ There are many computer languages. The language you learn in this book is a form of BASIC.

➤ A BASIC program must be converted to machine language before the computer can understand it. Visual Basic's compiler does this conversion.

➤ Writing a program is a lot like writing a text document. You must write several drafts before the program is complete.

➤ Programming with Visual Basic is as easy or as difficult as you want it to be.

Chapter 2

Cranking Up Visual Basic: What Does This Thing Do?

In This Chapter

➤ Get Visual Basic up and running

➤ Tour Visual Basic's main window

➤ Find the commands that control Visual Basic

So, here you are. You're all excited and ready to get to work. Your brand-new copy of Visual Basic is installed on your computer, and you swear you can actually hear it begging you to write a program. (Or is that your spouse nagging you to take out the trash?) There's only one problem. Not only do you not how to write a program, you don't even know how to get Visual Basic started or what to do with it when you do. Look at it this way: You've got a great excuse for not taking out the trash; you've got Visual Basic work to do!

Starting Visual Basic

When you installed Visual Basic (see Appendix A, "Installing Visual Basic," if you haven't), the Visual Basic installer not only copied a heap of files to your hard disk, but it also added Visual Basic to your Start menu. Starting Visual Basic is as easy as opening your Start menu, finding the Microsoft Visual Basic 6.0 folder, and then clicking on the Microsoft Visual Basic 6.0 entry in that folder, as shown here:

You can run Visual Basic from your Start menu.

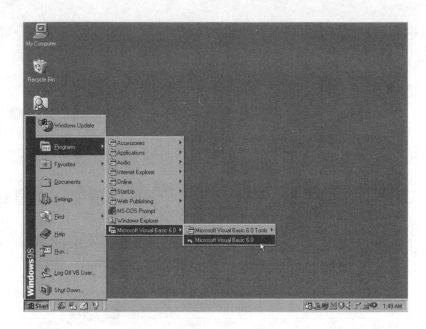

When you run Visual Basic, after a short wait, its main window pops up on your screen. That screen should look something like this:

Visual Basic's main window looks something like this.

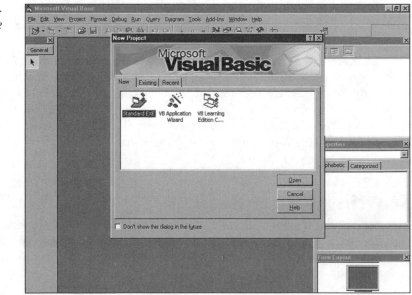

Starting and Loading Projects

That little window in the middle of the main screen is the New Project dialog box, which is politely waiting for you to decide exactly what kind of Visual Basic project

16

you want to start. As you can see, the dialog box displays (and proudly, I might add) three tabs that enable you to access projects in different ways. The New tab enables you to start a brand-new project. The Existing tab enables you to choose any Visual Basic project already on your disk. The following figure shows the Existing page:

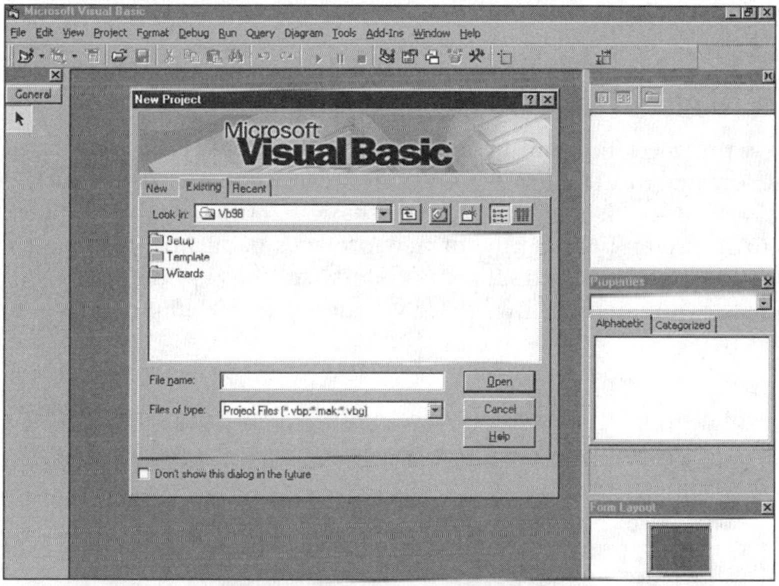

Use the Existing page's controls to locate a Visual Basic project on your disk drive.

The last tab, Recent, gives you quick access to any projects you may have worked on recently. That page looks like this:

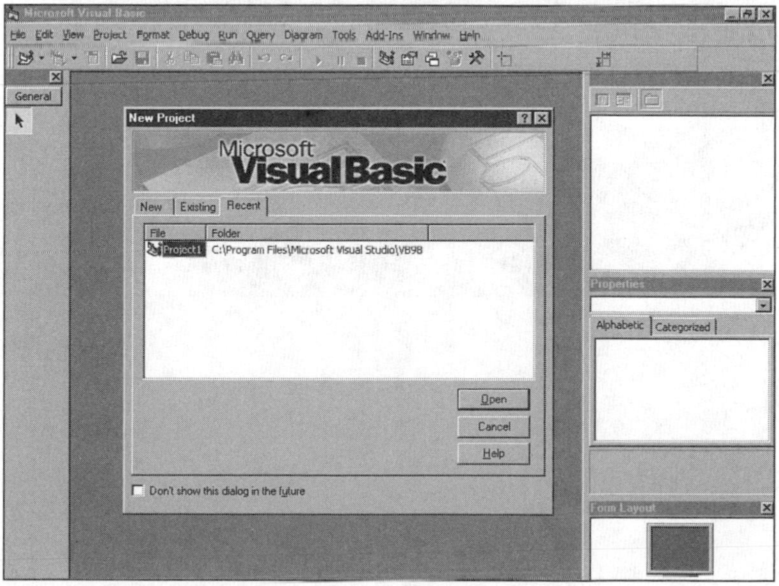

If you want to restart a project you worked on recently, go to the Recent page of the New Project dialog box.

The New Project dialog box is extremely patient, so there's no point in sitting there and gazing at it any longer. I assure you, it will win any staring contest. So, to get things started, double-click the Standard EXE icon on the New page of the New Project dialog box. This action informs Visual Basic that you want to create a brand-new program. Don't worry; Visual Basic doesn't know that you haven't learned to program yet, so it won't snicker at you.

The Parts of the Visual Basic Window

When you start that new project, a lot of other exciting stuff happens. First, a set of controls appears on the left side of the window in Visual Basic's toolbox. Also, your new program's starting window—called a *form* in Visual Basic—appears in the middle of the screen. And, as if that weren't enough, your new project's name and components appear in the Project window, and the form's property settings appear in the Properties window. The following figure shows these wonderful new elements of Visual Basic's main window:

Visual Basic's main window displays several different areas.

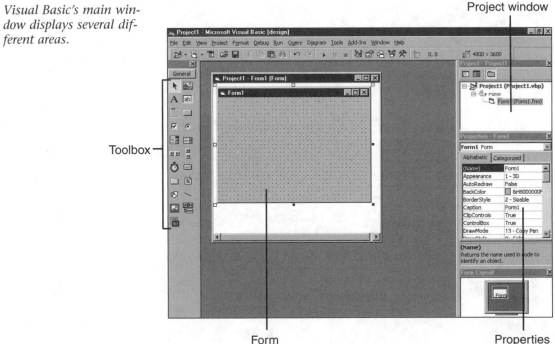

Project window

Toolbox

Form

Properties window

Now that you can see these marvelous wonders on the screen, you probably want to know what they are. If you don't, you're probably reading the wrong book. Everyone who thinks he's reading *Misbehaving Misses from Missouri* should now quietly exit the room; you're in the wrong class. The rest of you take a look at Visual Basic's toolbox.

See all those little icons? They represent controls that you can use with your program. Controls are objects like buttons, text boxes, labels, images, and shapes that you can position on your form in order to build your program's user interface. If all this sounds strange, don't worry about it. You'll learn how to build a program in the next chapter, "Creating Projects: This Stuff Really Works!"

The form part of Visual Basic's main display looks like a window inside a window. The window with "Project1" in its title bar is one of Visual Basic's own windows, but the window

What's a User Interface?

Almost all programs have a user interface, which is the part of the application that enables the user to interact with the program. A user interface usually includes various types of buttons, menus, dialog boxes, and other kinds of objects. By using the objects that make up the user interface, the user supplies commands and information to the program. Similarly, the program accesses the user interface in order to display information to the user.

inside the Project1 window—the one with "Form1" in its title bar—is your project's window. That is, when you run your program, this is the window that appears on the screen. Logically, then, this is also the window where you place the controls that make up your program's user interface.

The Project window gives you an overview of the objects in the currently loaded project. Usually, a form is one of these objects. You might, in fact, have more than one form in some projects. By clicking the plus and minus signs next to folders in the Project window, you can display more details about the project.

Finally, the Properties window displays the *properties* of the object that's currently selected in the form. Currently, the form itself is selected, so its properties appear in the Properties window. What are properties? You can think of properties as the attributes of an object. For example, your project's form has a property called Caption, which is the text that appears in the form's title bar. If you change the text for the Caption property, the text in the form's title bar changes too, as shown here:

A form's title bar holds the text from the Caption *property.*

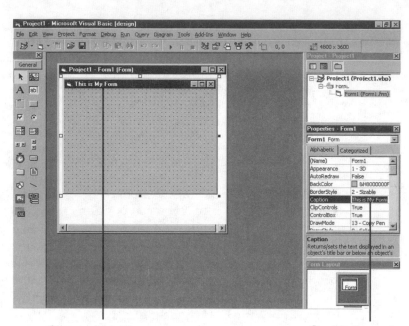

Changed caption   Caption property

The Code Window

Although Visual Basic enables you to build much of your project by placing controls from the toolbox onto the form, sooner or later, you have to settle down to writing some program source code. As you learned in Chapter 1, "An Introduction to Programming: A Walk on the Wild Side," programs comprise many lines of commands that tell the program what to do. In Visual Basic, you type these commands into the code window.

When you first start a new project, Visual Basic doesn't display the code window. To bring up the code window, just double-click the form. When you do, your Visual Basic window will look something like this:

Properties

Most controls and other Visual Basic objects have properties that determine how the object looks and acts. Many of Visual Basic's objects, in fact, share similar properties. For example, all objects have a Name property, which enables a program to refer to that object. Most objects also have properties that determine the object's size, position, text, colors, borders, and much more. You'll learn more about properties as you work with Visual Basic. You'll learn a lot about properties in Chapter 17, "Methods, Properties, and Events: An Object's Inner Workings."

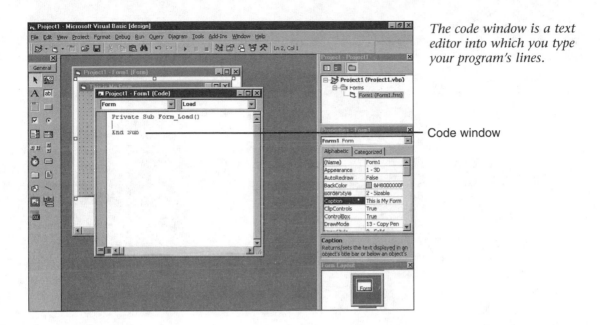

The code window is a text editor into which you type your program's lines.

Code window

The new window that appears is the code window. As you can see, Visual Basic is pretty smart and often tries to guess what you want to do. In this case, Visual Basic has started something called a procedure—a procedure named Form_Load. If you were actually writing a program, you would probably finish the Form_Load procedure by typing Visual Basic commands between the two lines that Visual Basic already provided for you. In fact, you'll see how to do this in the next chapter.

Menus and the Toolbar

Two important parts of the Visual Basic main window are the menu bar and the toolbar. The menu bar holds a series of menus, each of which contains commands you need to make Visual Basic do what you want. (To get Visual Basic to listen to you, you could try glaring threateningly at the screen, but the menus tend to work so much better.) For example, if you want to add a new form to your project, you could select the Project menu's Add Form command, as shown here:

The menu bar provides a home for Visual Basic's many commands.

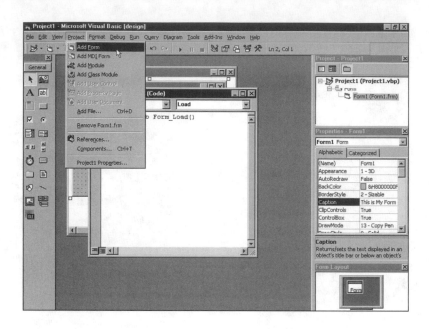

Many of the menu commands have *hotkeys* that you can use to select the command directly from the keyboard. For example, in the previous figure, you can see the keystroke Ctrl+D listed after the Add File command. This means that you can send Visual Basic the Add File command just by holding down your keyboard's Ctrl key and pressing D. You don't need to open the menu at all.

The toolbar provides access to many of Visual Basic's most commonly needed commands. Most of the buttons on the toolbar are just quick ways to select a command from the menus. For example, see the button on the toolbar that looks like a floppy disk? If you click this button, Visual Basic saves the currently open project. Clicking this button is the same as selecting the File menu's Save Project command, as shown here:

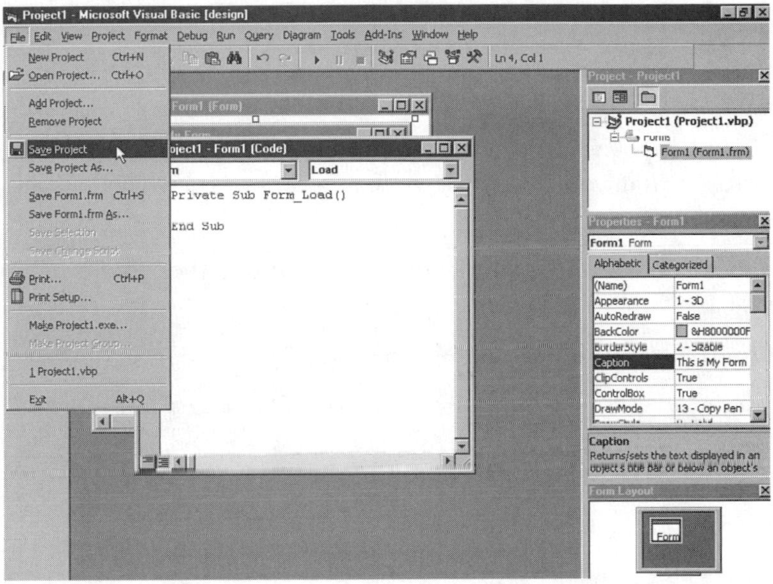

Some menu commands, such as Save Project, are represented as buttons on the toolbar.

If you're still paying attention, you might have noticed that the File menu's Save Project command has the same icon next to it as the icon used on the toolbar button. When you see an icon like this next to a command, you know that the command is also available in a toolbar—if you happen to have that particular toolbar turned on. (Visual Basic lets you turn different toolbars on and off.)

Now, wasn't that fun? Aren't you already starting to feel empowered? You should, because you've taken your first steps towards becoming a Visual Basic programmer.

The Least You Need to Know

➤ You can start Visual Basic from your Windows Start menu.

➤ When Visual Basic first appears, you can choose to start a new project, load any Visual Basic project from your disk drive, or load a project on which you've recently worked.

➤ Visual Basic's toolbox contains the controls you use to put together your program's user interface.

➤ A Visual Basic form represents your program's window.

➤ The Properties window displays the attributes of an object selected in the form.

➤ The Project window shows the main objects in your project. Usually, a project has at least one form.

➤ You type your program's commands into Visual Basic's code window.

➤ You can access many of Visual Basic's commands from the menu bar and the toolbar. Some commands even have hotkeys that enable you to select a command directly from your keyboard.

Chapter 3

Creating Projects: This Stuff Really Works!

In This Chapter

➤ Start a new Visual Basic programming project

➤ Use controls to build a user interface

➤ Write program source code

➤ Convert a program into an executable Windows application

Finally, it's time to actually do something with Visual Basic. In this chapter you'll learn the basic skills you need to create a simple program. This knowledge will be important to you as you explore the language itself in the next part of the book. This knowledge will also be important to you when you brag to your friends about your programming prowess.

Three Programming Steps

Creating a simple Visual Basic program is easier than goosing a sleeping cat. You need only complete three steps, after which you'll have a program that can be run outside of Visual Basic's programming environment, just like any other application you may have installed on your computer. The three steps are as follows:

1. Create the program's user interface
2. Write the program source code, which makes the program do what it's supposed to do
3. Compile the program into an executable file that can be run as a standalone application (able to run without being loaded into Visual Basic)

Of course, there are many details involved in each of these three steps, especially if you're writing a lengthy program. As you work, you'll complete these steps in the order in which they're listed above. However, you'll also frequently go back from step 2 to step 1 to fine-tune your user interface. You might even go back to step 2 from step 3 if you discover problems after compiling your program. Such is the nature of the programming beast.

In the rest of this chapter, you'll take a close look at each of the three Visual Basic program-development steps. When you complete these lessons, you'll either be totally fed up with Visual Basic or you'll be ready to move on to the next part of the book. I'm betting on the latter.

Step 1: Creating the User Interface

As you learned in the previous chapter, a program's user interface enables the user to interact with the program. The user interface comprises any objects that the user manipulates in order to give commands or information to the program. Such objects include buttons, menus, and text boxes, to name just a few.

Visual Basic makes it easy to create a user interface by providing a set of ready-to-go controls in a toolbox. All you have to do to create your user interface is start a new project and position the controls on the form, which is the object that represents the program's main window.

In this chapter, you'll create only a very simple user interface, learning just enough so you can understand the sample programs in the next section of the book. You won't get into more sophisticated programs until after you learn about the Visual Basic language itself. If you want to speed up this process, you could try using this book as a pillow and hope the information soaks in while you sleep. Probably, though, you'll just have to keep reading.

Go ahead and start Visual Basic. When you do, you see a screen that looks a lot like this:

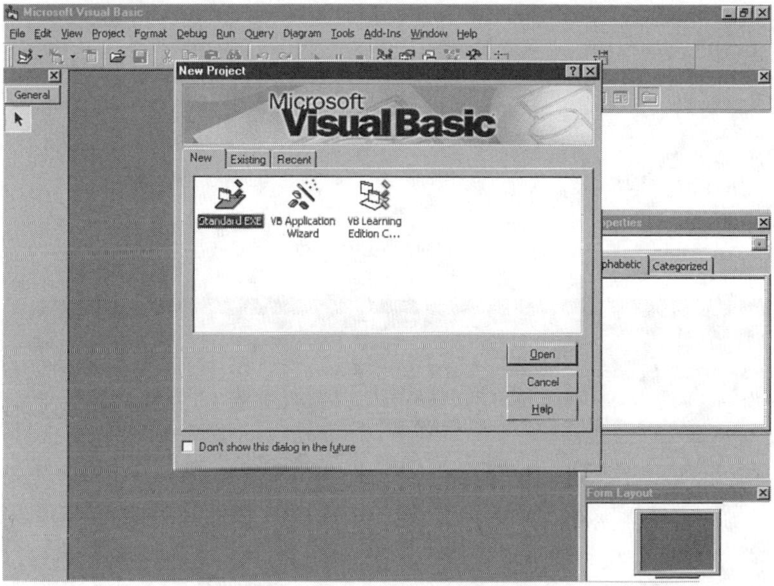

Visual Basic when it first appears.

Double-click the Standard EXE icon to start a new project. Visual Basic then creates a Form object for your program's window, as well as displays a bunch of goodies in the toolbox, Project window, and Properties window. The following figure shows how Visual Basic should look at this point:

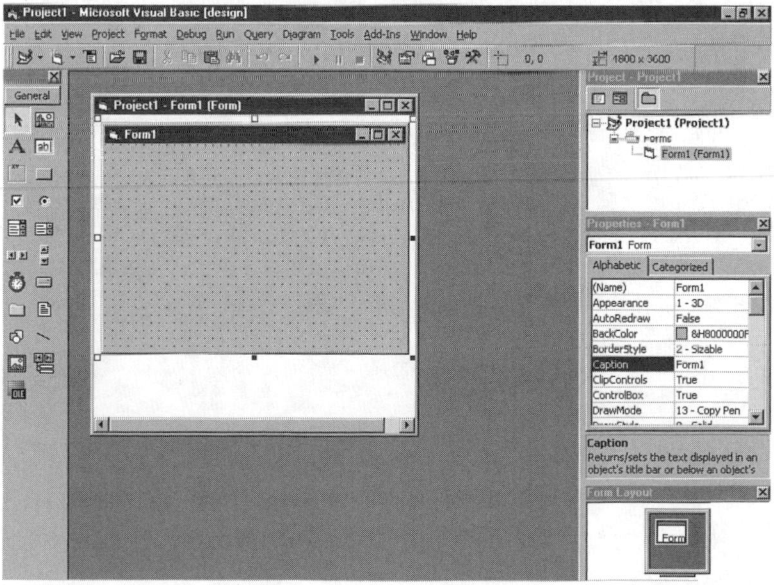

Visual Basic with a new project ready to go.

27

Do you see all those icons in Visual Basic's toolbox? Each icon represents one of the controls you can use to build your program's user interface. For your reference and profound pleasure, here's Visual Basic's toolbox with all its controls labeled:

Visual Basic's toolbox contains the controls you need to build your program.

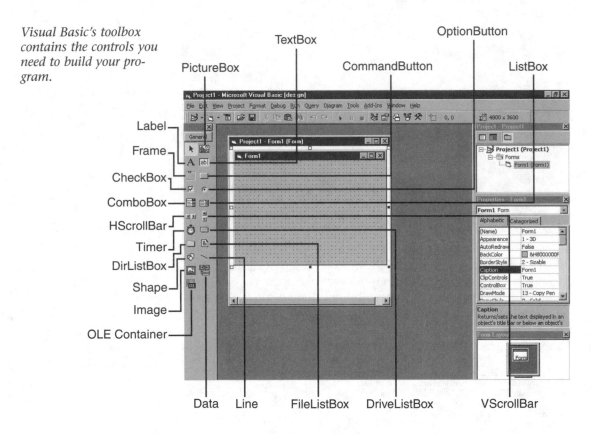

This chapter won't go into a lot of detail about each of the controls; you'll learn most of the details in Part IV, "Writing Windows Applications." Your goal right now is to get a general idea of how to create a Visual Basic program. (Or maybe you grabbed this book only because your boss just walked in. In that case, you have an entirely different goal.)

How about putting a button on your new form? You're not going to believe how easy this is. Just double-click the CommandButton control in Visual Basic's toolbox. When you do, a button magically appears on the form, as shown here:

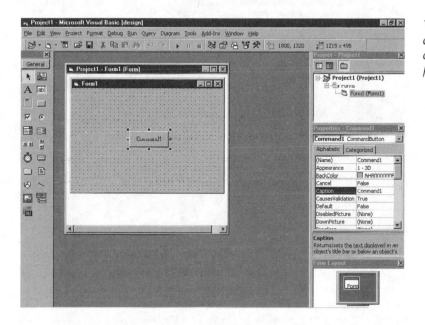

When you double-click a control in the toolbox, the control appears on the form.

The only way adding a button could be easier is by making Visual Basic telepathic!

See the eight small squares that border the button object? Those are the button's sizing handles. You can change the size of the button by placing your mouse pointer over one of the sizing handles, holding down the left mouse button, and dragging the handle. When you place your mouse pointer over a sizing handle, the mouse pointer changes to a new image that indicates the direction you can drag the handle.

For example, place your mouse pointer over the sizing handle in the center of the button's bottom edge. The mouse pointer changes into a double-headed arrow that points up and down. This arrow means that you can drag the button's bottom edge either up or down. Go ahead and drag the edge down, as shown here:

You can resize most controls by dragging their sizing handles.

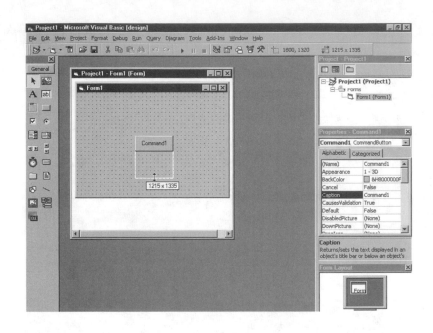

You should notice three things as you drag the button's edge. First, an outline follows the mouse pointer wherever you drag it. Second, the button's new size appears in a small box as you resize the button. Third, you're filled with a nice, tingly feeling as you realize that you just got one step closer to conquering Visual Basic.

When the button outline is the size you want the button to be, just release your mouse button. The button then redraws itself to the new size, as shown here:

Here's the button after it has been resized.

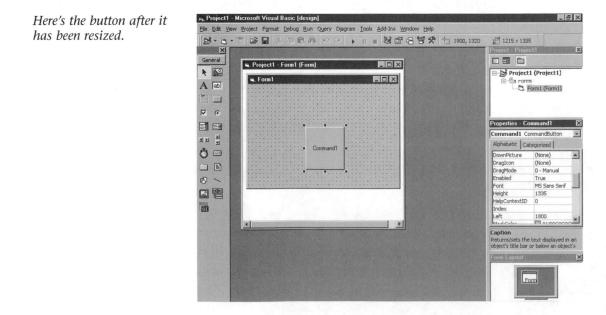

Adding the Program Source Code

You now have a button in a form, which is all fine and good except for the fact that the button does nothing. Don't believe it? Click the Start button (the button that looks like a small, blue triangle) on Visual Basic's toolbar (not the toolbox). (When your mouse pointer is over the correct button, a little box appears containing the word "Start.") When you click the Start button, Visual Basic runs your modest little program. You'll see a small window that looks like this:

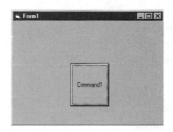

Your first Visual Basic program.

Go ahead and click your program's Command1 button. Nothing happens, right? OK, so the button looks like it pops in and out. All buttons do that. What's important to notice is that clicking the button doesn't make the program do anything useful. Of course, you're about to fix that little problem.

Click the End button (the one that looks like a small, blue square) in Visual Basic's toolbar to stop your program and get back to Visual Basic's main window. Now, double-click your form's Command1 button. Presto! Your project's code window pops up, as shown in the following figure:

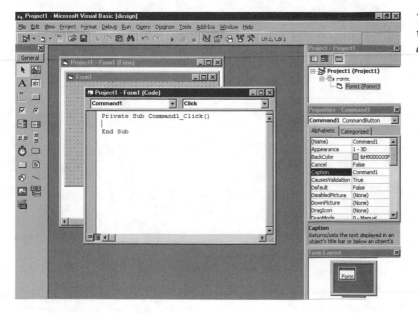

The code window appears whenever you double-click an object.

Current Events

Many of the things that happen in a Visual Basic program happen in response to events. An *event* is nothing more than something the user or the computer does to interact with your program. For example, when you clicked your program's Command1 button, you caused a Click event. To tell Visual Basic what to do with this event, you must complete the Command1_Click event procedure. You'll learn plenty of other events by the time you get to the end of this book.

When you double-clicked the CommandButton object, Visual Basic not only displayed the code window, but also started some program source code for you. This piece of source code is called a procedure. To put it simply, whenever a user clicks the Command1 button, Visual Basic goes to the Command1_Click procedure and performs all the commands the procedure contains. When you ran the program previously and clicked the button, Visual Basic did exactly what it was supposed to do and went to the Command1_Click procedure. Unfortunately, you hadn't yet placed commands in the procedure, so nothing happened.

You can change that easily, by adding the source code line

```
MsgBox "Visual Basic rocks!"
```

to the Command1_Click procedure, as shown here:

You type your own program code between the start and end of a procedure.

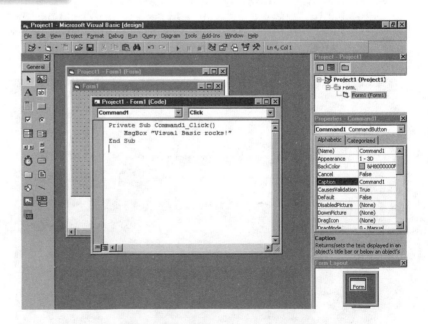

Now, run the program again (by clicking the Start button). When you click the Command1 button this time, a message box appears with the message "Visual Basic rocks!", as shown here:

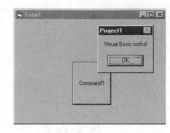

*Now your Command1
button actually does
something.*

As you might have already guessed, the MsgBox command tells Visual Basic to display
a message box. The text in the quotes after the MsgBox command is the text the message box should display. You'll see the MsgBox command a lot throughout this book.

In the following section, you'll see how to convert your Visual Basic program into a
standalone application. If you're using the Visual Basic Working Model that came
with this book, however, keep in mind that you can't create standalone applications.
Still, even if you're using the Working Model, read the following section to get an
idea of how this conversion process works.

Creating Your Program's Executable File

Now, if you're done patting yourself on the back and yelling for the family to come
and fuss over your first Visual Basic program, you can take the step that converts your
Visual Basic project into a full-fledged, standalone Windows application.

If you look in the File menu, you'll see a command called Make Project1.exe, as
shown here:

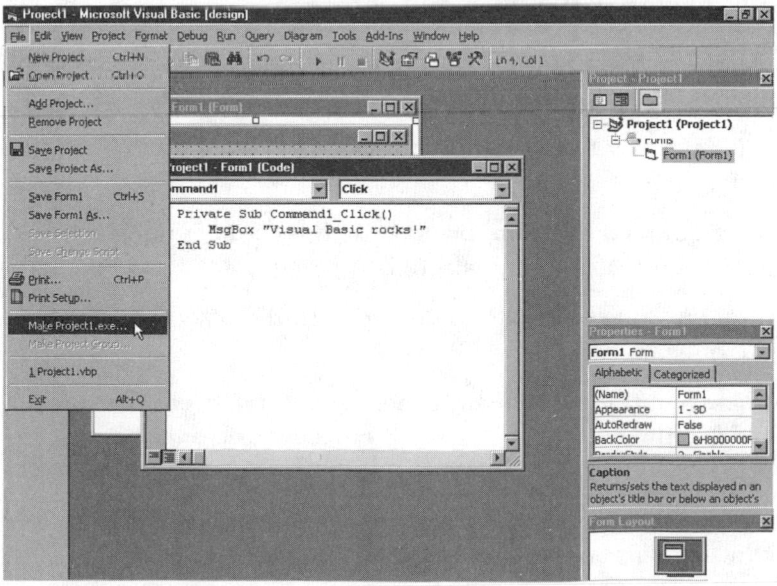

*The Make command
changes your program
into an executable file.*

33

A Matter of Execution

Not all files on your disk drive represent applications. Many are data files that other programs need to load. Files that end in .exe, however, are *executable files* that you can double-click to run. For example, Visual Basic 6.0's executable file is named Vb6.exe. If you find this file with Windows Explorer and double-click it with your mouse, you'll start Visual Basic, same as if you selected Visual Basic from your Start menu. Visual Basic can convert your program to an executable file, using a process called *compilation*.

Click the Make Project1 command, and when the Make Project dialog box appears, click the OK button. When you do, Visual Basic changes your program into an executable Windows application.

Now that Visual Basic has converted your program to an executable file, you don't need Visual Basic to run the program. To prove this, first save your program by clicking the Save Project button in the toolbar (that's the button that looks like a floppy disk), or you can select the File menu's Save Project command. Visual Basic prompts you for two filenames. The first is for your form. Click OK to select the default name of Form1.frm. The second file you need to save is your project settings. When the dialog box appears, accept the default project name of Project1.vbp.

Now you can exit from Visual Basic by pressing Alt+Q on your keyboard. Visual Basic vanishes from your screen and is now closed. Find the file Project1.exe, which should be in your Vb98 folder if you didn't change any of the defaults. Project1.exe is the executable file that Visual Basic created from your program. Double-click the file, and your Visual Basic application appears on the screen. Go ahead and click the Command1 button to display the message box. It works! Break out the champagne and cheese fondue!

The Least You Need to Know

➤ To create a Visual Basic application, you build a user interface, write the program source code, and then compile the program into an executable file.

➤ You build a user interface by placing controls from Visual Basic's toolbox on your program's form.

➤ You can resize a control (and the form) by dragging the control's sizing handles, which appear when the control is selected.

➤ One way to display the code window is to double-click the object for which you want to write program code.

➤ When the user clicks a button, Visual Basic generates a Click event. The program code you add to the button's Click event procedure determines what the button does.

➤ The File menu's Make command converts your Visual Basic program into a standalone Windows application.

Part 2
Writing Basic Program Code

Every programming language consists of keywords, symbols, and statements that work together to tell the computer how to complete many different kinds of tasks. To make your Visual Basic programs do what you want them to do, you have to know how to write Visual Basic commands. In this section, you'll learn the BASIC computer language, which is the language upon which Visual Basic is based.

Chapter 4

Variables and I/O: A Programming Secret Revealed

In This Chapter

➤ Understand input and output

➤ Learn to use the `Print`, `EndDoc`, and `Cls` commands

➤ Discover variables and how to declare them

➤ Use TextBox controls for input

➤ Use Label controls to give the user information

A computer wouldn't be of much use if you didn't have a way of getting data in and out of it. For example, to understand computer input and output, let's say you want to type that letter to your congressperson. Your first task is to get the characters that make up the letter into your computer's memory where you can manipulate them. You can't just dictate the letter as you would to a secretary. You have to use one of the computer's input devices—in this case, the keyboard—to type your letter, placing it into memory one character at a time.

When you finish typing and editing your letter, you need a way to get it out of the computer's memory so the congressperson can read it. You need another kind of device—an output device—to which you can send the letter to get it into a form that is useful. You probably want to use a printer, but you might also save your letter onto a disk and send the disk to the recipient. Then he could just load the letter into his computer's memory and read it onscreen.

Input or Output?

As you now know, input devices, such as your keyboard and your mouse, transfer data from you to your computer. Output devices, such as printers and monitors, transfer data from the computer back to you. Some devices, however, such as disk drives, are both input and output devices. This is because they can transfer data in both directions. For example, you can save data from your computer to a disk, and you can also load the data back from the disk into your computer.

The process of moving data in and out of a computer is called, appropriately enough, input and output (or I/O, for short). There are all kinds of input and output, but you need to know only a couple to get started with Visual Basic. In this chapter, you'll learn to ask a user for data and accept that data from the keyboard. You'll also learn to print the data on your computer's screen or on your printer.

Computer Programs and I/O

The program that is currently running controls most input and output. If you load a program that doesn't use the keyboard, the program will not notice your keystrokes—no matter how much you type. Likewise, if a program wasn't designed to use your printer, you have no way of accessing the printer when running that program. Obviously, then, if it's up to a program to control your computer's input and output, every programming language must contain commands for input and output. In fact, a programming language without I/O commands would be about as useful to you as a book of matches would be to a fish. By providing commands for putting data into the computer and getting data back out again, a computer language allows you to create interactive programs.

Interactive programs allow two-way communication between the user and the computer. For example, the computer might output a question to the user by printing the question onscreen. The user might then answer the question by typing on his or her keyboard.

Visual Basic, like any other computer language, features several commands for controlling input and output. The Print command, for example, allows you to make text appear on the computer's screen. You might want to do this in order to ask the user a question or to show the user a piece of information he asked for.

Suppose you want to print a simple message on the screen. Try this: Get Visual Basic cranked up, and start a new project. Place a CommandButton control at the bottom of the form, double-click the button to display its Click procedure in the code window, and complete the procedure like this:

```
Private Sub Command1_Click()
    Form1.Print "Here's some text output."
    Form1.Print "Here's some more text output."
    Form1.Print "And here's still more text output."
End Sub
```

When you run the program and click the button, you see the screen shown here:

Windows applications display text in their windows.

As you can see, each `Print` command creates a single line of text onscreen, in the form's window. The text the command prints is the text that you place after the word `Print`. This text, called a *string literal*, must be enclosed in quotation marks.

What's the `Form1` in front of the `Print` command? `Print` is actually a command that belongs to the Visual Basic Form object. By placing the name of the Form object (`Form1`, in this case) followed by a dot in front of the `Print` command, Visual Basic knows where to look for the `Print` command. If you want to get technical about it, `Print` isn't really a command at all, but rather something called a *method*. You'll learn a lot about methods later in this book, especially in Chapter 18, "Methods, Properties, and Events: An Object's Inner Workings." For now, just think of `Print` as a command.

Text in Your Programs

A *string* is a group of text characters. A *string literal* is text that you want the computer to use exactly as you type it. You tell the computer that a line of text is a string literal by enclosing the text in quotation marks. You'll run into strings and string literals a lot as you program with Visual Basic or any other computer language.

Now, suppose you wanted the text printed on your printer instead of onscreen? In Visual Basic, this task is easy to do. Just change all the `Form1.Print` commands in the program to `Printer.Print`. You should also make a couple of other changes, as shown here:

```
Private Sub Command1_Click()
    Form1.Print "Printing..."
    Printer.Print "Here's some text output."
    Printer.Print "Here's some more text output."
    Printer.Print "And here's still more text output."
    Printer.EndDoc
    Form1.Cls
End Sub
```

Notice the first line in this program. It displays the word `Printing...` onscreen. Without this line, the program's user would not know what the computer was doing until text started appearing on the printer. Your program should always tell the user what it's doing (if it's not immediately obvious), especially when it's doing processing that takes more than a few seconds to complete. Nothing is quite as alarming to a computer user as watching a computer that seems to be doing nothing. You can spot alarmed computer users easily: They're the ones pounding their monitors, punching their computer's reset button, and screaming words we can't print in this book.

Next, notice that by changing the Form1 to Printer in the Print commands, the program sends the text to the printer rather than to the screen. You can see now why it's important to place an object name in front of a command. In this case, the object names tell Visual Basic which text to send to the screen and which text to send to the printer.

After printing the text to the printer, the program executes the Printer object's EndDoc command. This command causes the printer to finish printing and to eject the page from the printer.

Finally, notice the last line (before the End Sub). The Form object's Cls command clears the form's window, which causes the word Printing... that appeared during the printing process to vanish. In fact, your computer system might send the text to the printer so fast that Printing... seems to just blink on and off.

Now you know how to use Visual Basic to ask a computer user a question, which is one form of output. But how can you get the user's answer into your program? As you might have guessed, Visual Basic has a way to get typed input from the user. You need to add a TextBox control to your form. But before you can learn about the TextBox control, you need to know about variables.

Variables

When you input data into a computer, the computer stores that data in its memory. You can think of your computer's memory as millions of little boxes, each holding a single value. Normally, each little box is numbered, starting at zero. The actual number of boxes in your computer depends upon how much memory you have installed. Your computer's memory is organized something like this:

Computer memory is a lot like a bunch of numbered boxes into which a program can store values.

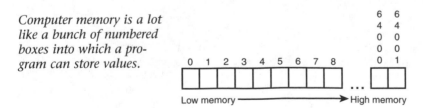

When you input data into your computer, your computer stuffs the data into one of those little boxes that make up its memory. But in which box should the value be stored, and how can you refer to that box in a way that makes sense within a program? This is where variables come in.

Variables are really just memory boxes with names. Because you, the programmer, supply the names, you can name your variables almost anything you want, making your programs easier to read and understand. Later in your program, you can store values into the memory box by referring to its name. For example, to keep track of the score in a game, you might have a variable named score. Whenever the player's score changes, you can put the new score value into the variable named score. In this way, you've set aside a little piece of memory that contains data you need in your program.

You must, however, follow certain rules when creating variable names. First, a variable name must be no longer than 255 characters. (If you need more characters than that, I suggest you look up the word "concise" in your dictionary.) Second, the name must start with a letter. The other characters can be letters, numbers, or the underscore character. (You can't use spaces in a variable name.) Because Visual Basic isn't case sensitive, you can use any combination of upper- and lowercase letters in a variable name—the variable names Score, score, and SCORE all mean the same thing to Visual Basic. Finally, you can't use a Visual Basic keyword as a variable name.

Here are some valid variable names:

```
Total

Money_Spent

FirstName

name23

AMOUNT
```

Here are some invalid variable names:

```
3456

current.balance

Date Paid

Print
```

Variables and Input

To get user input into your Visual Basic programs, you can use something called a TextBox control. Suppose, for example, you're writing a program that needs to know the number of cars in a parking garage. Suppose also that when the user runs the program, the first thing he or she must do is input the current car count.

To solve this problem, try this: Start a new Visual Basic project. Then place a TextBox control and a CommandButton control on the form (refer to the following figure). Double-click the CommandButton control to display its `Click` procedure in Visual Basic's code window. Complete the `Click` procedure like this:

```
Private Sub Command1_Click()
    cars = Text1.Text
    Form1.Print "You have " & cars & " cars."
End Sub
```

Now, run the program, type a number into the text box (after deleting the "Text1" that's already there), and click the button. When you do, Visual Basic jumps to the button's `Click` procedure, where the program grabs your input from the text box, and prints the results in the window, as shown in this figure:

A program can easily display data that's been stored in a variable.

What happened here? Look at the first line of the `Click` procedure (not counting the line with the procedure's name). The line `cars = Text1.Text` takes the contents of the text box and places it into a variable named `cars`. To see how this works, you first need to know that the TextBox control's name is `Text1`. (Visual Basic automatically assigned this name to the control. Later in this book, you'll see how to rename objects.) It just so happens that a TextBox control has variables of its own. These special variables—called *properties*—enable the TextBox control to store information about itself. One of these pieces of information is the text the control contains, which the control stores in its `Text` property. You can copy the text into your own variable by using the equals sign.

The word `cars` is a variable name, which is used to identify the little box in memory where Visual Basic stores the response. Suppose you type the number **8** in response to the program. Your computer's memory might then look something like this figure:

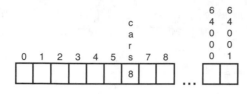

Visual Basic assigns a memory location to a variable.

In this figure, Visual Basic has assigned the variable cars to memory location 6 and has placed the value 8 into that location. Luckily, you don't have to worry about where Visual Basic puts variables in memory; Visual Basic handles all that for you.

How about that last line in the program? Pretty fancy-looking Print command, wouldn't you say? This shows how powerful the Print command can be. In this case, the Print command displays not only string literals, but also the value stored in the variable cars. See the ampersands? By using ampersands, you can build a line of text from different elements. In the Print command above, the line of text displayed onscreen comprises three elements: the string literal "You have ", the variable cars, and the string literal " cars". The ampersands tell the Print command to place each of these elements one after the other on the same line.

Declaring Variables

Variables can exist as many different types. You'll learn about variable types in the next chapter, but for now you can think of variables

More About Variables and Literals

Notice that Visual Basic can easily tell the difference between the string literal "cars" and the variable cars. Now you know why the quotation marks are so important. In fact, without the quotation marks, Visual Basic would interpret each word following the Print command as a variable, rather than as a string.

as holding either numeric values or text. When you wrote the previous program, you didn't tell Visual Basic too much about the variable cars, so Visual Basic waited to see what the program was going to do with it. When the program assigned the TextBox control's text to the variable, Visual Basic made cars into a string variable (one that can hold text) and copied the control's text into the variable.

Technically, only a string variable can hold text and only a numerical variable can hold numerical values. This might not seem to be the case with Visual Basic because Visual Basic is so smart about figuring out how a program uses its variables. However, this cleverness comes with a price: When Visual Basic has to figure out how to use a variable, it takes longer for Visual Basic to assign a value to the variable. For this reason, it's not a bad idea to declare your variables before you use them.

When you declare a variable, you not only tell Visual Basic the variable's name, but also how the variable is to be used. For example, the following is a rewritten version of the previous `Click` procedure:

```
Private Sub Command1_Click()
    Dim cars As Integer
    cars = Text1.Text
    Form1.Print "You have " & cars & " cars."
End Sub
```

Notice the line `Dim cars As Integer`. This line tells Visual Basic that the program will use the variable `cars` to store integer data. (If you remember your math, you know that an integer is any whole number.) Now, when Visual Basic transfers the text from the TextBox control, it changes the text from a string to a numerical value and stuffs the result into `cars`.

This is all well and good, but what happens if the user types non-numerical characters into the TextBox control? For example, what if the user typed **ten** into the box instead of **10**? There's no way that Visual Basic can change the string `ten` into a numerical value, so Visual Basic generates an error, which looks like this:

Visual Basic displays errors when something goes wrong in your program.

A type-mismatch error tells you that the program tried to store the wrong type of data into a variable. You can never store a string in a numerical variable. For example, these Visual Basic lines cause an error:

```
' Dont' do this!
Dim value As Integer
value = "This is a string literal"
```

You can, however, create a variable for holding text, by declaring the variable's type to be String. Here's a version of the Click procedure that declares cars as a string variable:

```
Private Sub Command1_Click()
    Dim cars As String
    cars = Text1.Text
    Form1.Print "You have " & cars & " cars."
End Sub
```

This version of the procedure works just like the previous one, with one small difference. It doesn't matter whether the user types a string or a number into the text box. In both cases, the result is a string that is stored in cars. You might find it confusing that the value 10 can be both a numerical value and a text value. But you have to remember that there's a big difference between the text character "1" and the value 1. When numbers are part of a string, Visual Basic treats them just the same as any other character, such as "A" or "?". The downside is that a program cannot perform mathematical operations with numbers that are stored as strings. Numbers in a string are not really numbers at all, any more than letters are numbers.

What's in a Name?

As you write your Visual Basic programs, watch out for misspelled variable names. Misspelling a variable name creates program bugs that are difficult to find. For example, suppose you have in your program a variable named TotalNumbers. As you type the lines of your program, you accidentally spell this variable as Total_Numbers. To Visual Basic, TotalNumbers and Total_Numbers are different variables, each with its own value.

One way around this problem is to add the line Option Explicit to all your Visual Basic programs. This line tells Visual Basic that every variable name must be declared before it can be used. Then, if you accidentally misspell a variable name, Visual Basic will recognize the misspelled name as an undeclared variable and generate an error. Place the Option Explicit line at the very top of the project's code window, outside of any procedures in the program.

Storing Text Data

In some cases, it only takes one memory location (one of those little boxes you learned about) to store a number. However, strings are often made up of more than one character, and only one character can fit in any memory location. This means string data actually takes up much more space in your computer's memory than numerical values do. Exactly how much space can be hard to predict because Visual Basic stores extra information about the string along with the string. Every string takes up a little more memory than the number of characters in the string. For example, the string "This is a test" takes up a little more than 14 memory locations.

Labeling Your Text Boxes

A TextBox control without a label is as confusing as a David Lynch film. After all, unless you tell the user what you expect him to enter, how will he know what to do? (This, of course, doesn't apply to programs written for mind readers.) Because you frequently need to prompt for information in programs, Visual Basic provides a special control, called a Label control, for labeling items in a window.

You can easily add a label to the program you've been working on in this chapter. First, place a Label control on the form, dragging it into place above the TextBox control. Then, change the Label control's Caption property to Enter the number of cars:. You can make this change by clicking the label to select it, and then changing the value of the Caption property in the Properties window, as shown in this figure:

Change the label's text in the Properties window.

Change the Caption property here

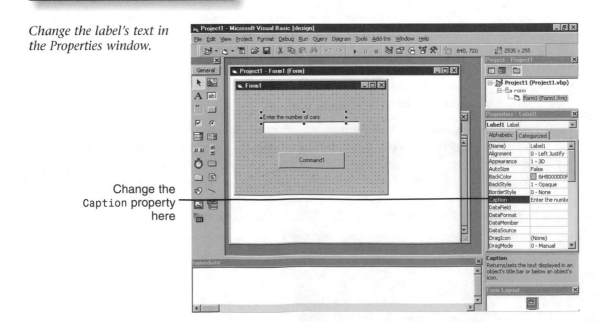

(If you like, you can also erase the string "Text1" from the text box by deleting the text from the TextBox control's Text property in the Properties window.) This figure shows the program in its final form:

Now the text box has a label so the user knows what to type.

Fun with Input and Output

Now that you've learned a little about Visual Basic input and output, how about finishing up with a program that puts this new knowledge to the test? First, start a new Visual Basic project, and place three TextBox controls, two Label controls, and one CommandButton control like this:

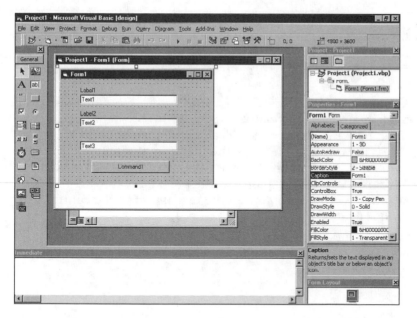

Position your controls as shown here.

(Be sure to place the controls in order from top to bottom so that the TextBox controls are in the order Text1, Text2, and Text3.)

Next, clear all the text from the TextBox controls' Text properties. Then, change the first label's Caption property to Enter first name: and the second label's Caption property to Enter last name:. Finally, double-click the CommandButton control to display its Click procedure, and complete the procedure as follows:

```
Private Sub Command1_Click()
    Dim firstName As String
    Dim lastName As String

    firstName = Text1.Text
    lastName = Text2.Text
    Text3.Text = "Hello, " & firstName & " " & lastName
End Sub
```

Now, run the program, and type your first and last name into the appropriate text boxes. Press the button, and a personalized greeting appears in the third text box, as shown in the following figure:

This chapter's final program says hello.

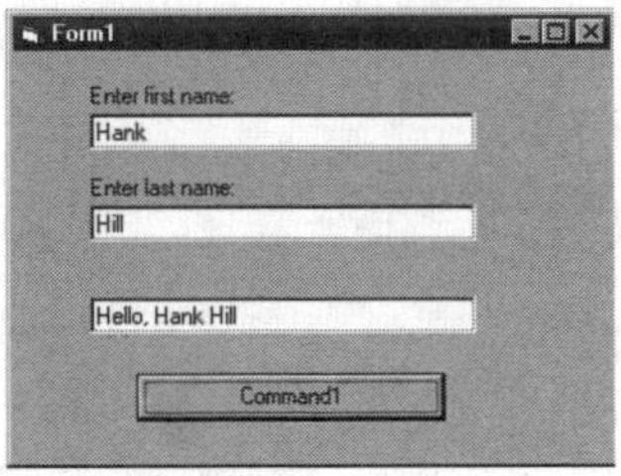

You should be able to figure out most of what's going on in this program's Click procedure. The first two lines tell Visual Basic that the variables firstName and lastName will be holding text data. The next two lines copy the text from the TextBox controls into your new string variables. The final line is something new. There, rather than copying text from a TextBox control's Text property, the program is copying text *to* a TextBox control's Text property. This action makes the text appear in the control, as you can see in the previous figure.

No Error Too Small

Novice programmers often don't realize how fussy Visual Basic is about tiny errors, such as missing or incorrect punctuation. Remember: Every character in a program is important. Be careful not to overlook any or to mistype any. Such mistakes can cause Visual Basic to display an error or result in unpredictable program bugs. Most big companies can tell you horror stories about how a single missing semicolon or comma caused them thousands of dollars worth of problems.

The Least You Need to Know

➤ Input and output devices transfer data to and from a computer.

➤ The Print command prints a line of text on the screen or a printer.

➤ String literals must be enclosed in quotation marks.

➤ Your computer's memory can be thought of as a series of little boxes, with each box holding a single value.

➤ Variables are named places in memory where a program can store data.

➤ Numeric variables can hold only numeric values. String variables can hold only text (or numbers that the computer treats as text).

➤ You can use TextBox controls to get input from a program's user. You should use Label controls to label text boxes.

➤ A TextBox control's Text property holds the text in the control, whereas a Label control's Caption property holds the text displayed in the label.

Chapter 5

Visual Basic Mathematics: It's Easier Than You Think!

> ## In This Chapter
>
> ➤ Use variables in mathematical expressions
>
> ➤ Understand arithmetic operations
>
> ➤ Discover the order of operations
>
> ➤ Learn about different data types

You've probably heard that programming a computer requires lots of math. And if you're like most people, all those formulas and equations you learned in high school now look stranger than an ostrich at a square dance. Guess what? Most programs require only simple mathematical calculations—addition, subtraction, multiplication, and division—the same stuff you do every day.

Moreover, when you're writing a program, you won't have to wear down pencils adding long columns of numbers or fry your brain trying to figure out 35,764 divided by 137. The computer can do the calculations for you. If you know how to use basic arithmetic operations to solve simple problems, you know all the math necessary to write a computer program. (Well, most computer programs, anyway; don't expect to be able to write the next Quake without a college degree in mathematics.) Computer programming is more logical than mathematical. It's just a matter of common sense. (So, if you have trouble remembering to come in out of the rain, computer programming might not be for you.)

Still, you can't avoid math entirely. Heaven knows, your humble author has tried. Computers, after all, are number-crunching machines that like nothing better than spitting out the results of hundreds, thousands, or even millions of calculations. It's up to you, the wise programmer, to give the computer the commands it needs to perform these calculations. In this chapter, you'll learn to do just that.

Variables and Math

In Chapter 4, "Variables and I/O: A Programming Secret Revealed," you learned about variables—the little boxes in memory in which your program stores numbers. A computer program can also use values that never change called literals. Unlike a literal such as the number 3, variables can represent almost any value—except maybe the balance on my Visa card (a number so large even a computer has a tough time remembering it). Variables are extremely valuable entities. Because variables represent numbers, you can use them in mathematical operations.

For example, suppose you run a small video store, and you want to know how many tapes you have. You might think to yourself, "I've got 20 copies of *Naughty Banshees from Venus*, 50 copies of *Dances with Muskrats*, and 10 copies of *Ren and Stimpy's 60-Minute Workout*. So, I've got 80 videotapes." If you want to use the computer to solve this mathematical problem, you could load Visual Basic and type the command Print 20+50+10 into Visual Basic's immediate-command window. The computer would print the answer 80, as you can see in this figure:

You can type mathematical calculations into Visual Basic's Immediate window.

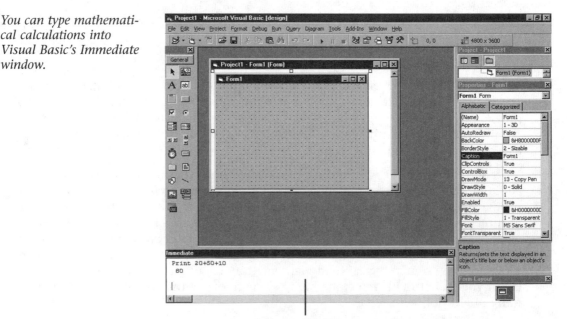

Immediate window

Just as you would suspect, the + symbol means addition in a computer program.

There's a better way, however, to solve the videotape problem—one that works with any number of videotapes. This new method uses variables in mathematical operations. As you've learned, you can name a variable just about anything you like. (Yes, you can even call a variable lateForDinner.) Names such as naughty, dances, and stimpy are completely acceptable. Beginning to see the light?

Try this: Start a new Visual Basic project, and place four Label controls, three TextBox controls, and one CommandButton control as shown in the following figure:

Displaying the Immediate Window

If your Visual Basic setup doesn't show the Immediate window, just press Ctrl+G or select the View menu's Immediate Window command.

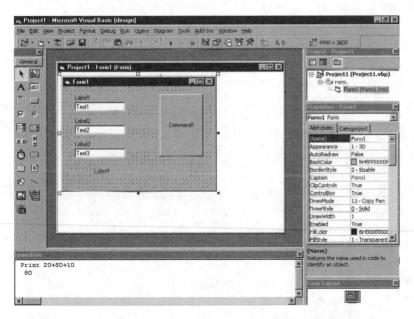

Position the controls as shown here.

Now, double-click the Form object, and type the following code into the code window (Visual Basic will have started the Form_Load procedure for you):

```
Option Explicit

Private Sub Form_Load()
    Label1.Caption = "Enter # of Naughty Banshees:"
    Label2.Caption = "Enter # of Dances with Muskrats:"
```

```
        Label3.Caption = "Enter # of Ren and Stimpy:"
        Label4.Caption = "Total number of video tapes:"
        Text1.Text = "0"
        Text2.Text = "0"
        Text3.Text = "0"
        Command1.Caption = "Calculate"
    End Sub

Private Sub Command1_Click()
        Dim naughty As Integer
        Dim dances As Integer
        Dim stimpy As Integer
        Dim tapes As Integer

        naughty = Text1.Text
        dances = Text2.Text
        stimpy = Text3.Text
        tapes = naughty + dances + stimpy
        Label4.Caption = "Total number of video tapes: " & tapes
    End Sub
```

Sizing Controls

If a Label control isn't big enough to hold its caption, you can resize the control by clicking it and then dragging the control's sizing handles. You can do the same thing to resize your program's form or any other control. However, you can only do this type of resizing when you're designing the program, not when the program is running.

The line Option Explicit tells Visual Basic that all variables in the program must be declared before they're used. The Form_Load procedure sets the various controls' Caption and Text properties to the text the controls need to display. Visual Basic jumps to the Form_Load procedure the instant you run the program, making it a great place to set things up in your program. Finally, the Command1_Click procedure, which Visual Basic jumps to when the user clicks the button, gets the values typed into the text boxes, adds the values together, and uses the fourth Label control's Caption property to display the result of the calculation.

Now that you've written you program, go ahead and run it. When you do, type three values into the text boxes, and then click the Calculate button. The computer zaps your entries into the variables naughty, dances, and stimpy (converting the values from strings to integers) Then the program adds the variables and plunks the total into another variable called tapes. Finally, the program uses the fourth Label control's Caption property to display the numbercontained in tapes, as shown in the following figure:

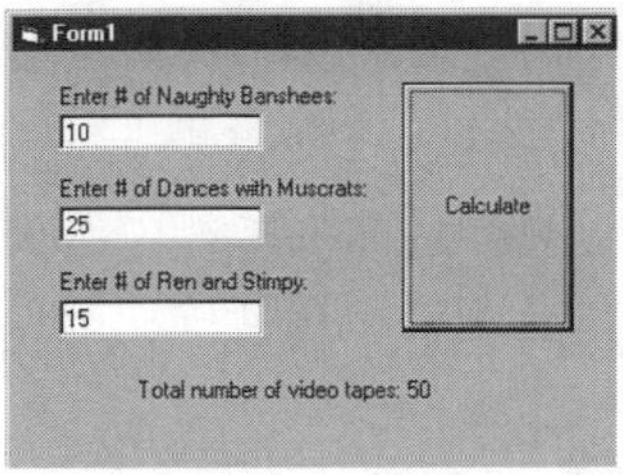

This program adds the number of video tapes.

Now you know the following two things:

1. You have 50 videotapes in your store.
2. With movie titles like these, you'll be out of business faster than you can say, "Dances with WHAT?"

By using a program similar to this one, you can get a new tape total anytime you like. Just provide your program with new counts for each movie.

Beyond Addition

Of course, computers can do more than add. They can perform any basic arithmetic operation. Visual Basic even has functions for figuring out things such as square roots and absolute values. If you don't know what a square root or an absolute value is, don't hit the panic button; you still won't have trouble programming your computer. Just don't plan to write an algebra tutorial anytime soon.

Let's assume that your videotape store is still thriving, despite its horrible selection and the fact that the local chapter of Citizens Against Painfully Stupid Movies has a contract out on your head. Suppose you now want to find the total value of your inventory, as well as the average cost per tape. To find the total value of your inventory, multiply each title's price by the number of copies you own. Perform this calculation for all titles, and then add those amounts together to get the total value. To find the average value per tape, divide the total value by the total number of tapes.

To build this program, start a new Visual Basic project, and place eight Label controls, six TextBox controls, and one CommandButton control as shown here:

*Position the controls as
shown here.*

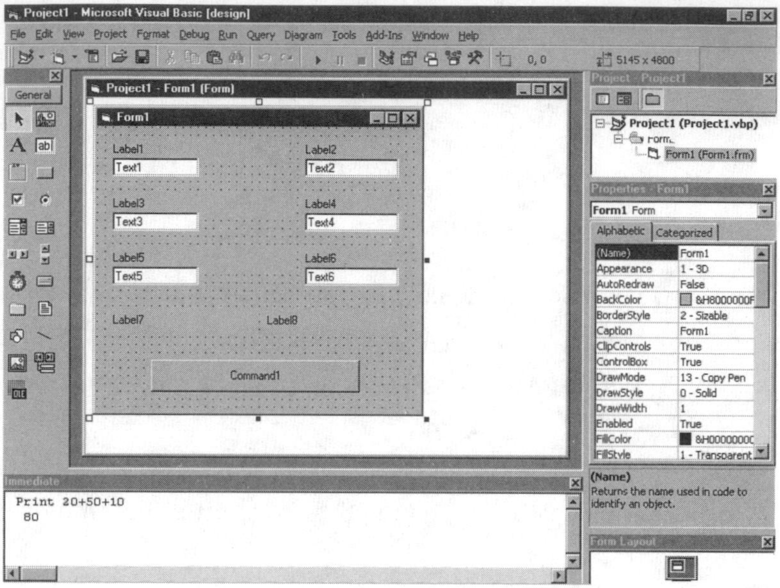

Now, double-click the Form object, and type the following code into the code window (Visual Basic will have started the Form_Load procedure for you):

```
Option Explicit

Private Sub Form_Load()
    Label1.Caption = "# of Naughty Banshees:"
    Label2.Caption = "Price each:"
    Label3.Caption = "# of Dances with Muscrats:"
    Label4.Caption = "Price each:"
    Label5.Caption = "# of Ren and Stimpy:"
    Label6.Caption = "Price each:"
    Label7.Caption = "Total value:"
    Label8.Caption = "Average value:"
    Text1.Text = "0"
    Text2.Text = "0"
    Text3.Text = "0"
    Text4.Text = "0"
    Text5.Text = "0"
    Text6.Text = "0"
End Sub

Private Sub Command1_Click()
    Dim quantity As Integer
    Dim price As Single
    Dim totalNumTapes As Integer
    Dim totalValue As Single
```

```
    Dim averageValue As Single

    quantity = Text1.Text
    totalNumTapes = quantity
    price = Text2.Text
    totalValue = quantity * price
    quantity = Text3.Text
    totalNumTapes = totalNumTapes + quantity
    price = Text4.Text
    totalValue = totalValue + quantity * price
    quantity = Text5.Text
    totalNumTapes = totalNumTapes + quantity
    price = Text6.Text
    totalValue = totalValue + quantity * price
    averageValue = totalValue / totalNumTapes

    Label7.Caption = "Total value: " & totalValue
    Label8.Caption = "Average value: " & averageValue
End Sub
```

After typing in the code, run the program, and enter appropriate values into each of the text boxes. Then, click the Calculate button to see the total value of the video tapes and the average value for a tape, as shown here:

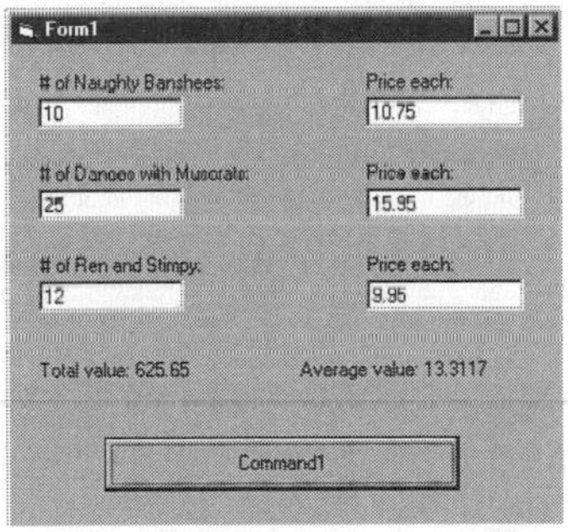

This program calculates the total and average value of video tapes.

When you run this program, Visual Basic begins at the Form_Load procedure, where it sets the various controls' Text and Caption properties. When you click the Calculate button, Visual Basic jumps to the Command1_Click procedure, where the program gets the quantity and price of the first video title. These values are temporarily stored in the variables quantity and price. The quantity is then placed in the variable totalNumTapes. The total value for all tapes with that title is calculated by multiplying the price of the tape by the quantity; that total is stored in the variable totalValue.

57

Next, the program gets the quantity and price of the second title. After the program retrieves that information, it adds the quantity for the second title to `totalNumTapes` (which already contains the quantity for the first title). This total is the combined quantity for the first two titles. The program calculates the total value for the two titles by multiplying the second tape's price by its quantity and adding that amount to `totalValue`.

Recycling Variables

Notice how the program reuses the variables `price` and `quantity`. You don't need to save the price and quantity of each tape after you've added them to the running totals, so you can use `price` and `quantity` as input variables for every tape.

The program processes the third tape the same way. Then, the program calculates the average value for each tape by dividing `totalValue` by `totalNumTapes`. Finally, the program displays the results by setting Label7 and Label8's `Caption` property.

Yes, this program is a bit longer than the first one, but it still uses only basic arithmetic. It's longer because it performs more calculations than the first example.

If you look at the program carefully, you'll see some new ideas. First, the program declares a few of the variables as `Single`, rather than `Integer`. A `Single` value holds a *floating-point* number, which is a number with whole-number and decimal portions. For example, 26.82 is a floating-point number.

Second, you might have seen something strange about `totalNumTapes`. Specifically, what the heck does the line

```
totalNumTapes = totalNumTapes + quantity
```

do? How can the same variable be on both sides of an equation? Why do I keep asking these dumb questions?

First, you have to stop thinking that the equals sign (=) always means equals. It doesn't. In Visual Basic arithmetic operations, this symbol actually means "takes the value of," which makes it an assignment operator. (Even in programming, however, the equals sign still can mean "is equal to," as you'll learn in Chapter 7, "`If`, `Then`, and `Else`: Decisions, Decisions, Decisions.")

You also must understand that Visual Basic interprets statements from the right side of the equals sign to the left side. So, the program adds `totalNumTapes` and `quantity` first, and then assigns the result of that addition back to `totalNumTapes`—that is, the result is stored in `totalNumTapes`, wiping out the value that was there previously.

Confused? Suppose `totalNumTapes` is equal to 7 and `quantity` is equal to 3. When the program sees the line `totalNumTapes = totalNumTapes + quantity`, it adds 7 to 3 and pops the value `10` into `totalNumTapes`. Using this method, you can add values to a variable that already holds a value. You'll do this often in your programs.

As you can see, a Visual Basic program uses an asterisk (*) to represent multiplication, not an X as you might expect. Division is represented by the forward slash character (/) because the computer keyboard doesn't have a division symbol. You could try painting a division symbol on one of your keys, but you'll still have to use the slash character in your programs.

Variables and Their Assignments

Visual Basic uses an assignment operator to assign a value to a variable. In Visual Basic the assignment operator is an equals sign, but other computer languages might use different assignment operators. In Pascal, for example, the assignment operator is a colon followed by an equals sign (:=).

The following table shows all of Visual Basic's arithmetic operators:

Operator	Name	Use
+	Addition	Sum values
−	Subtraction	Subtract values
*	Multiplication	Multiply values
/	Division	Divide values
\	Integer division	Determine the whole number result of division
^	Exponentiation	Raise a value to a power
MOD	Modulus	Determine the remainder of division

The next table shows some examples of mathematical operations using the arithmetic operators.

Operation	Result
5+8	13
12−7	5
3*6	18
10/3	3.333333
10\3	3
2^3	8
10 Mod 3	1

Mathematical Operations with Visual Basic

When you use regular division, denoted by the forward slash character (/), you are performing the type of division you learned in school. You might end up with a result like 2 (such as in the operation 4/2) or a result like 2.4 (such as in the operation 12/5).

When you useinteger division, denoted by the backslash character (\), your answer will always be an integer because Visual Basic drops any part of the result that lies to the right of the decimal point. This means that, with integer division, the operation 12\5 results in 2, rather than 2.4.

The Mod operator performs division, too, but it only gives you the remainder of the division. For example, 4 goes into 14 three times with a remainder of 2, so the operation 14 Mod 4 yields a result of 2. As a beginning programmer, you probably won't have a lot of use for this operator.

Finally, the exponentiation operator (^) is used to raise numbers to a power. When you raise a number to a power, you multiply the number times itself the number of times indicated by the exponent (the number after the ^ character). For example, 10^2 is the same as 10 * 10, which equals 100. The operation 5^3 is the same as 5 * 5 * 5, which equals 125.

Order of Operations

Another curious line in the previous program is the following:

```
totalValue = totalValue + price * quantity
```

This program line is similar to the line that calculates the total number of tapes, but it contains both an addition and multiplication operation. This brings up the important topic of operator precedence, or as it's more commonly known, the order of operations.

If you were to add totalValue to price and then multiply the sum by quantity, you would get an incorrect result. Operator precedence dictates that all multiplication must take place before any addition. So in the preceding line, totalValue is calculated by first multiplying price times quantity and then adding that product to totalValue.

Don't forget about operator precedence; if you do, your calculations won't be accurate, and your programs won't run correctly.

The order of operations for Visual Basic is exponentiation first; then multiplication, division, integer division, and Mod; finally, addition and subtraction. Operations of the same precedence are evaluated from left to right. For example, in the expression 3 * 5 / 2, 3 is first multiplied by 5, which gives a result of 15. This result is then divided by 2, giving a result of 7.5. The Visual Basic operator precedence is summarized in the following table:

Order	Operator	Name
1	^	Exponentiation
2	* / \ MOD	Multiplication, division, integer division, and modulus
3	+ −	Addition and subtraction

You can change operator precedence by using parentheses. For example, suppose you wanted the addition in the line

```
totalValue = totalValue + price * quantity
```

to be calculated before the multiplication. You could rewrite the line as

```
totalValue = (totalValue + price) * quantity
```

Any operation enclosed in parentheses is performed first. Consequently, Visual Basic adds totalValue and price first, and then multiplies the sum by quantity.

Data Types

You'll be happy to know you're almost finished with the math stuff. Before you move on, you have to explore only one more topic: data types. You've already had a little experience with data types, but you probably didn't pay too much attention at the time.

When you used numeric variables and string variables, you were using variables of two different data types. Numeric variables can hold only numbers and string variables can hold only text strings. What you haven't learned is that numeric variables can be divided into manyother data types, including integers, long integers, single-precision, and double-precision.

Avoiding Operator Confusion

When writing a program line that contains many arithmetic operations, you might want to use parentheses to more clearly indicate the order of operation. For example, the formula totalValue = totalValue + (price * quantity) is easier to read than the original formula totalValue = totalValue + price * quantity.Both formulas, however, yield the same result.

When a Number's Not a Number

Although numeric variables can hold only numbers and string variables can hold only text strings, that doesn't mean a string variable can't hold a character that represents a number. For example, when assigned to a numeric variable, the number 3 represents a value that can be used in arithmetic operations. However, the character 3 assigned to a string variable is just a text character—no different from any other text character, such as A or Z. Although a string variable can hold number characters, those characters cannot be used directly in mathematical operations.

Until now, you've been more concerned with giving your numeric variables appropriate names; you haven't worried so much about what type of value the variables would hold. You could ignore data types for the most part because Visual Basic is so smart about determining and converting data types on its own. But what if you want to be sure that a variable always contains a certain type of data, no matter what type of assignment operation it's involved in? For example, what if you want to add two floating-point numbers, but you want to store the result as an integer? What are floating-point numbers and integers, anyway?

An integer is any whole number, such as 23, 76, –65, or 1200. Notice that none of these numbers contain a decimal portion. Notice also that none of them are smaller than –32,768 or greater than 32,767. A Visual Basic integer must fall into this range.

What if you need to use a number that doesn't fit into the integer range? You can use a long integer. A long integer resembles an integer in that it can hold only a whole number. However, the range of a long integer is much larger: –2,147,483,648 to 2,147,483,647, to be exact. Unless you're trying to calculate the national debt or count the number of times Elizabeth Taylor has been married, you're not likely to need values larger than these.

Numbers that contain a decimal portion are called floating-point numbers. Like integers, they come in two flavors. A single-precision floating-point number is accurate down to six decimal places (for example, 34.875637). A double-precision floating-point number, on the other hand, is accurate down to 14 decimal places (for example, 657.36497122357638). Floating-point numbers in Visual Basic can be very tiny or incredibly large.

Avoid Laziness

When writing a program, you might be tempted to make all your integer variables long integers and all your floating-point variables double-precision. When you do this, you no longer need to worry about whether your values go out of range. However, this technique has two drawbacks. First, long integers and double-precision floating-point numbers take up more memory space than their smaller counterparts. Second, your computer takes longer to access and manipulate these larger values, so using them can significantly slow down your programs. Use long integers and double-precision values only when you really need them.

Visual Basic also provides a couple of unusual data types, called Variant and Currency. A Variant variable can contain almost any type of data, leaving it to Visual Basic to figure out the best way to store the data. In fact, Variant is the default Visual Basic data type. When you declare a variable with no data type, Visual Basic makes it a Variant. For example, the following lines both declare a variable of the Variant data type:

Literals and Data Types

Like a variable, a literal has a data type. The difference is that the data type is implicit. For example, 10 is an integer, 23.7564 is a single-precision real number, and "Alexander" is a string. You can tell what the data type is just by looking at the value, and so can Visual Basic.

```
Dim value1
Dim value2 As Variant
```

Keep in mind, however, that when you use Variant data types, Visual Basic has to do more work to figure out how it should handle the value. This causes Variant data types to use up more memory than something like an integer and also slows your program down a tiny bit. As a general rule, it's a good idea to avoid the Variant data type as much as you can.

The Currency data type is another floating-point type of number. A Currency value can hold values in the range of –922337203685477.5808 to 922337203685477.5807 (over 922 trillion). That's almost big enough to hold the value of Bill Gates' net worth!

Mixing Data Types

If you look back at the previous sample program, you might notice the following line:

```
totalValue = quantity * price
```

Here, Visual Basic multiplies a floating-point number, `price`, and an integer, `quantity`. Seems like the old case of apples and oranges, doesn't it? In a way, it is. You must be careful when mixing data types in expressions, to be sure you get the result you expect. The data type you'll end up with is the one on the left of the equals sign. In this case, the variable on the left of the equals sign, `totalValue`, is a single-precision floating-point number (the `Single` data type), so the result of the multiplication will be a single-precision floating-point number.

Unless the expression contains only integers, be especially careful when assigning results of a calculation to an integer. You could get an incorrect result. For example, the line

```
result = 13.5 * 3.3
```

makes `result` equal to 45, not 44.55 as you might expect. Why? The variable `result` is an integer, so it cannot hold a floating-point number like 44.55. When Visual Basic solves this expression, it first multiplies 13.5 times 3.3 to get the result of 44.55. Visual Basic then rounds this answer to the nearest integer, which is 45, because you've asked it to store the answer as an integer. Visual Basic assumes that you know what you're doing and gives you no warning of the conversion.

The Least You Need to Know

➤ Computer programming requires more logic than math. However, you can't avoid some mathematical operations in your programs.

➤ Variables can hold any value you assign to them, whereas literals never change. Because variables can change value in your programs, you can use them to represent numbers whose values you don't know ahead of time.

➤ You can perform all normal arithmetic operations with Visual Basic, including addition (+), subtraction (–), multiplication (*), and division (/). Other operations available are integer division (\), exponentiation (^), and modulus (Mod).

➤ When used in arithmetic expressions, the equals sign (=) acts as an assignment operator.

➤ All arithmetic expressions in Visual Basic follow the standard rules of operator precedence (order of operations).

➤ Variables and literals in a Visual Basic program can be one of many data types, including integer, long integer, single-precision floating-point, double-precision floating-point, and string.

Chapter 6

Strings and Text: A Frank Textual Discussion

In This Chapter

➤ Join strings together

➤ Calculate the length of a string

➤ Manipulate substrings

➤ Convert between strings and numbers

Pictures of bathing beauties (or well-oiled hunks) may be more fun to look at than a screen full of words and numbers; the simple truth, however, is that most information displayed on your computer screen is in text form. This fact separates computer users into two groups: those who would rather hang out at the beach, and those who understand that computers were designed to help humans deal with large amounts of information—information most often presented in text form.

Because text displays are so important in computing, Visual Basic has a number of functions and commands that manipulate text. These functions enable you to join two or more strings into one, find the length of a string, extract a small portion of a string, and convert numbers to strings or strings to numbers. In this chapter, you'll learn to use many of Visual Basic's string-handling functions. If you're still more interested in bathing beauties, shut down your computer and go back to the *Sports Illustrated* swimsuit issue. The rest of you, follow me.

Joining Strings

You'll often have two or more strings in your programs that you must combine into one. For example, you might have a user's first name and last name in two separate strings. In order to get the user's entire name into a single string, you have to concatenate (join together end-to-end) the two strings. Use Visual Basic's concatenation operator, which is the ampersand on your keyboard, to handle this string-handling task. To join three strings, for example, type the following:

```
string1 & string2 & string3
```

Simply joining the strings, however, is not a complete program statement; you also must tell Visual Basic where to store the new string. To do this, use Visual Basic's assignment operator, the equals sign (=). The assignment operator for strings works just like the assignment operator for numeric variables. For example, to make the string variable insult equal to the text string Your breath is strong enough to lift a horse, use the following command:

```
insult = "Your breath is strong enough to lift a horse"
```

To see how all this works, look at these lines:

```
Dim str1 As String
Dim str2 As String
Dim str3 As String
str1 = "This is "
str2 = "a test."
str3 = str1 & str2
Form1.Print str3
```

These lines first declare three string variables and assign strings to two of the variables, str1 and str2. Then, the sixth line joins the first two strings together and assigns the result to the third string variable, str3.

The Length of a String

Every string has a length, which is the number of characters contained in that string. For example, the string Why did the chicken cross the road? has a length of 35 because it contains 35 characters. (Spaces are characters, too.) The string Because the farmer was chasing him with a hatchet. has a length of 50. Theoretically, a string can have any length, from 0 to infinity. In Visual Basic, however, a string is much more conservative and can be any length from 0 to 32,767 characters.

Empty Strings

An empty string is a string that contains 0 characters. How can a string contain 0 characters? When you assign a string variable to an empty string, you get a string with a length of 0, as shown in the following example: string1 = "".

Notice that there are no characters between the quotation marks. This creates an empty string. At first, you might think creating an empty string makes about as much sense as drinking from an empty glass. But sometimes you might want to initialize a string variable this way so that you know the string contains no old data.

Sometimes in your program, you might need to know the length of a string. To find the length of a string variable, use Visual Basic's Len function, as in the following:

```
length = Len(string1)
```

Here, the function's single argument, string1, is the string for which you want the length. The Len function returns the length of the string as a numerical value that can be used anywhere you can use a numeric value.

What the heck is a function, anyway? A *function* is simply a command that performs a specific task and then sends a result (returns a value) back to your program. (The result returned from a function is called a *return value*.) For example, in the previous paragraph, you learned that Len is a function that calculates the number of characters in a string. After doing this calculation,

No Keywords for Names

Notice that the previous paragraph refers to a string variable called string1. Why is there a number after the name? The number is actually part of the variable's name, and is required because String is a Visual Basic keyword. Remember: You can't use Visual Basic keywords as variable names, so you must change (or add) at least one character to set the variable name apart from the keyword or function name. Please refer to Chapter 4, "Variables and I/O: A Programming Secret Revealed," if you need to review the rules of creating variable names.

A Functional Definition

A *function call* in Visual Basic consists of a function name followed by parentheses that contain the function's arguments. A function call always returns a single value (sends a value back to your program), which you usually store in a variable. For example, in the case of the Len function, the return value is the number of characters in the string used as the argument. In other words, when you use the Len function, the function sends the string's character count back to your program.

Len sends the number of characters back to you, so you can use it in your program. Usually, you assign a function's return value to a variable.

Visual Basic features two types of functions. The first type includes Visual Basic's built-in functions such as Len, Abs (absolute value), and Sqr (square root). Visual Basic boasts dozens of built-in functions that you can use in your programs. Visual Basic also lets you write your own functions, which usually comprise several program lines that perform a specific task. You'll learn about this second type of function in Chapter 13, "Procedures and Functions: Breaking Things Down."

To get a better idea of how the Len function works, try this: Start a new Visual Basic project, and place four Label controls, two TextBox controls, and one CommandButton control as shown here:

Position the controls as shown here.

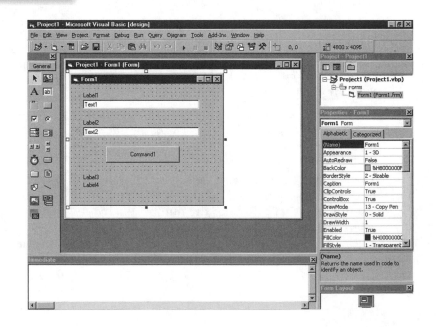

Double-click the Form object to display the code window, and then type the following lines. (Visual Basic will have already started the Form_Load procedure for you.)

```
Option Explicit

Private Sub Form_Load()
    Label1.Caption = "First name:"
    Label2.Caption = "Last name:"
    Label3.Caption = "Full name:"
    Label4.Caption = "Name length:"
    Command1.Caption = "Process Names"
    Text1.Text = ""
    Text2.Text = ""
End Sub

Private Sub Command1_Click()
    Dim firstName As String
    Dim lastName As String
    Dim fullName As String
    Dim nameLength As Integer
    firstName = Text1.Text
    lastName = Text2.Text
    fullName = firstName & " " & lastName
    nameLength = Len(fullName)
    Label3.Caption = "Full name: " & fullName
    Label4.Caption = "Name length: " & nameLength
End Sub
```

In the previous lines, the Option Explicit tells Visual Basic that all variables in the program must be declared before they're used. The Form_Load procedure sets the various controls' Caption and Text properties to the text the controls need to display. As you might remember, Visual Basic jumps to the Form_Load procedure the instant you run the program, so it's a good place to assign starting values to controls' properties. Finally, the Command1_Click procedure, which Visual Basic jumps to when the user clicks the button, performs the following actions:

➤ Declares the variables needed in the procedure

➤ Retrieves the names typed into the text boxes

➤ Joins the names together

➤ Uses the third and fourth Label controls' Caption properties to display the final name and the length of the name

Try the program yourself. Run the program, and then type a first name and last name into the appropriate boxes. Click the Process Names button, and the program displays the full name and the name's length, as shown in the following figure:

This program can count the number of characters in a name.

Extracting a Substring

Bits and Pieces

A substring is a portion of a larger string. For example, the string "mour Twit" is a substring of "Seymour Twitdum."

Just as you can join strings to create a larger string, so too can you separate strings into smaller strings called *substrings*. Visual Basic has several special string-handling functions that were created especially to extract whatever portion of a string you need. These string-handling functions are Left, Right, and Mid.

The Left function returns a specified number of characters in a string beginning with the leftmost, or first, character of the string. This is similar to what happens when the hatchet-wielding farmer catches up with his runaway chicken—except cutting a substring from another string is a lot less messy than separating a chicken from its head.

To use Left, you might type a command such as the following:

```
string2 = Left(string1, 7)
```

This function call has two arguments. The first argument is the string from which you want to extract a substring; the second argument is the number of characters, counting from the first character in the string, that you want to include in the substring. So, the previous example returns the first seven characters of the variable string1. If string1 was the phrase Yo ho ho and a bottle of rum, Left would return the string Yo ho h. The lines you might type to create and display the substring are as follows:

```
Dim string1 As String
Dim string2 As String
string1 = "Yo ho ho and a bottle of rum."
string2 = Left(string1, 7)
Form1.Print string2
```

The function `Right` returns a specified number of characters in a string starting from the rightmost, or last, character of the string. So, the statement

```
string2 = Right(string1, 7)
```

returns the last seven characters of the variable `string1`. If `string1` was the phrase `Visual Basic is way cool!`, the previous call to `Right` would return the string `y cool!`. Here are the lines that accomplish that task:

```
Dim string1 As String
Dim string2 As String
string1 = "Visual Basic is way cool!"
string2 = Right(string1, 7)
Form1.Print string2
```

Finally, the function `Mid`, which has two forms, allows you to extract text from any position in a string. In fact, you can use `Mid` to do anything you can do with the `Left` and `Right` functions—and much more. In other words, if you can remember only one string-handling function, `Mid` is the one to remember. If you can't remember even one string-handling function, forget Visual Basic and join the bikini-gazers at the beach.

In the first form of `Mid`, you supply as arguments the source string (the string from which you will cut your substring) and a starting position. The function then returns a substring consisting of all the characters from the starting position to the end of the string. One example is the following program line:

```
string2 = Mid(string1, 7)
```

In this case, if `string1` was `I'd rather be at the beach`, `string2` would be equal to `ther be at the beach` after the call to `Mid`. (The "t" in "rather" is the seventh character in `string1`.) Here's the complete example:

```
Dim string1 As String
Dim string2 As String
string1 = "I'd rather be at the beach"
string2 = Mid(string1, 7)
Form1.Print string2
```

In the second form of `Mid`, you supply as arguments the source string, a starting position, and the length of the substring you want. The function then returns a string composed of all the characters from the starting position up to the requested length. Assuming that `string1` still equals `I'd rather be at the beach`, the line

```
string2 = Mid(string1, 7, 4)
```

would make `string2` equal to `ther`.

To show how the Mid function can take the place of the Left or Right function, consider that the following two lines produce exactly the same result:

```
string2 = Left(string1, 8)
string2 = Mid(string1, 1, 8)
```

Likewise, the next two lines also produce the same result:

```
string2 = Right(string1, 8)
string2 = Mid(string1, Len(string1)-7)
```

To get a little practice with substrings, try this: Start a new Visual Basic project, and place four Label controls, one TextBox control, and one CommandButton control as shown here:

Position the controls as shown here.

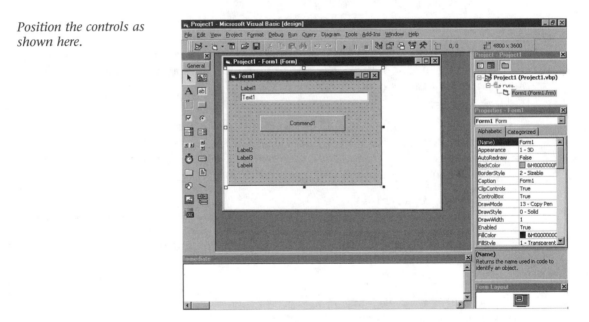

Double-click the Form object to display the code window, and type the following lines. (Visual Basic will have already started the Form_Load procedure for you.)

```
Option Explicit

Private Sub Form_Load()
    Label1.Caption = "Enter string:"
    Label2.Caption = ""
    Label3.Caption = ""
    Label4.Caption = ""
```

```
    Text1.Text = "This is a test."
    Command1.Caption = "Get Substrings"
End Sub

Private Sub Command1_Click()
    Dim string1 As String
    Dim string2 As String
    Dim string3 As String
    Dim string4 As String

    string1 = Text1.Text
    string2 = Left(string1, 5)
    string3 = Right(string1, 5)
    string4 = Mid(string1, 3, 5)

    Label2.Caption = "First five characters are " & _
        "'" & string2 & "'"
    Label3.Caption = "Last five characters are " & _
        "'" & string3 & "'"
    Label4.Caption = "Five characters in the middle are " & _
        "'" & string4 & "'"
End Sub
```

In the previous lines, the Option Explicit tells
Visual Basic that all variables in the program
must be declared before they're used. The
Form_Load procedure sets the various controls'
Caption and Text properties to the text the controls need to display. Finally, the
Command1_Click procedure, which Visual Basic
jumps to when the user clicks the button, performs the following actions:

➤ Declares the variables needed in the procedure

➤ Gets the string typed into the text box

➤ Calls the Left, Right, and Mid functions to
extract substrings from the string1 string

➤ Uses the remaining Label controls'
Caption properties to display the substrings

Dividing Long Program Lines

In the previous program listing, you
might notice the underscore character (_). The underscore tells Visual
Basic that the current program line
continues on the next line. By using
the underscore character (preceded
by a space character), you can
divide unusually long program lines
into smaller chunks.

Try the program yourself. Run the program, and then type some text into the text
box. Click the Get Substrings button, and the program displays the results, as shown
in the following figure:

This program can extract and display substrings.

Almost Foolproof Strings

When you run the previous program, try entering a string that's fewer than five characters. Because, in this program, the `Left` and `Right` string–handling functions assume a string length of at least five characters, and the function `Mid` assumes a string length of at least seven characters, you might expect the program to drop dead if you give it a string shorter than it expects.

But Visual Basic's string functions are smart little devils. If you give them values that don't make sense, they usually can still figure out how to handle the situation. For example, if the string you typed was `This`, the `string2`, `string3`, and `string4` substrings would be `This`, `This`, and `is`, respectively. Despite Visual Basic's clever-ness, you should watch out for this kind of error.

Finding Substrings

Now that you know how to extract a substring from a larger string, you might won-der how you can find the exact substring you want. Suppose, for example, you have a string containing a list of names, and you want to find the name Twitdum. The func-tion `InStr` (which stands for "in string") was created for just this task. (Well, actually, it was created to find any string, not just `Twitdum`.)

Like the function `Mid`, `InStr` has two forms. One form of `InStr` enables you to find the first occurrence of a substring by providing the function with the source string (the string to search through) as well as the substring for which to search. For exam-ple, the following line finds the position of the substring `Twitdum` in `string1`:

```
P = InStr(string1, "Twitdum")
```

When you find the position of the string, simply use Mid to extract the actual string. (If InStr cannot find the requested substring, it returns a value of 0.) In the above case of Twitdum, you would use Mid to extract the substring like this:

```
string2 = Mid(string1, P, 7)
```

After finding the first occurrence of a substring, you might want to search the rest of the string for another occurrence. After all, your name list might contain more than one Twitdum. (It's such a common name, after all.) To continue searching, you use the second form of the InStr function. This second form takes as arguments not only the string to search and the substring for which to search, but also the starting position of the search.

You could use the value returned in P to continue searching the string, as in the following:

```
P = InStr(P + 1, string1, "Twitdum")
```

Notice that the starting position, which is the function's first argument, is P + 1, not just P. If you used P, the function would find the same substring it just found. An error like this in your program can be very hard to detect.

The following program demonstrates how all this substring-search stuff works. To build the program, start a new Visual Basic project, double-click the form to display the code window, and then complete the Form_Load procedure like this:

```
Option Explicit

Private Sub Form_Load()
    Dim string1 As String
    Dim string2 As String
    Dim msg As String
    Dim position As Integer

    string1 = "SmithTwitdumFreemanTwitdumRothTwitdum"
    position = InStr(string1, "Twitdum")
    string2 = Mid(string1, position, 7)
    msg = "The first occurrence of " & "'" & string2 & "'"
    msg = msg & " is at position " & position
    msg = msg & vbCrLf & vbCrLf

    position = InStr(position + 1, string1, "Twitdum")
    string2 = Mid(string1, position, 7)
    msg = msg & "The second occurrence of " & _
        "'" & string2 & "'"
```

```
        msg = msg & " is at position " & position
        msg = msg & vbCrLf & vbCrLf

        position = InStr(position + 1, string1, "Twitdum")
        msg = msg & "The third occurrence of " & _
            "'" & string2 & "'"
        msg = msg & " is at position " & position
        MsgBox msg

    End
End Sub
```

This program requires no input. Just run it and compare the message shown in the message box with the program listing. (Click the message box's OK button to close the message box and end the program.) The following figure shows the message box the program displays:

A message box displays the results of all the fancy string handling.

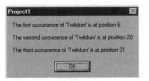

A few things about this program might have you scratching your head (no, you don't have lice), so it might be a good idea to go through it a little at a time. First, the following lines declare the variables used in the procedure:

```
Dim string1 As String
Dim string2 As String
Dim msg As String
Dim position As Integer
```

The next line in the program sets the source-string variable to its starting value:

```
string1 = "SmithTwitdumFreemanTwitdumRothTwitdum"
```

With the source-string variable ready to go, the program can call the InStr function to look for the first occurrence of the name Twitdum, like this:

```
position = InStr(string1, "Twitdum")
```

Next, the program assigns the located substring to the string2 variable by using, as one of the Mid function's arguments, the position value returned by the InStr function:

```
string2 = Mid(string1, position, 7)
```

The next three lines start building the message that the program will display in its message box:

```
msg = "The first occurrence of " & "'" & string2 & "'"
msg = msg & " is at position " & position
msg = msg & vbCrLf & vbCrLf
```

There's some curious stuff going on in these lines. First, notice how the program can build a long string message by continually adding text to the msg string. This technique is similar to the way you learned to add values to a integer value with a line like this:

```
value = value + 1
```

Also, see the two instances of vbCrLf? You might be wondering what language that is. The value vbCrLf is a symbol that Visual Basic uses to represent two special characters, a carriage-return and a linefeed. To put it simply, when you add this symbol to a string, you're starting a new line. By using two of these symbols, the program starts a new line twice, which puts a blank line after the preceding text string.

Getting back to the program, most of the rest of the procedure finds the next two occurrences of the name Twitdum and continues to build the msg string, which will be displayed in the message box.

And speaking of message boxes, the following line, found near the end of the procedure, is where the program displays the message box:

```
MsgBox msg
```

As you can see, to display a message in a message box, all you need to do is to type the MsgBox command followed by the string you want to display.

Finally, the procedure ends appropriately enough with the End command:

```
End
```

This one word is all you need to end the program. Because the End command terminates the program inside the Form_Load procedure, the form never even appears on the screen. From the user's point of view, the program does nothing more than display a message box and then end.

Passing Strings to MsgBox

As you've learned, the MsgBox statement can display a line of text (and other types of data). In the previous example, the line of text was stored in a variable called msg. However, if the line of text you want to display is a string literal, rather than the contents of a variable, don't forget that you need to enclose the string in quotes, like this: MsgBox "This is your text."

Changing Case

As you know, alphabetic characters in Visual Basic can be typed either in uppercase or lowercase letters. Sometimes, you might want your strings to be displayed all in one case or the other. To change all characters in a string to either uppercase or lowercase, use Visual Basicís handy UCase (which stands for "uppercase") and LCase (which stands for "lowercase") functions.

There's not a heck of a lot to say about these functions; they just do what they do. For example, look at these lines:

```
Dim myString As String
Dim lcString As String
Dim upString As String
myString = "This Is a Test"
lcString = LCase(myString)
ucString = UCase(myString)
```

After Visual Basic executes these commands, the lcString variable will contain the string this is a test and the ucString variable will contain the string THIS IS A TEST. 'Nuff said?

Converting Numbers to Strings

You probably remember that there's a big difference between numerical values and text strings, even if the text string contains numeric characters. Numerical values, such as the number 5 or the integer variable number, can be used in mathematical operations. Strings, however, cannot. Luckily, Visual Basic includes a handy function, Val (which stands for "value"), that lets you convert number strings into numerical values that can be used in mathematical operations. You can also change numerical values into strings with the Str function—something you might want to do with the result of a calculation. (Str stands for "string.")

To convert a number string into a numerical value, use the Val function like this:

```
number = Val(string1)
```

The variable string1 is the string you want to convert to a numerical value. Keep in mind that Val can convert only string characters that represent numbers: digits, decimal points, and minus signs. The following statement makes number equal to 3.4:

```
number = Val("3.4Apples")
```

In this example, because the characters that compose the word "Apples" are not numerical characters, Val can do nothing with them and ignores them. If Val cannot convert the string at all, as in the case of number = Val("Apples"), it returns a value of 0.

You should also know that Val ignores spaces in strings, and that it understands number strings in scientific notation form. The following table shows a summary of the results of the Val function when it is used with different strings. (If you don't know about scientific notation, don't worry. Just be aware that the last example in the table shows a string using this number form.)

Function Call	Result
Val("34")	34
Val("56.23")	56.23
Val("23.6&HYG")	23.6
Val("2 3 4")	234
Val("-76")	-76
Val("764,345")	764
Val("0")	0
Val("SJuHGd")	0
Val("HFGYR345")	0
Val("nine")	0
Val("3.4D+4")	34000

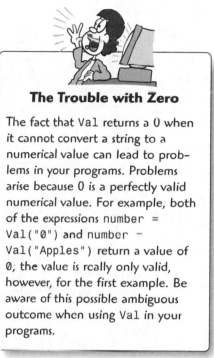

The Trouble with Zero

The fact that Val returns a 0 when it cannot convert a string to a numerical value can lead to problems in your programs. Problems arise because 0 is a perfectly valid numerical value. For example, both of the expressions number = Val("0") and number = Val("Apples") return a value of 0; the value is really only valid, however, for the first example. Be aware of this possible ambiguous outcome when using Val in your programs.

Converting strings to numerical values is only half the story. You might also need to go the other way and convert a numerical variable into a string. You might, for example, want to convert a numerical value to a string so you can add it to a text document. You can do this conversion by calling the Str function, which looks like this:

```
string1 = Str(number)
```

Here, number is the numerical value you want to change into string form. For example, the program statement

```
string1 = Str(34.45)
```

makes string1 equal to the string 34.45.

Spacing Out

When the function Str converts a numerical value into a string, it always reserves a space for the value's sign. Strings created from positive numbers always have a leading space, and strings created from negative numbers always begin with a minus sign.

Now that you know all about Val and Str, I'll let you in on a little secret. Visual Basic is smart enough to do many conversions for you automatically. For example, the following two lines produce the same result, except that the second line doesn't add the leading space to myString:

```
myString = Str(100)
myString = 100
```

These lines also do exactly the same thing, making the integer variable value equal to 35:

```
value = 35
value = "35"
```

The Least You Need to Know

➤ You can use the ampersand operator (&) to join strings together. This process is called concatenation.

➤ The equals sign (=) can be used with strings just as it is used with numerical values. Specifically, you use the assignment operator to set a string variable to a specific string value.

➤ The length of a string is the number of characters contained in the string. An empty string contains no characters and so has a length of 0.

➤ The Len function returns, as a numerical value, the length of a string.

➤ A substring is a portion of a larger string.

➤ The functions Left, Right, and Mid enable a program to extract substrings from other strings.

➤ The function InStr returns the position of a substring within a string.

➤ You can use the functions LCase and UCase to convert strings to lowercase and uppercase, respectively.

➤ The function Val converts number strings to numerical values. The function Str does the opposite, converting numerical values to strings.

Chapter 7

If, Then, and Else: Decisions, Decisions, Decisions

In This Chapter

➤ Use branching to change program flow

➤ Learn about If, Else, and ElseIf

➤ Discover relational operators

➤ Work with logical operators

In previous chapters, you learned much about the way Visual Basic works. You now know how to type programs, how to input and output data, how to perform mathematical operations, and how to handle strings. But these techniques are merely the building blocks of a program. To use these building blocks in a useful way, you have to understand how computers make decisions.

In this chapter, you learn how your programs can analyze data in order to decide what parts of your program to execute. Until now, your programs have executed their statements mostly in sequential order, starting with the first line and working, line by line, to the end of the program. Now it's time to learn how you can control your program's flow—the order in which the statements are executed—so that you can do different things based on the data your program receives.

If the idea of computers making decisions based on data seems a little strange, think about how you make decisions. For example, suppose you're expecting an important letter. You go out to your mailbox and look inside. Then you choose one of the following two actions:

➤ If there's mail in the mailbox, you take it into the house.

➤ If there's no mail in the mailbox, you complain about the postal system.

In either case, you've made a decision based on whether or not there is mail in the mailbox.

Computers use this same method to make decisions (except that they never complain, and they don't give a darn how late your mail is). You will see the word "if" used frequently in computer programs. Just as you might say to yourself, "If the mail is in the mailbox, I'll bring it in," so a computer uses "if" to decide what action to take.

Program Flow and Branching

Program flow is the order in which a program executes its code. Your programs so far in this book have had sequential program flow. Truth is, almost all program code executes sequentially. However, virtually every program reaches a point where a decision must be made about a piece of data. The program must then analyze the data, decide what to do about it, and jump to the appropriate section of code. This decision-making process is as important to computer programming as pollen is to a bee. Virtually no useful programs can be written without it.

When a program breaks the sequential flow and jumps to a new section of code, it is called *branching*. When this branching is based on a decision, the program is performing *conditional branching*. When no decision-making is involved and the program always branches when it encounters a branching instruction, the program is performing *unconditional branching*.

To continue with the mailbox example, suppose you went out to the mailbox and found your mail, but decided to complain about the Post Office anyway. Because the poor mail carrier was destined to be the focus of your wrath whether or not the mail was delivered on time, your complaining is unconditional. No matter what, after going to the mailbox, you complain.

The If/Then Statement

Most conditional branching occurs when the program executes an If/Then statement, which compares data and decides what to do next based on the result of the comparison. If the comparison works out one way, the program performs the statement following the Then keyword. Otherwise, the program does nothing and drops to the next program line. This gives each comparison two possible outcomes.

For example, in older DOS programs, you've probably seen programs that print menus on the screen. To select a menu item, you often type its selection number. When the program receives your input, it checks the number you entered and decides what to do.

To see what I mean, try this: Start a new Visual Basic project (a Standard EXE), and then place a Label control, a TextBox control, and a CommandButton control on the form, as shown here:

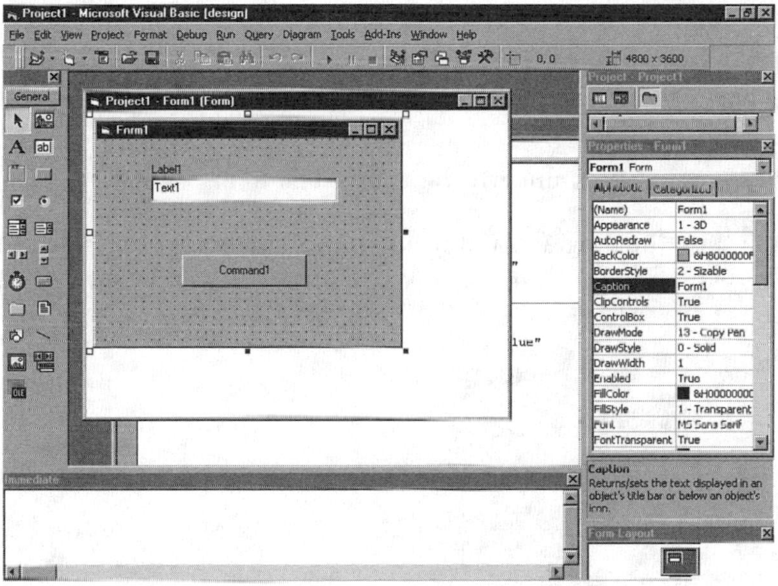

Position the controls on your form as shown here.

Now, double-click the form to display the code window, and type the following lines. (Visual Basic will have already started the Form_Load procedure for you.)

```
Option Explicit

Private Sub Form_Load()
    Label1.Caption = "1 = Red, 2 = Green, 3 = Blue"
    Text1.Text = ""
    Command1.Caption = "Process Selection"
End Sub

Private Sub Command1_Click()
    Dim choice As Integer
    Dim entry As String

    entry = Text1.Text
    choice = Val(entry)
```

```
        If choice = 1 Then MsgBox "You chose red."
        If choice = 2 Then MsgBox "You chose green."
        If choice = 3 Then MsgBox "You chose blue."
    End Sub
```

In these lines, `Option Explicit` tells Visual Basic that all variables in the program must be declared before they're used. The `Form_Load` procedure sets the various controls' `Caption` and `Text` properties to the text the controls need to display. Finally, the `Command1_Click` procedure, which Visual Basic jumps to when the user clicks the button, performs the following actions:

➤ Declares the variables needed in the procedure

➤ Retrieves the text typed into the text box

➤ Converts the text value to an integer

➤ Uses `If`/`Then` statements to determine which message box to display

Try the program yourself. Run the program, and then type a value from 1 to 3 into the text box. Click the Process Selection button, and the program displays a message box that tells you the color you selected, as shown in the following figure:

This program shows how a program can make decisions.

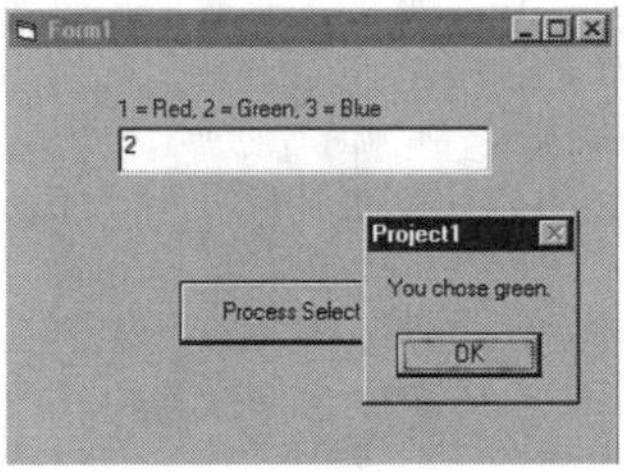

One thing to notice about this program is what happens if you type a value other than a number from 1 to 3. If you type anything else (including non-numerical characters), no message box appears because the variable `choice` will not contain one of the three values the program checks for in the `If`/`Then` statements. This causes the program to skip over all the `If`/`Then` statements and jump to the end of the procedure.

As you now know, the preceding program shows a menu and lets you enter a menu selection. The program then uses a series of `If`/`Then` statements to compare the value you entered with the acceptable menu choices. See the equals signs in the `If`/`Then` statements? These are not assignment operators; they are relational operators, which enable the program to compare two or more values. Look at the first `If`/`Then` statement in the program:

```
    If choice = 1 Then MsgBox "You chose red."
```

If this line were written in English, it would read "If the value of the variable choice equals 1, then show You chose red." The other If/Then statements in the program have similar meanings.

A simple If/Then statement includes the keyword If followed by a Boolean expression. You follow the Boolean expression with the keyword Then and, finally, with the statement that you want executed if the Boolean expression is true.

As I said, a Boolean expression is an expression that evaluates to either true or false. For example, the expression 3 + 4 = 7 is true, whereas the expression 6 + 1 = 9 is false. A Boolean expression usually compares a variable to a constant or to another variable, such as num + 1 = 7 or num1 – 10 = num2.

How do If/Then statements work? Let's say that when you run the previous program, you type the value 1 into the text box. When the program gets to the first If/Then statement, it checks the value of choice. If choice equals 1 (which it does, in this case), the program shows the message You chose red. and then drops down to the next If/Then statement. This time,

About Relational Operators

Relational operators such as the equals sign enable you to compare two pieces of data. By comparing variables to literals, for example, you can check variables for specific values. The most common relational operator is the equals sign, which checks whether two expressions are equal. However, there are also relational operators for such relationships as less than, greater than, and not equal. (You'll see these operators later in this chapter.) When you use relational operators to compare two values, you are writing a Boolean expression, which is an expression that is either true or false.

the program compares the value of choice with the number 2. Because choice doesn't equal 2, the program ignores the Then part of the statement and drops down to the next program line, which is another If/Then statement. The variable choice doesn't equal 3 either, so the program ignores the Then portion of the third If/Then statement.

Suppose you enter the number 2 into the text box. When the program gets to the first If/Then statement, it discovers that choice is not equal to 1, so it ignores the Then part of the statement and drops down to the next program line, which is the second If/Then statement. Again, the program checks the value of choice. Because choice equals 2, the program can execute the Then portion of the statement; the message You chose green. appears. Program execution drops down to the third If/Then statement, which does nothing because choice doesn't equal 3.

Multi-Line If/Then Statements

The previous program demonstrated the simplest If/Then statement. This simple statement usually fits your program's decision-making needs just fine. Sometimes, however, you want to perform more than one command as part of an If/Then statement. To perform more than one command, press Enter after Then, write the commands you want to add to the If/Then statement, and end the block of commands with the End If keywords. Here's a revised version of the Command1_Click procedure from the previous program that uses multi-line If/Then statements:

The Value of the Truth

The conditional expression in an If/Then statement, no matter how complex, always evaluates to either true or false. True and false are actual values: true equals any non-zero value, and false equals 0. Consequently, the statement If 1 Then Form1.Print "True!" prints the message True!; but the statement If 0 Then Form1.Print "False!" does nothing. In the first statement, the value 1 is considered true, so the program executes the Then part of the statement. In the second statement, the 0 is considered false, so the program ignores the Then portion of the statement.

```
Private Sub Command1_Click()
    Dim choice As Integer
    Dim entry As String

    entry = Text1.Text
    choice = Val(entry)

    If choice = 1 Then
        MsgBox "You chose red."
        Form1.BackColor = vbRed
    End If

    If choice = 2 Then
        MsgBox "You chose green."
        Form1.BackColor = vbGreen
    End If

    If choice = 3 Then
        MsgBox "You chose blue."
        Form1.BackColor = vbBlue
    End If
End Sub
```

This version of the Command1_Click procedure is similar to the previous one. The primary difference is that the program not only displays the message box, but also changes the form's background color to the selected color. The three If/Then statements compare the user's selection with the possible choices. When an If/Then statement's conditional expression evaluates to true, the program executes the lines between the If and the next End If.

What's happening in this version of the
`Command1_Click` procedure? Suppose you run
the program and enter the number 2. When the
program gets to the first If/Then statement, it
compares the value of choice with the number
1. Because these values don't match (or, as programmers say, the statement doesn't evaluate to
true), the program skips over every program
line until it finds an End If statement, which
marks the end of the block of code that goes
with the If.

This brings the program to the second If/Then
statement. When the program evaluates the
conditional expression, it finds that choice
equals 2, and it executes the Then portion of the
If/Then statement. This time the Then portion
is not just one command, but two. The program
displays a message box and, after the user dismisses the message box, changes the form's
background color to green (the color selected
from the menu). Finally, the program reaches
End If, which marks the end of the If/Then statement.

This brings the program to the last If/Then
statement, which the program skips over
because choice doesn't equal 3.

You might think it's a waste of time for the program to evaluate other If/Then statements after
it finds a match for the menu item you chose.
You'd be right, too. When you write programs,
you should always look for ways to make them
run faster; one way to make a program run
faster is to avoid all unnecessary processing. But
how, you might ask, do you avoid unnecessary
processing when you have to compare a variable with more than one value?

One way to keep processing to a minimum is to
use Visual Basic's ElseIf clause. Before you

Indenting for Easy Reading

Notice that some program lines in
the most recent Command1_Click
procedure are indented. By indenting the lines that go with each If
block, you can more easily see the
structure of your program. The
procedure also uses blank lines to
separate blocks of code that go
together. The computer doesn't care
about the indenting or the blank
lines, but these features make your
programs easier for you, or another
programmer, to read.

One After the Other

In the sample program, a message
box appears when the user selects a
color choice. The window's background color doesn't change until
the message box is dismissed because
the message box statement comes
before the statement that changes
the background color. A program's
execution can't continue after a
message box appears until the user
dismisses the message box.

learn about ElseIf, however, let's look at the simpler version, Else. This keyword enables you to use a single If/Then statement to choose between two outcomes. When the If/Then statement evaluates to true, the program executes the Then part of the statement. When the If/Then statement evaluates to false, the program executes the Else portion. When the If/Else statement evaluates to neither true nor false, it's time to get a new computer! Following is a program that demonstrates how Else works. Just replace the program lines you already typed with these:

Visual Basic Colors

You've probably figured out by now that BackColor is the property of the Form object that determines the form's background color. By setting this property's value, the program changes the window's color. The vbRed, vbGreen, and vbBlue values are color values that Visual Basic has already defined for you. Other color values include vbBlack, vbYellow, vbMagenta, vbCyan, and vbWhite.

```
Option Explicit

Private Sub Form_Load()
    Label1.Caption = "Enter name:"
    Text1.Text = ""
    Command1.Caption = "Process Selection"
End Sub

Private Sub Command1_Click()
    Dim name As String

    name = Text1.Text

    If name = "Fred" Then
        MsgBox "Hi, Fred!"
    Else
        MsgBox "Hello, stranger!"
    End If
End Sub
```

In these lines, Option Explicit tells Visual Basic that all variables in the program must be declared before they're used. The Form_Load procedure sets the various controls' Caption and Text properties to the text the controls need to display. Finally, the Command1_Click procedure, which Visual Basic jumps to when the user clicks the button, performs the following actions:

➤ Declares the variable needed in the procedure

➤ Retrieves the text typed into the text box

➤ Uses an If/Then/Else statement to determine which message box to display

Run the program, and then type a name into the text box. Click the Process Selection button. If you typed **Fred**, the program gives you a personalized greeting, as shown in the following figure; otherwise, the program displays the message Hello, stranger!.

This program recognizes the name Fred.

As you can see, the program executes the Else clause only when the If/Then statement is false. If the If/Then statement is true, the program ignores the Else clause.

This program also demonstrates how to compare strings. Strings are compared just as numerical values are: by using the equals sign, which, in the case of an If/Then statement, is a relational operator. You will compare strings often in your programs, especially programs that require text input from the user. By using string comparisons, you can catch an incorrect response to a prompt and display an error message to inform the user of the incorrect entry.

Simply, Else provides a default outcome for an If/Then statement. A default outcome doesn't help much, however, in an If/Then statement that must associate program code with more than two possible outcomes. Suppose you want the program to recognize your friends' names, too. No problem. First, get some friends; then use Visual Basic's ElseIf keyword, as shown here:

```
Private Sub Command1_Click()
    Dim name As String

    name = Text1.Text
    name = UCase(name)

    If name = "FRED" Then
        MsgBox "Hi, Fred!"
    ElseIf name = "SARAH" Then
        MsgBox "How's it going, Sarah?"
    ElseIf name = "TONY" Then
        MsgBox "Hey! It's my man Tony!"
    Else
        MsgBox "Hello, stranger."
    End If
End Sub
```

This version of the Command1_Click procedure retrieves the user's name from the text box, and then changes the name to all uppercase letters. Next, the If/Then statement checks for the name "FRED". If the user entered **FRED**, the program prints Fred's message. Otherwise, the ElseIf clauses check for other names and print an appropriate message if a match is found. If none of the names match the user's input, the program executes the Else clause, displaying a generic message in the message box.

Here is a new Command1_Click procedure for the color menu program, one that uses ElseIf and Else clauses. You should now know enough about computer decision-making to figure out how it works:

```
Private Sub Command1_Click()
    Dim choice As Integer
    Dim entry As String

    entry = Text1.Text
    choice = Val(entry)

    If choice = 1 Then
        MsgBox "You chose red."
        Form1.BackColor = vbRed
    ElseIf choice = 2 Then
        MsgBox "You chose green."
        Form1.BackColor = vbGreen
    ElseIf choice = 3 Then
        MsgBox "You chose blue."
        Form1.BackColor = vbBlue
    Else
        MsgBox "Invalid selection."
    End If
End Sub
```

Helping the User

When you need to get string input from the user, it's often a good idea to change the input to all upper- or lowercase. This enables the program to recognize a word no matter the case in which the user types it. For example, in the new Command1_Click procedure, the program converts the user's input to uppercase before comparing it to the names in the If and ElseIf clauses. With this method, Fred can type his name any way he likes: **Fred**, **fred**, **FRED**, or even **fRed**. One of your goals as a programmer should be to make your programs as easy to use as possible. Allowing the user to enter a string in any form is one way to do this.

Relational Operators

The previous programs in this chapter used only the equals operator to compare values. Often you'll need to compare values in other ways. You might, for example, want to know if a value is less than or greater than another value. Visual Basic features an entire set of relational operators you can use in If/Then statements and other types of comparisons. These operators include not only the equals sign (=), but also not equal to (<>), less than (<), greater than (>), less than or equal (<=), and greater than or equal (>=). The relational operators are summarized in the following table:

Operator	Meaning	Examples
=	Equals	3=(4-1) or "FRED"="FRED"
<>	Not equal	5<>(3+3) or "FRED"<>"SAM"
<	Less than	3<23 or "A"<"B"
>	Greater than	41>39 or "BART">"ADAM"
<=	Less than or equal	5<=6 or "ONE"<="ONE"
>=	Greater than or equal	10>=10 or "TWO">="THREE"

To see how relational operators are used, load your last Visual Basic program from this chapter and replace all the code in the code window with the following lines:

```
Option Explicit

Private Sub Form_Load()
    Label1.Caption = "Enter a number no larger than 50: "
    Text1.Text = ""
    Command1.Caption = "Process Selection"
End Sub

Private Sub Command1_Click()
    Dim Number As Integer
    Dim entry As String

    entry = Text1.Text
    Number = Val(entry)

    If Number < 10 Then
        MsgBox "Less than 10."
    ElseIf Number < 20 Then
        MsgBox "Greater than 9 and less than 20."
    ElseIf Number < 30 Then
        MsgBox "Greater than 19 and less than 30."
    ElseIf Number < 40 Then
        MsgBox "Greater than 29 and less than 40."
    ElseIf Number < 50 Then
        MsgBox "Greater than 39 and less than 50."
    ElseIf Number = 50 Then
```

```
            MsgBox "Your number is 50."
        Else
            MsgBox "Out of the acceptable range."
        End If
    End Sub
```

This program asks the user to enter a number no greater than 50. After the user types the number, the program uses an `If/Then` statement with a series of `ElseIf` clauses to determine the range within which the number falls. For this determination, the program uses the less-than operator (<). If the selected number is less than the specified numerical literal in the `If` or `ElseIf` clauses, the program prints an appropriate message to the user. If the number is larger than the specified literal, the program moves on to the next clause and again makes the comparison, this time with a higher numerical literal. Finally, if the number turns out to be larger than the allowed maximum of 50, the program prints an error message.

Go ahead and run the program, and type a value into the text box. After you type the number, the program determines the number's range and prints a message informing you of this range, as shown here:

This program can analyze and report on the values you enter.

This program doesn't just demonstrate the use of the less-than operator; it keeps you off the streets by having you do a lot of typing! More important, though, the program further illustrates the way a block of `If` and `ElseIf` clauses works.

Suppose when you run the program, you type the number 9. When the program gets to the `If` clause, it compares 9 to 10 and discovers that 9 is less than 10. (And to think you paid hundreds of dollars for a machine to tell you that.) The `If` clause then evaluates to true, and the program prints the message `Less than 10`.

Look at the block of `ElseIf`'s that go along with the `If`. Isn't 9 also less than 20? Moreover, isn't 9 also less than 30, 40, and 50? Why then, when you enter the number 9, don't you also see the messages associated with all of these `ElseIf`'s, as well as the message associated with the `If`? And why, when you drop a piece of buttered bread, does it always land butter-side down? (Just thought I'd ask.)

The answer to the first question has to do with the way the If/ElseIf block works. (The answer to the second question is beyond today's science, so we'll just ignore it.) Once an If or ElseIf evaluates to true, the program skips the rest of the statements in the block—or, as programmers say, the program branches to the next statement after the block. In the case of your new program, there is no statement after the block so the program simply exits the procedure.

Logical Operators

A single comparison in an If/Then statement often isn't enough to determine whether data matches your criteria. How can you be sure, for example, that the user enters a number within a specific range? You could hold a gun to the user's head as he's typing the data. Although this might ensure that data is entered properly, it requires that you stay by the computer at all times. Hardly practical. A better way to ensure that data is in the correct range is to use logical operators in your If/Then statements.

Let's say your program asks the user to enter a number between 0 and 50, inclusive. To discover whether a number is within this range, you must check not only that the number is greater than or equal to 0, but also that the number is less than or equal to 50. To help handle these situations, Visual Basic features four logical operators—And, Or, Xor, and Not—that can be used to combine expressions in an If statement.

The And operator requires all expressions to be true in order for the entire expression to be true. For example, the expression

```
(3 + 2 = 5) And (6 + 2 = 8)
```

is true because the expressions on both sides of the And are true. However, the expression

```
(4 + 3 = 9) And (3 + 3 = 6)
```

Relational Operators and Strings

When using relational operators with strings, the value of each letter in a string is relative to its alphabetic order. In other words, the letter "A" is less than the letter "B," the letter "B" is less than the letter "C," and so on. When comparing lowercase letters and uppercase letters, however, the lowercase letters have a greater value than their uppercase counterparts. Therefore, "a" is greater than "A," and "b" is greater than "B," but "c" is greater than "b." Finally, just as when you organize words into alphabetical order, when a program compares strings, the letters on the left have greater significance than those on the right. For example, Mick is less than Mike to Visual Basic.

Where's the Logic?

The logical operators And, Or, Xor, and Not are called logical operators because they use computer logic to join two or more Boolean expressions into a larger Boolean expression. (Remember: Boolean expressions always evaluate to true or false.)

is false, because the expression on the left of the And is false. Remember this when combining expressions with And: If any expression is false, the entire expression is false.

The Or operator requires only one expression to be true in order for the entire expression to be true. For example, the expressions

```
(3 + 6 = 2) Or (4 + 4 = 8)
```

and

```
(4 + 1 = 5) Or (7 + 2 = 9)
```

are both true because at least one of the expressions being compared is true. Note that in the second case both expressions being compared are true, which also makes an Or expression true.

The Xor (exclusive Or) operator requires one and only one expression to be true in order for the entire expression to be true. For example, the expression

```
(3 + 6 = 2) Xor (4 + 4 = 8)
```

is true because only the (4 + 4 = 8) expression is true. The expression

```
(4 + 1 = 5) Xor (7 + 2 = 9)
```

however is false, because both expressions are true. (Confused yet?)

The Not operator reverses (or negates) the value of a logical expression. For example, the expression

```
(4 + 3 = 5)
```

is not true; however, the expression

```
Not (4 + 3 = 5)
```

is true because the Not operator reverses the (4 + 3 = 5) expression's false outcome to true.

Take a look at the following expression:

```
(4 + 5 = 9) And Not (3 + 1 = 3)
```

Is this expression true or false? If you said true, you understand the way the logical operators work. The expressions on either side of the And are both true, so the entire expression is true. The following table summarizes how you use the logical operators:

Operator	Meaning
And	True if both sides of the expression are true
Or	True if one or both sides of the expression are true
Xor	True if only one side of the expression is true
Not	Reverses true to false and vice versa

Of course, you wouldn't write expressions like

```
(4 + 5 = 9) And Not (3 + 1 = 3)
```

in your programs. They would serve no purpose because you already know how the expressions evaluate. However, when you use variables, you have no way of knowing in advance how an expression may evaluate. For example, is the expression

```
(num < 9) And (num > 2)
```

true or false? You don't know without being told the value of the numerical variable num. By using these logical operators in your If/Then statements, though, your program can do the evaluation, and, based on the result—true or false—take the appropriate action.

The following new Command1_Click procedure demonstrates how logical operators work. In your Visual Basic program, replace the old procedure with the new one:

```
Private Sub Command1_Click()
    Dim Number As Integer
    Dim entry As String

    entry = Text1.Text
    Number = Val(entry)

    If (Number < 0) Or (Number > 50) Then
        MsgBox "The number " & Number & " is out of range!"
    Else
        MsgBox "The number " & Number & " is in range."
    End If
End Sub
```

When you run the program, it asks you to enter a number between 0 and 50. (Well, actually, it still asks for a number no greater than 50, but we'll let that little technicality go by.) If you type a number that is out of that range, the program lets you know. Although this version of the Command1_Click procedure is similar to the previous one, it works very differently. After the user types a number, the program uses a single If/Then statement to determine whether the number is within the acceptable range. If the number is out of range, the program prints an error message, as shown here:

This program reports all invalid entries.

The Infamous GoTo

Most of this chapter has been dedicated to conditional branches. If you recall, however, programmers can also use unconditional branches. This type of branching can be accomplished by using the GoTo instruction, which forces program execution to branch to a specific line number or label. Because line numbers in BASIC programs are now obsolete, you don't have to worry about how to use them—you'll probably never need them. You may, however, want to use labels.

Here's a new Command1_Click procedure that demonstrates the GoTo command:

```
Private Sub Command1_Click()
    Dim Number As Integer
    Dim entry As String

    entry = Text1.Text
    Number = Val(entry)

    If Number <= 100 Then GoTo lessthan
    MsgBox "Your number is greater than 100."
    End

lessthan:
  MsgBox "Your number is less than or equal to 100."
End Sub
```

This procedure uses the GoTo instruction to branch to a specific place in the program. The destination of the branch is marked by the label lessthan.

In this procedure, after getting a number from the user, the If/Then statement checks whether the number is less than or equal to 100. If it is, the program executes the Then portion of the statement, which is a GoTo statement. GoTo sends program execution to the label lessthan, at which point the program prints an appropriate message. If the number the user enters is greater than 100, the If/Then statement's conditional expression evaluates to false. In this case, program execution drops down to the next line, the program displays a message, and the End statement ends the program.

In this program, notice that when the label's name follows the GoTo, it doesn't include a colon; however, the actual label in the program does include a colon.

Go Where?

Although the GoTo statement might seem like a handy thing to have around, programmers have misused it so much in the past that most avoid it like nuclear waste. Overuse of GoTo can turn a program into a tangled, unreadable mess. A modern, structured language like Visual Basic has little need for the GoTo instruction. In fact, GoTo is usually used only for handling errors, which you'll learn about in Chapter 15, "The Art of Bug Extermination: Raid for the New Millennium."

The Least You Need to Know

➤ Program flow is the order in which a program executes its statements.

➤ When a computer program branches, it jumps to a new location in the code and continues execution from there.

➤ An If/Then statement compares the values of data and decides what statements to execute based on that evaluation.

➤ The Else and ElseIf clauses allow If/Then statements to handle many different outcomes.

➤ The End If keywords mark the end of a multi-line If/Then statement, including multi-line statements with ElseIf and Else clauses.

➤ The relational operators, equals (=), does not equal (<>), less than (<), greater than (>), less than or equal (<=), and greater than or equal (>=), enable programs to compare data in various ways.

➤ Logical operators (And, Or, Xor, and Not) enable an If/Then statement to evaluate more than one expression, yet they still resolve the expressions to a single true or false.

Chapter 8

EENIE, MEENIE
MINY, MO...

Select Case:
Another Way to
Decide

In This Chapter

➤ Replace If/Then statements with Select Case statements

➤ Use a Select Case statement to make decisions based on the value of variables of most data types

➤ Discover the Is keyword for examining a variable for a range of values

---

Thanks to the If/Then statements you just learned, your computer programs can now make decisions. Go ahead and ask your computer to decide between the fish tie and the *Simpsons* tie. Nothing happened? That could be because the computer doesn't care for your taste in ties, or, more likely, it's because a computer doesn't usually make those kinds of decisions (which isn't saying that a computer can't, given the right programming). Computer programs usually make much simpler decisions, and another way they can make such decisions is with the Select Case statement.

Introducing Select Case

The If/Then statement is only one way a computer can make decisions. Using a Select Case statement gives the same results. The best way to learn how to use a

Select Case statement is to compare it to an If/Then statement. For example, in the previous chapter, you wrote a Command1_Click procedure that looks like this:

```
Private Sub Command1_Click()
    Dim name As String

    name = Text1.Text
    name = UCase(name)

    If name = "FRED" Then
        MsgBox "Hi, Fred!"
    ElseIf name = "SARAH" Then
        MsgBox "How's it going, Sarah?"
    ElseIf name = "TONY" Then
        MsgBox "Hey! It's my man Tony!"
    Else
        MsgBox "Hello, stranger."
    End If
End Sub
```

You can rewrite this procedure using a Select Case statement, and get rid of all those Ifs, Thens, ElseIfs, and Elses. Such a procedure might look like this:

```
Private Sub Command1_Click()
    Dim name As String

    name = Text1.Text
    name = UCase(name)

    Select Case name
        Case "FRED"
            MsgBox "Hi, Fred!"
        Case "SARAH"
            MsgBox "How's it going, Sarah?"
        Case "TONY"
            MsgBox "Hey! It's my man Tony!"
        Case Else
            MsgBox "Hello, stranger."
    End Select
End Sub
```

This new procedure is about the same size as the original. However, it's a bit easier to see what's going on because the decision-making is more concise, using fewer keywords and expressions.

Digging into Select Case

Now that you've taken a gander at Select Case, I suppose you're going to insist on an explanation. Here goes. As you can see, Select Case starts with the line

    Select Case name

The first two words, Select Case, tell Visual Basic that you're starting a Select Case statement. (Sorry, but sometimes technical books have to state the obvious in order to get to the meatier stuff. Bear with me.) The name part of the line tells Visual Basic that the computer will be making a decision based on the contents of the variable name.

That neatly brings you to the next line, which looks like this:

    Case "FRED"

This is just a quick way of saying

    If name = "FRED" Then

> ### A Common Use
>
> Because a Select Case statement tends to be much more concise than an If/Then statement, programmers usually use a Select Case statement when the program must decide between many different possible outcomes. For example, if a program must examine a variable for a value between 1 and 20 and execute different program lines for each possible value, a Select Case statement sure saves on the typing!

See how a Select Case statement is more concise than an If/Then statement? A line with five keywords, expressions, and operators reduces to one keyword and a value.

Now, if name happens to equal "FRED" (Yay, Fred!), the program executes the line or lines following the Case clause, which in this case would be the following:

    MsgBox "Hi, Fred!"

If name doesn't equal "FRED", the program drops down to the next Case clause and checks to see whether name equals "SARAH":

    Case "SARAH"
        MsgBox "How's it going, Sarah?"

Our main man Tony, who's no less important than Fred and Sarah, gets his own Case clause, as well:

    Case "TONY"
        MsgBox "Hey! It's my man Tony!"

If someone other than Fred, Sarah, or Tony types his name into the program's text box, the Case Else clause leaps into action, making sure that everyone gets some sort of greeting:

```
Case Else
    MsgBox "Hello, stranger."
```

Finally, the program tells Visual Basic that the Select Case statement is over with this line:

```
End Select
```

Digging Even Deeper

You wouldn't have to burn up too much brain fuel to realize that Select Case statements work with more than strings. Sure enough, Select Case statements can also handle other types of data, such as integers and floating-point values. As an example, consider the following Command1_Click procedure from the previous chapter:

```
Private Sub Command1_Click()
    Dim choice As Integer
    Dim entry As String

    entry = Text1.Text
    choice = Val(entry)

    If choice = 1 Then
        MsgBox "You chose red."
        Form1.BackColor = vbRed
    ElseIf choice = 2 Then
        MsgBox "You chose green."
        Form1.BackColor = vbGreen
    ElseIf choice = 3 Then
        MsgBox "You chose blue."
        Form1.BackColor = vbBlue
    Else
        MsgBox "Invalid selection."
    End If
End Sub
```

You might recall that this particular version of Command1_Click gets a number from a text box and sets the form's background color based on that number. If you don't recall this procedure, you can check back with Chapter 7, "If, Then, and Else: Decisions, Decisions, Decisions." If you don't recall even what "Microsoft" means, you should probably take a break and get a snack.

For those of you who aren't heading for the kitchen, you can rewrite the previous Command1_Click procedure like this:

```
Private Sub Command1_Click()
    Dim choice As Integer
    Dim entry As String

    entry = Text1.Text
    choice = Val(entry)

    Select Case choice
        Case 1
            MsgBox "You chose red."
            Form1.BackColor = vbRed
        Case 2
            MsgBox "You chose green."
            Form1.BackColor = vbGreen
        Case 3
            MsgBox "You chose blue."
            Form1.BackColor = vbBlue
        Case Else
            MsgBox "Invalid selection."
    End Select
End Sub
```

This procedure not only demonstrates using a Select Case statement with an integer, but also shows how you can have more than one program line associated with each Case clause. Here, except for the Case Else, each Case shows a message box and then changes the form's background color. You can have as many lines as you want with each Case, although you'll probably want to limit the line count to something less than the number of pages in the latest Tom Clancy novel.

Ranges and Select Case

So far, all your Select Case statements (all two of them) have checked a variable for a specific value. Select Case, though, can be more flexible than that; a program can use a Select Case statement to check for a range of values.

What's that strange feeling? Why, it's a sample program coming on! Start a new Visual Basic project (a Standard EXE), and place a Label control, a TextBox control, and a CommandButton control on the form, as shown here:

Position your controls as shown here.

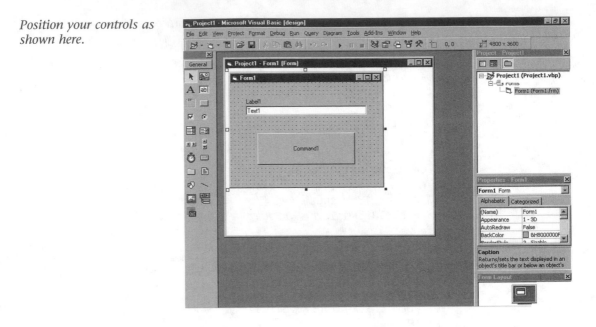

Next, double-click the form to bring up the code window, and type the following program lines (Visual Basic will have already started the Form_Load procedure for you):

```
Private Sub Command1_Click()
    Dim value As Integer
    value = Text1.Text
    Select Case value
        Case Is < 4
            MsgBox "Your value is less than 4."
        Case Is < 8
            MsgBox "Your value is less than 8."
        Case Is < 11
            MsgBox "Your value is less than 11."
        Case Else
            MsgBox "Your value is out of range."
    End Select
End Sub

Private Sub Form_Load()
    Label1.Caption = "Enter a value from 1 to 10:"
    Text1.Text = "1"
    Command1.Caption = "Check Value"
End Sub
```

After typing the program lines, save your work, and then run the program. When the application's window appears, type a number from 1 to 10 into the text box and click the Check Value button. When you do, the program displays a message box describing where your number falls in the 1 to 10 range. The following figure shows the program after the user has clicked the Check Value button:

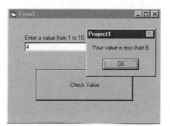

This program can check value ranges with a Select Case *statement.*

The only real difference between this Select Case statement and the others you've written is the way each Case clause examines the variable's value:

```
Case Is < 4
```

Now, thanks to the Is keyword, the Case clauses can determine whether the value fits some specified criteria. In the case of the preceding code, if value is less than 4, the program executes the lines that make up the body of the Case clause and then skips over the remaining Case clauses. Otherwise, as always, the program moves on to the next Case.

Using Relational Operators

You can use all kinds of relational operators along with a Case clause's Is keyword. For example, the clause Case Is >= 10 works just fine, as does Case Is <> 4. You can even do something strange like Case Is = 10. Why is this strange? Because it's the same as writing Case 10.

The Least You Need to Know

➤ A Select Case statement can replace most If/Then statements.

➤ A Select Case statement is more concise than its If/Then counterpart.

➤ A program can, with a Select Case statement, examine variables containing most any type of data, including strings, integers, and floating-point values.

➤ The Select Case statement, with the use of the Is keyword, can examine variables for a range of values.

Chapter 9

Looping with For/Next: Counting the Computer Way

A computer handles repetitive operations especially well—it never gets bored, and it can perform a task as well the 10,000th time as it did the first. Consider, for example, a disk file containing 10,000 names and addresses. If you tried to type labels for all those people, you would be seeing spots before your eyes in no time. A computer, on the other hand, can spit out all 10,000 labels tirelessly—and with nary a complaint to the union.

Every computer language must have some form of looping command to instruct a computer to perform repetitive tasks. Visual Basic features three types of looping: For/Next loops, Do-While loops, and Do-Until loops. In this chapter, you learn to use

Around and Around We Go

In computer programs, looping is the process of executing a block of statements repeatedly. Starting at the top of the block, the statements are executed until the program reaches the end of the block, at which point the program goes back to the top and starts over. The statements in the block can be repeated any number of times, from once to forever.

the first of these powerful programming techniques. In the following chapter, you'll learn about the other two.

The For/Next Loop

Probably the most often used loop in Visual Basic is the For/Next loop, which instructs a program to perform a block of code a specified number of times. You could, for example, use a For/Next loop to instruct your computer to print those 10,000 address labels. Because you don't currently have an address file, however, let's say you want to print your name on the screen ten times. To see one way to accomplish that task, start a new Visual Basic project, and place a Label, TextBox, and CommandButton controls on the form as shown here:

Position the controls as shown in this figure.

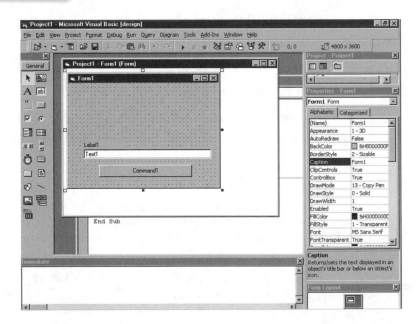

After placing the controls on the form, double-click the CommandButton to bring up the code window. Type the following program lines. (Visual Basic will have already started the Command1_Click procedure for you.)

```
Private Sub Command1_Click()
    Dim name As String

    name = Text1.Text

    Form1.Print name
    Form1.Print name
    Form1.Print name
    Form1.Print name
    Form1.Print name
    Form1.Print name
    Form1.Print name
    Form1.Print name
    Form1.Print name
    Form1.Print name
End Sub

Private Sub Form_Load()
    Label1.Caption = "Enter name:"
    Text1.Text = ""
    Command1.Caption = "Display Name"
End Sub
```

When you run the program, type a name into the text box, and then click the Display Name button. When you do, the program prints the name ten times in the form's window, as shown in the following figure:

Any name you enter appears ten times in the window.

Look at the program listing. See all those Print commands? As a computer programmer, whenever you see program code containing many identical instructions, a little bell should go off in your head. When you hear this little bell, you should do one of two things:

1. Answer your phone.

2. Say to yourself, "Hmmmm. This looks like a good place for a loop."

Having many lines in your program containing identical instructions makes your program longer than necessary and wastes memory. It also shows poor programming style. Unless you want your programming friends to snicker behind your back, learn to replace redundant program code with program loops.

The previous program's Command1_Click procedure can be streamlined easily by using a For/Next loop, and here's how:

```
Private Sub Command1_Click()
    Dim x As Integer
    Dim name As String

    name = Text1.Text

    For x = 1 To 10
        Form1.Print name
    Next x
End Sub
```

Replace the previous program's Command1_Click procedure with this new one. When you run the program, the output will be identical to the first program's, but now the program is shorter and contains no redundant code.

Look at the program line beginning with the keyword For. The loop starts with this line. The word For tells Visual Basic that you're starting a For/Next loop. After the word For is the loop-control variable x. The loop-control variable, which can have any legal numerical-variable name, is where Visual Basic stores the current loop count. See the number after the equals sign? Visual Basic uses this number to begin the loop count. The number after the keyword To is the last value of x in the loop. That is, as the loop runs, x will take on values from 1 to 10, as you'll see in the following paragraphs.

In the new Command1_Click, when the For loop begins, Visual Basic places the number 1 in the variable x. The program then drops down to the next line, which prints the user's name. The line

```
Next x
```

tells Visual Basic to increment (increase by one) the loop-control variable and start again at the top of the loop. So, x becomes 2, and the program returns to the For line. The program then compares the value in x with the number following the keyword To. If the loop count (in x) is less than or equal to the number following To, the program executes the loop again. In the case of Command1_Click, this process continues until x is greater than 10.

Whew! Got all that? If you just woke up, rub the fuzzies from your eyes and read the previous paragraph a couple times to make sure it sinks in. If you still can't stay awake, take a nap.

Suppose you want to modify the program to print your name only five times. What would you change? If you answered, "I'd change the 10 in the For line to 5," you win the Programmer of the Week award. If you answered, "I'd change my socks," start reading this chapter from the beginning.

Adding the Step Clause

The previous example of a For/Next loop increments the loop counter by 1. But suppose you want a For/Next loop that counts from 5 to 40 by fives? You can do this by adding a Step clause to your For/Next loop, as shown in the following example:

```
Private Sub Command1_Click()
    Dim x As Integer
    Dim name As String

    name = Text1.Text

    For x = 5 To 40 Step 5
        Form1.Print name & " -- Loop counter value: " & x
    Next x
End Sub
```

Up and Down

In computer programs, variables are often incremented and decremented. When you *increment* a variable, you add some value to it. When you *decrement* a variable, you subtract some value from it. If the value of the increment or decrement is not explicit, it's assumed that the value is 1. For example, the statement "The program increments the variable num by 5" means that num is increased in value by 5. On the other hand, the statement "The program increments num" usually means that num is increased by 1.

Replace the previous Command1_Click procedure with this one, and then run the program. When you enter a name and click the button, you see a window something like this:

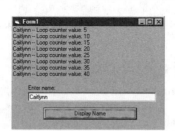

This program displays both a name and the value of the loop counter.

As you can see, the program prints both your name and the current value of the loop variable eight times.

Look closely at the new `Command1_Click` procedure. Unlike the previous programs, this loop doesn't start counting at 1. Rather, the loop variable begins with a value of 5. Then, thanks to the `Step 5` clause, Visual Basic increments the loop variable by 5 each time through the loop. So, x goes from 5 to 10, from 10 to 15, and so on up to 40, resulting in eight loops.

Here's how you can use the `Step` clause to count backwards:

```
Private Sub Command1_Click()
    Dim x As Integer
    Dim name As String

    name = Text1.Text

    For x = 40 To 5 Step -5
        Form1.Print name & " — Loop counter value: " & x
    Next x
End Sub
```

When you replace the previous `Command1_Click` with this new one, a program run looks something like this:

Now the program counts in reverse.

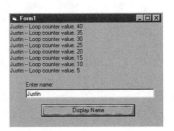

Notice in the program that the loop limits are in reverse order; that is, the higher value comes first. Notice also that the `Step` clause specifies a negative value, which causes the loop count to be decremented (decreased) rather than incremented.

Using Variables in Loops

Just as with most numerical values in a program, you can substitute variables for the literals you've used so far in your `For`/`Next` loops. In fact, you'll probably use variables in your loop limits as often as you use literals, if not more. To see how this works, start a new Visual Basic project, and place two Label controls, two TextBox controls, and a CommandButton control on the form as shown here:

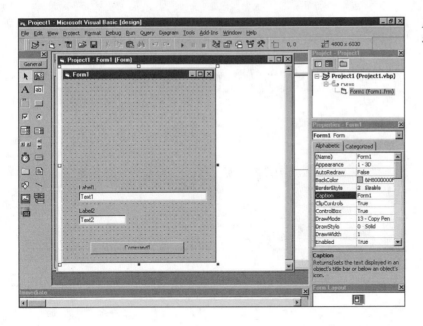

Position the controls as shown in this figure.

After placing the controls on the form, double-click the form to bring up the code window. Type the following program lines (Visual Basic will have already started the Form_Load procedure for you):

```
Private Sub Command1_Click()
    Dim x As Integer
    Dim name As String
    Dim count As Integer

    name = Text1.Text
    count = Text2.Text

    For x = 1 To count
        Form1.Print name & " — Loop counter value: " & x
    Next x
End Sub

Private Sub Form_Load()
    Label1.Caption = "Enter name:"
    Label2.Caption = "Enter loop count:"
    Text1.Text = ""
    Text2.Text = ""
    Command1.Caption = "Display Name"
End Sub
```

When you run this program, enter—in the appropriate text boxes—your name and the number of times you want your name printed. When you click the button, the

115

program prints your name the requested number of times. As you can see in the code listing, you can have the program print your name any number of times (well, up to 32,766 times, if you want to get technical about it) because the loop's upper limit is contained in the variable count; count gets its value from you at the start of each program run. Here's what the program looks like after it's run:

Print your name as many times as you like.

```
Form1                           _ □ ✕
Stephen – Loop counter value: 1
Stephen – Loop counter value: 2
Stephen – Loop counter value: 3
Stephen – Loop counter value: 4
Stephen – Loop counter value: 5
Stephen – Loop counter value: 6
Stephen – Loop counter value: 7
Stephen – Loop counter value: 8
Stephen – Loop counter value: 9
Stephen – Loop counter value: 10
Stephen – Loop counter value: 11
Stephen – Loop counter value: 12



Enter name:
Stephen

Enter loop count:
12


            Display Name
```

Using variables in For/Next loops makes your programs more flexible and produces a powerful programming construct. As you'll soon see, you can use variables with other types of loops, too. In fact, you can use a numerical variable in a program in most places a numerical value is required. You can even use numerical variables in salads, but they taste bitter and leave a nasty film on your tongue.

Strings and Integers

In the previous program, you might have noticed that the value used for the variable count comes from a text box and so starts off life as a string. How can a string be used as an integer variable? Well, it really can't. When Visual Basic sees the line count = Text2.Text, it already knows that count is supposed to be an integer, so it converts the string for you. Watch out, though, if you type something other than digits into the text box. If you do Visual Basic will proudly present you with an error when it tries to convert a non-numerical string to an integer.

116

Just a Variable

The loop-control variable in a For/Next loop (for example, the x in For x = 1 To 10) is nothing special; it's just a typical variable. The only difference between this variable and the other variables you've been using is that Visual Basic knows that it can use the loop-control variable for its own purpose, which is to keep track of the loop count. Because the loop-control variable is a plain ol' variable, you can even assign values to it yourself. However, the practice of directly changing a loop-control variable's value is greatly discouraged.

The Least You Need to Know

➤ Repetitive operations in a computer program can be handled efficiently by program loops, including For/Next loops, Do-While loops, and Do-Until loops.

➤ A For/Next loop instructs a program to execute a block of commands a given number of times.

➤ In the For/Next loop For x = num1 To num2, the variable x is the loop's control variable. The loop limits are the values of num1 and num2.

➤ By adding a Step clause to a For/Next loop, you can make the loop-control variable count up or down in any increment or decrement. For example, the loop For x = 20 to 10 Step -2 counts backwards by twos, from 20 to 10.

➤ You can use a numeric variable for either of the two loop limits in a For/Next loop.

Chapter 10

Looping with Do, While, and Until: Around and Around We Go

Zip Zip

In This Chapter

➤ Learn about Do While loops

➤ Discover how to use Do Until loops

➤ Program Do/Loop While and Do/Loop Until loops

In the previous chapter, you got an introduction to program loops. Specifically, you learned about For/Next loops, which enable a program to perform a set of actions a certain number of times. Visual Basic, however, provides four other types of looping techniques, including Do While, Do Until, Do/Loop While, and Do/Loop Until loops. (And you hoped you were finished with this looping nonsense!) In the following pages, you'll learn how these types of loops can beef up your Visual Basic programs. Or, for the health conscious, "fish" up your Visual Basic programs.

The Do While Loop

Unlike a For/Next loop, which loops the number of times given in the loop limits, a Do While loop continues executing as long as its control expression is false. The control expression is a Boolean expression much like the Boolean expressions you used with If statements. In other words, any expression that evaluates to true or false can be used as a control expression for a Do While loop.

To see a Do While loop in action, first start a new Visual Basic project, and then place two Label controls, one TextBox control, and one CommandButton control on the form, like this:

Position the controls as shown in this figure.

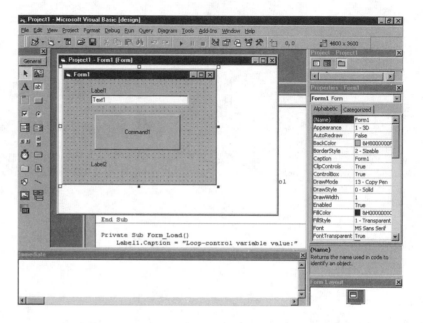

After placing the controls on the form, double-click the form to bring up the code window. Type the following program lines into the code window (Visual Basic will have already started the Form_Load procedure for you):

```
Private Sub Command1_Click()
    Dim control As Long

    On Error Resume Next
    control = Text1.Text
    Form1.BackColor = vbWhite

    Do While control <> 0
        control = Text1.Text
        Label2.Caption = _
            "Current variable value: " & control
        If Form1.BackColor = vbWhite Then
            Form1.BackColor = vbRed
        Else
            Form1.BackColor = vbWhite
        End If
        DoEvents
    Loop
```

```
        MsgBox "looping complete"
    End Sub

    Private Sub Form_Load()
        Label1.Caption = "Loop-control variable value:"
        Label2.Caption = "Current variable value: "
        Text1.Text = "5"
        Command1.Caption - "Start Loop"
    End Sub
```

Run the program, and click the Start Loop button to start the Do While loop located in the Command1_Click procedure. This Do While loop continually changes the form's background color, as well as retrieves the value currently entered into the application's text box. Enter any value you like in the text box. The program loads the value into the control variable and updates the Label control at the bottom of the window to show the current value of control. The Do While loop continues until you enter the value 0 into the text box, as shown here:

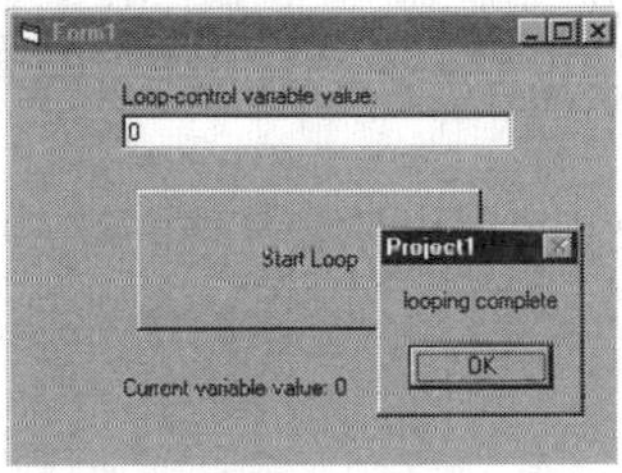

A value of 0 stops the loop and displays a message box.

To fully understand this program's Command1_Click procedure, you need to stop staring at the running program with that stunned expression (yeah, the program is kind of cool) and examine the procedure line by line.

The line

```
    Dim control As Long
```

declares the variable control as a long integer, which enables it to accept the large values you might enter into the text box.

Next, the line

```
    On Error Resume Next
```

tells Visual Basic to keep running even if a runtime error occurs. This line is important because the Do While loop is constantly grabbing the contents of the text box and converting the contents to a numerical value. If you backspace to get rid of the current value in the text box, for a couple of seconds the text box will be empty, which means when the program tries to grab and convert the contents, Visual Basic will generate an error. The On Error Resume Next command ensures that you never even know that an error occurred. (You'll learn more about this error stuff in Chapter 15, "The Art of Bug Extermination: Raid for the New Millennium.")

Next, the line

```
control = Text1.Text
```

sets the control variable's starting value, which, by default, is 5, the value that the text box starts with.

Next, the line

```
Form1.BackColor = vbWhite
```

sets the form's background color to white, after which the line

```
While control <> 0
```

starts the While loop, because control doesn't equal 0. If the program started with the value 0 entered into the text box, the Do While loop would never start. If you were to read the previous line in English, you would say, "while control doesn't equal 0."

The lines between the While and the Loop lines are the lines that the program executes every time the loop repeats. Inside the loop, the line

```
control = Text1.Text
```

gets a new value for the control variable, after which the lines

```
Label2.Caption = _
    "Current variable value: " & control
```

display the control variable's current value in the program's second Label control.

After setting the caption, the loop decides whether to set the form's background color to white or red, like this:

```
If Form1.BackColor = vbWhite Then
    Form1.BackColor = vbRed
Else
    Form1.BackColor = vbWhite
End If
```

As long as the loop runs, this If/Then statement keeps changing the form's background color between white and red so that you can actually see the loop running.

The following line is essential to the program's operation:

```
DoEvents
```

If this line were missing, you would never be able to enter a value into the text box, because the Do While loop runs so fast that no other input is possible—for any program, not just the sample program! This problem occurs because Windows, in order to manage running applications, relies on a series of messages being passed back and forth between Windows and currently running programs. The DoEvents command tells the Do While loop to wait a little while so that other Windows messages can get through. If you take the DoEvents line out of the program, the program will seem to die and sit idle on the screen. In fact, you'll have to press Ctrl+Alt+Delete to end the program, because even Visual Basic loses all control of the system.

At the end of the loop, the line

```
Loop
```

tells Visual Basic it has reached the end of the Do While loop. At this point, Visual Basic goes back to the Do While line to take another look at the value of control. If control still doesn't equal 0, the loop runs again. On the other hand, if control does equal 0, the Do While loop ends, and the program jumps to the next line after the loop:

```
MsgBox "looping complete"
```

This line simply displays a message box, letting you know that the While loop has stopped.

The Do Until Loop

Visual Basic also features another type of loop, called a Do Until loop, which is very similar to a Do While loop. For example, the previous program's Command1_Click procedure could have been rewritten with a Do Until loop, like this:

```
Private Sub Command1_Click()
    Dim control As Long
```

Getting the Right Start

Notice how the program sets the variable control to a value before the Do While loop starts. This is important because it ensures that the value in control starts at a value other than 0. If control did happen to start at 0, the program would never get to the statements within the Do While loop because the loop's control expression would immediately evaluate to true. Mistakes like this make programmers growl and answer the phone with, "What do you want, butthead?"

Initializing Variables

Initializing a variable means setting it to its starting value. In Visual Basic, all numeric variables are automatically initialized to 0. If you need a variable to start at a different value, you must initialize it yourself.

```
    On Error Resume Next
    control = Text1.Text
    Form1.BackColor = vbWhite

    Do Until control = 0
        control = Text1.Text
        Label2.Caption = _
            "Current variable value: " & control
        If Form1.BackColor = vbWhite Then
            Form1.BackColor = vbRed
        Else
            Form1.BackColor = vbWhite
        End If
        DoEvents
    Loop

    MsgBox "looping complete"
End Sub
```

Do you see the difference between the original Do While loop and the Do Until loop? Both loops continue until their control expressions become true. However, the control expressions in the two loop types have reverse logic. Specifically, in the previous program with the Do While loop, the loop continues until control does not equal 0. The version with the Do Until continues looping until control does equal 0, just the opposite of the Do While case.

The Do/Loop While Loop

In both cases, the Do While and Do Until loops check their control expression before the loop runs for even the first time. This means both these loop types might not loop at all. If the control expression starts off true, the entire loop is skipped. What if you want to write a Do While-type of loop, but want to be sure it executes at least once? Then you could use a Do/Loop While loop.

The only real difference between a Do While loop and a Do/Loop While loop is that in the latter case, the loop checks its control expression after the loop runs instead of before. For example, here's your familiar Command1_Click procedure, rewritten with a Do/Loop While loop:

```
Private Sub Command1_Click()
    Dim control As Long

    On Error Resume Next
    Form1.BackColor = vbWhite
```

```
    Do
        control = Text1.Text
        Label2.Caption = _
            "Current variable value: " & control
        If Form1.BackColor = vbWhite Then
            Form1.BackColor = vbRed
        Else
            Form1.BackColor = vbWhite
        End If
        DoEvents
    Loop While control <> 0

    MsgBox "looping complete"
End Sub
```

The Do/Loop Until Loop

As you might have guessed, Do/Loop While has a cousin called Do/Loop Until. These two types of loops are just as similar as their counterparts (second cousins?) Do While and Do Until. The only difference is that these loops check their control expressions at the end of the loop rather than at the start. Here's yet another version of the Command1_Click procedure, one that shows how to use the Do/Loop Until loop:

```
Private Sub Command1_Click()
    Dim control As Long

    On Error Resume Next
    Form1.BackColor = vbWhite

    Do
        control = Text1.Text
        Label2.Caption = _
            "Current variable value: " & control
        If Form1.BackColor = vbWhite Then
            Form1.BackColor = vbRed
        Else
            Form1.BackColor = vbWhite
        End If
        DoEvents
    Loop Until control = 0

    MsgBox "looping complete"
End Sub
```

Getting the Right Start

Different looping methods work best in different programming situations. Although experience is the best teacher, you should keep some things in mind when selecting a looping construct. When you want a loop to run a specific number of times, the For/Next loop is usually the best choice. When you want a loop to run until a certain condition is met, the Do While and Do Until loops work best. Finally, if you want to be sure the loop runs at least once, you should use the Do/Loop While or Do/Loop Until loop.

Infinite Loops

New programmers are infamous for creating loops that never end. For example, if you write a Do While loop whose control expression can never become true, your loop will loop forever. When this happens, it'll look to you as though your program has locked up your machine (your computer has stopped dead in its tracks and will accept no input). But, really, your program is looping frantically, with no hope of ever moving on. Often, the only way out of this predicament is to type Ctrl+Alt+Delete to terminate the program.

The Least You Need to Know

➤ A Do While loop continues to run until its control expression becomes true. Because this type of loop checks the control expression before running the loop, a Do While loop can run zero or more times.

➤ A Do Until loop also continues to run until its control expression becomes true and checks the control expression before running the loop. A Do Until loop can run zero or more times.

➤ A Do/Loop While loop runs until its control expression becomes true, but it checks the control expression at the end of the loop instead of at the beginning. This difference means that a Do/Loop While loop always executes its statements at least once.

➤ A Do/Loop Until loop works exactly like a Do/Loop While loop, but enables you to use the opposite logic in the control expression. This type of loop also always executes its statements at least once.

Chapter 11

Arrays: Tricky Problems with Clever Solutions

In This Chapter

➤ Learn to create arrays

➤ Use arrays with loops

➤ Understand numerical and string arrays

➤ Create arrays of controls

As you've learned by now, using variables makes your programs flexible. Thanks to variables, you can conveniently store data in your programs and retrieve it by name. You can also get and store input from your program's user. The best thing about variables is that they can constantly change value. They're called variables, after all, because they're variable!

Until now, you've learned about various types of numerical variables, including integers, long integers, single-precision variables, and double-precision variables. You also know about string variables, which can hold text. Now that you have a good understanding of these data types, it's time to explore one last data type, a handy data structure called an array.

An Introduction to Arrays

Often in your programs, you'll want to store many values that are related in some way. Suppose you manage a bowling league, and you want to keep track of each player's average. One way to do this is to give each player a variable in your program. The following program shows how to accomplish this task.

To build the program, start a new Visual Basic project, and position four Label controls, four TextBox controls, and one CommandButton control, as shown here:

Position the controls as shown in this figure.

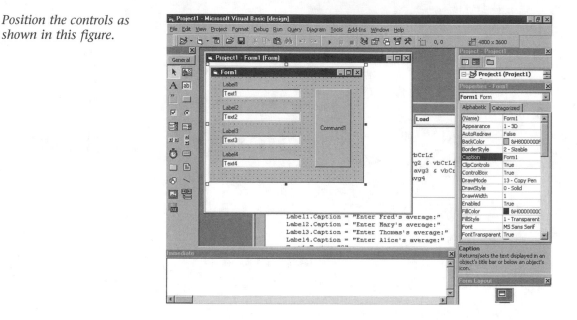

After placing the controls on the form, double-click the form to bring up the code window. Type the following program lines into the code window (Visual Basic will have already started the Form_Load procedure for you):

```
Private Sub Command1_Click()
    Dim avg1 As Integer
    Dim avg2 As Integer
    Dim avg3 As Integer
    Dim avg4 As Integer

    avg1 = Text1.Text
    avg2 = Text2.Text
    avg3 = Text3.Text
    avg4 = Text4.Text

    MsgBox "Fred's Score: " & avg1
    MsgBox "Mary's Score: " & avg2
    MsgBox "Thomas's Score: " & avg3
    MsgBox "Alice's Score: " & avg4
End Sub

Private Sub Form_Load()
    Label1.Caption = "Enter Fred's average:"
```

```
        Label2.Caption = "Enter Mary's average:"
        Label3.Caption = "Enter Thomas's average:"
        Label4.Caption = "Enter Alice's average:"
        Text1.Text = "0"
        Text2.Text = "0"
        Text3.Text = "0"
        Text4.Text = "0"
        Command1.Caption = "Show Scores"
    End Sub
```

Run the program, and enter bowling scores into the four text boxes. Then click the Show Scores button to display the scores, one at a time, in a message box. As you can see from the program's Command1_Click procedure, when you click the button, the program does nothing more than retrieve the scores from the text boxes and display them in a message box, as shown here:

The message box formats and displays the scores you enter.

Nothing too tricky going on here, right?

Remember in a previous chapter when you learned to keep an eye out for repetitive program code? (Well, I wouldn't suggest actually keeping an eye out. Eyeballs tend to dry out quickly and are easily knocked off your desk.) How about all those repetitive statements in the Command1_Click procedure? The procedure declares four very similar variables, as well as gets the values for those variables in a very similar way. Moreover, the program displays the values of all four scores in almost exactly the same way. If you could find some way to make a loop out of this code, you would need only one line to input all the data and only one line to display the averages for all four bowlers. You could, in fact, use a For/Next loop that counts from one to four.

But how can you use a loop when you're stuck with four different variables? The answer is an array. An *array* is a variable that can hold more than one value. When you first studied variables, you learned that a variable is like a box in memory that holds a single value. Now, if you take a bunch of these boxes and put them together, what do you have? (No, the answer isn't "a bunch of variables smooshed together.") You would have an array. For example, to store the bowling averages for your four bowlers, you would need an array that can hold four values. You could call this array avg. You could also call this array TheseAreTheBowlersAverages, but who wants to do all that typing?

Now you have an array called avg that can hold four bowling averages. But how can you retrieve each individual average from the array? You could run out on your front lawn in your skivvies, wave a plucked chicken over your head, and shout praises to the gods of computing. However, an easier way—and one that doesn't amuse the neighbors quite so much—is to add something called a subscript to the array's name.

The Meaning of Zero

The number zero is insanely important to computers, as you'll discover as you do more and more programming. Computers don't consider 1 to be the first positive whole number, but rather 0. This is why the first value in an array is stored at a subscript of 0.

A *subscript* is a number that identifies the box in which an array value is stored. For example, to refer to the first average in your avg array, you would write avg(0). The subscript is the number in parentheses. In this case, you're referring to the first average in the array. To refer to the second average, you would write avg(1). The third and fourth averages are avg(2) and avg(3).

If you're a little confused, look at the following figure, which shows how the avg array might look in memory. In this case, the four bowling averages are 145, 192, 160, and 203. The value of avg(0) is 145, the value of avg(1) is 192, the value of avg(2) is 160, and the value of avg(3) is 203.

An array looks something like this in memory.

AVG(0)	AVG(1)	AVG(2)	AVG(3)
145	192	160	203

An Elementary Definition

The little memory boxes that make up an array are called *elements* of the array. For example, in an array named numbers, numbers(0) is the first element of the array, numbers(1) is the second element, and so on.

Using a Variable as a Subscript

As you've learned, most numerical constants in a Visual Basic program can be replaced by numerical variables. Suppose, then, you were to use the variable x as the subscript for the array avg. Then (based on the averages in the previous figure), if the value of x were 1, the value of avg(x) would be 192. If the value of x were 3, the value of avg(x) would be 203.

Now take one last gigantic intuitive leap (c'mon, you can do it), and think about using your subscript variable x as both the control variable in a For/Next loop and the subscript for the avg array. If you use a For/Next loop that counts from 0 to 3, you can use a single line (not including the For and Next lines) to show all four players' averages. The following new version of your Command1_Click procedure shows how this is done:

```
Private Sub Command1_Click()
    Dim avg(3) As Integer
    Dim x As Integer

    avg(0) = Text1.Text
    avg(1) = Text2.Text
    avg(2) = Text3.Text
    avg(3) = Text4.Text

    For x = 0 To 3
        MsgBox "Bowler's Score: " & avg(x)
    Next x
End Sub
```

This version of Command1_Click first declares an array that can hold four values (subscripts 0 through 3), which in programmer speak is a *four-element array*. The procedure then loads the array from the values entered into the text boxes. Finally, the For/Next loop displays the averages one by one, using the variable x as the array's subscript (sometimes called an *index*).

Array Size

When you declare your arrays, make sure you have enough room for the data you need to store. After you declare an array, Visual Basic will not allow you to store or retrieve values beyond the end of the array. For example, if you declare an array as numbers(10) and then try to access numbers(11), your program will come to a crashing halt and give you a subscript-out-of-range error. Note that you can change the size of an array using the ReDim statement. If you're interested in this advanced feature of arrays, check ReDim out in your Visual Basic online documentation.

Do you understand how the program works? In the For/Next loop, the variable x starts with a value of 0. So, the first message box displays the value of avg(0). The next time through the loop, x equals 1, so the message box displays the value in avg(1). This continues until x becomes 4, and the For/Next loop ends.

Zeroing in on Elements

As you now know, arrays can actually have what's called a *zeroth element*. That is, you can actually start storing data in element 0 of an array. To make arrays start at element 1 instead of element 0, you need to add the `Option Base 1` statement to the beginning of your program. Then, an array that's been dimensioned as `numbers(3)` has three elements: `numbers(1)`, `numbers(2)`, and `numbers(3)`.

Control Arrays

In the last version of the `Command1_Click` procedure, you managed to use an array so you can store the bowling scores into a single variable and retrieve and display the values with a single line in a loop. However, getting the values into the array requires that the program extract information from four different text boxes, and there's no way to refer to those text boxes within a loop as you can with the `avg` array.

Or is there?

You'll be pleased to know that Visual Basic enables you to create an array of controls. For example, you can create an array that contains all four of the TextBox controls, enabling the program to use a subscript in a loop to refer to a control. To see how this works, start a new Visual Basic project, and place four Label controls and a CommandButton control on the form as shown in this figure:

Position the controls as shown here.

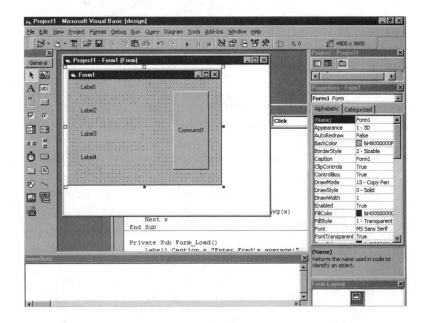

Now you're ready to create your TextBox-control array. To do this, first place a TextBox control on the form as shown here:

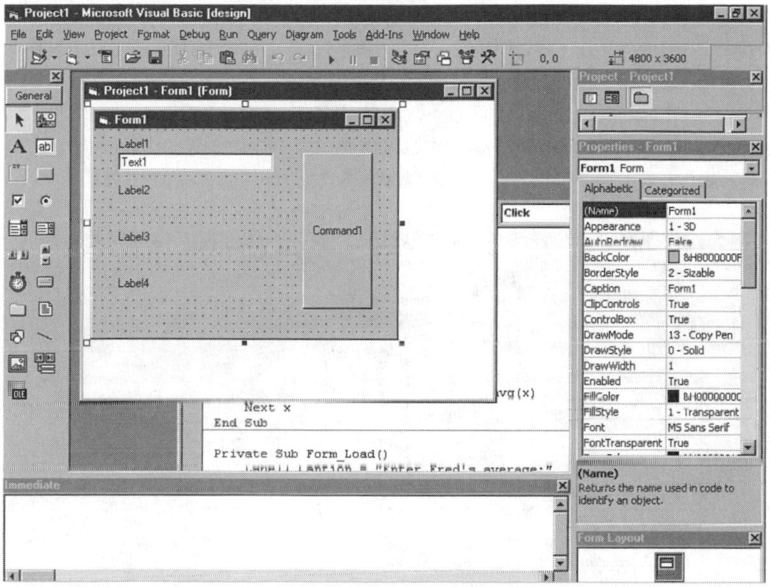

The TextBox control will be the first control in the array.

Now, with the TextBox control still selected, press Ctrl+C to copy the control to the Windows Clipboard. Then, press Ctrl+V to paste the control from the Clipboard to the form. When you do, Visual Basic asks whether you want to create a control array, as shown here:

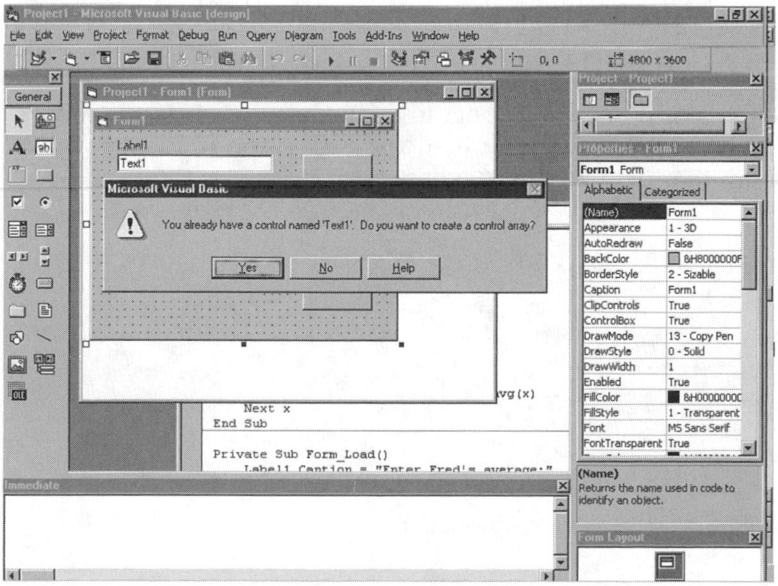

Visual Basic asks whether you want to create a control array.

Click the Yes button, and a new TextBox control appears on the form. Drag this TextBox into place beneath the second Label control. Press Ctrl+V again and another TextBox appears. Place this TextBox beneath the third Label control. Finally, press Ctrl+V one more time to create the fourth TextBox control in your TextBox array. Position this final control beneath the fourth Label control. Notice how all four TextBox controls have the same name, Text1, as shown in the following figure:

All four TextBox controls now have the same name.

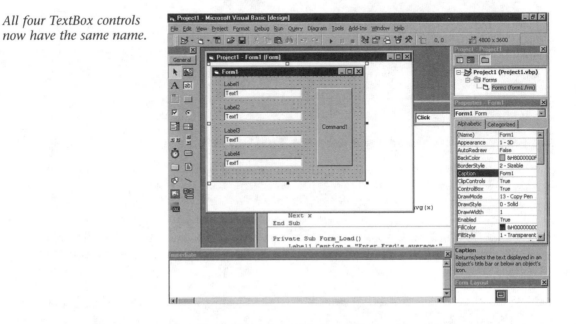

The TextBox controls have the same name because they are all part of a TextBox-control array called Text1. Your program can refer to each control in the same way the program referred to values in the avg array, by using a subscript. So, your program can refer to the controls in the Text1 array as Text1(0), Text1(1), Text1(2), and Text1(3).

This TextBox-control array enables you to make your Command1_Click procedure even more compact, like this:

```
Private Sub Command1_Click()
    Dim avg(3) As Integer
    Dim x As Integer

    For x = 0 To 3
        avg(x) = Text1(x).Text
        MsgBox "Bowler's Score: " & avg(x)
    Next x
End Sub
```

Now the program can both retrieve the bowler's scores from the text boxes and display the scores all inside a single For/Next loop. Your Command1_Click procedure is now about half the size it used to be. Pretty impressive. Imagine what a difference arrays can make when the program needs to work with 1,000 bowlers' scores!

String Arrays

The previous program shows how handy arrays can be, but there's something missing from the program. First, there's no built-in Mario game, so using this program for long periods of time is downright boring. More to the point, though, the bowlers' names are missing when the program displays the scores. You can get around this problem easily, by creating an array to hold strings. (You can get over the Mario problem by taking a Nintendo break.) Replace the previous program's Command1_Click and Form_Load procedures with the following lines:

```
Private Sub Command1_Click()
    Dim avg(3) As Integer
    Dim x As Integer
    Dim names(3) As String

    names(0) = "Fred"
    names(1) = "Mary"
    names(2) = "Thomas"
    names(3) = "Alice"

    For x = 0 To 3
        avg(x) = Text1(x).Text
        MsgBox names(x) & "'s Score: " & avg(x)
    Next x
End Sub

Private Sub Form_Load()
    Dim x As Integer

    Label1.Caption = "Enter Fred's average:"
    Label2.Caption = "Enter Mary's average:"
    Label3.Caption = "Enter Thomas's average:"
    Label4.Caption = "Enter Alice's average:"

    For x = 0 To 3
        Text1(x).Text = "0"
    Next x

    Command1.Caption = "Show Scores"
End Sub
```

When you run the program now, it looks and acts almost the same. However, now most of the program's data is handled in arrays. Look closely at the Command1_Click procedure. The procedure declares a string array that can hold four strings, like this:

```
Dim names(3) As String
```

Next, the procedure loads the array with the bowlers' names:

```
names(0) = "Fred"
names(1) = "Mary"
names(2) = "Thomas"
names(3) = "Alice"
```

The new For/Next loop now accesses the names array to get the name that's associated with the current score, which enables the message box to show both the name and the score:

```
For x = 0 To 3
    avg(x) = Text1(x).Text
    MsgBox names(x) & "'s Score: " & avg(x)
Next x
```

The following figure shows how the new message boxes look:

The message boxes now display both the name and the score.

138

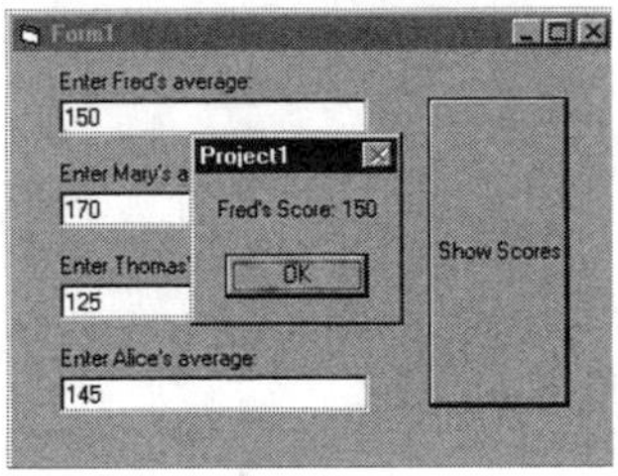

The Least You Need to Know

➤ Arrays allow you to store many values under a single variable name.

➤ An array's subscript, which is a number within parentheses appended to the array's name, identifies each element of the array. A subscript is sometimes called an index.

➤ By using a numerical variable for an array's subscript, you can easily access each element of the array within a loop.

➤ To tell Visual Basic how large an array should be, you declare the array with a Dim statement.

➤ Visual Basic can create not only arrays of values, but also arrays of controls.

Chapter 12

File Handling: The Ol' Data I/O Shuffle

In This Chapter

➤ Open and close files

➤ Save data to a file

➤ Load data from a file

➤ Add data to an existing file

As you've used your computer, you've no doubt noticed that most applications save and load data to and from your hard disk. The applications you write with Visual Basic don't have to be any different; they, too, can save information to a disk file. If you've been trying to save data from your Visual Basic programs by photographing the screen, you're going to love this chapter!

Steps in Accessing a File

Simple file handling is actually an easy process, after you get the hang of it. However, you need to perform three steps to be sure that your program's data gets properly tucked away in that binary home called a file. Those steps are as follows:

1. Open the file
2. Send data to the file or read data from the file
3. Close the file

In the following sections, you'll cover each of these steps in detail.

Opening a File

Probably the most complicated part of managing file I/O (input/output, remember?) is opening the file in the proper mode. You see, not only can files be used to save and load data, but they also can be used to save and load specific kinds of data in specific ways. For example, there's a big difference between opening a file to read a line of text and opening a file to read a database record, even though a file must be opened in both cases. Specifically, you can open a file in one of five different modes:

➤ Append

➤ Binary

➤ Input

➤ Output

➤ Random

Before you reach for the Valium, let me assure you these mode thingies are not as confusing as they might seem to be. First, because you're just starting out, you can forget about the Binary and Random modes. You'll leave those puppies to a more advanced book that covers things like databases, records, and binary files. Feeling better already, right?

The remaining modes are easy to understand. To prove that claim, you're about to open a file in Output mode, which makes good sense. You can't, after all, load data from a file until you've saved data to the file. Here's the Visual Basic statement that opens a file in the Output mode:

```
Open "c:\MyFile.dat" For Output As #1
```

The keyword Open tells Visual Basic that you're about to open a file. (Programs lines like Open My Mail really annoy Visual Basic.) The string that follows the Open keyword is the path and name of the file you want to open. In this case, the file is called MyFile.dat and is located in the root directory of drive C.

Now comes the part that determines the file mode. See the For Output? That tells Visual Basic you want to open the file in the Output mode. This mode enables a program to save data to the disk file. In this case, the file is MyFile.dat. If the file doesn't already exist, Visual Basic creates it. If the file does exist, Visual Basic gets the file ready to accept output from your program, which includes erasing the current contents of the file.

Examine that last sentence carefully! Yes, the sentence includes 15 E's, which is the most commonly used letter in the English language. However, you didn't really need to examine the sentence *that* closely. What you do need to notice is the phrase "…which includes erasing the current contents of the file." To state the point again, *if you use the Output mode to open an existing file, Visual Basic erases the previous contents of the file.*

That's all there is to opening a file, except for that mysterious As #1 tacked on the end of the line. Every time your program opens a file, the program needs a way to refer to the file. The same way your friends might refer to you as Mack, Sarah, Willie, or "Hey, Einstein," your Visual Basic program must refer to the open file with a number. In this case, that number is 1. You could try writing Open "C:\MyFile.dat" For Output As Willie, but it's unlikely to work and will annoy Willie.

Saving Data to the File

Your file is now open, sitting there patiently on your disk drive like a kitten waiting for a scratch behind the ears. The file, however, will sit there waiting patiently for attention long after the kitten has wandered away in boredom. I wouldn't suggest that you try to scratch your file behind the ears, but it might be a good idea at this point to put some data into the file, something you can do with a Visual Basic command like this:

```
Print #1, "This is a test"
```

As you undoubtedly realize, the keyword Print, which you've run into before in other contexts, tells Visual Basic you want to print data to a file. Visual Basic knows you're printing to a file rather than to the screen, thanks to the #1 after the Print keyword. The number is the same number the program used to open the file. Remember the As #1 part of the Open statement? That's the culprit.

Punctuation Is Important!

When you are typing program lines, make sure you get all the punctuation right. Leaving out something as simple as a comma can bring your program to a crashing halt. For example, don't forget the comma in the Print statement, between the file number and the data to save.

After the file number, you place a comma and follow it with the data you want to save to the file. In this case, the data is the string "This is a test". After Visual Basic has performed this command, your file will contain the string, no fuss or muss.

Closing the File

When you put a bird in a cage, you finish the task by closing the cage door. A file and its data are similar. After you place data into the file, you must close the file; otherwise, you might wind up losing data. Data doesn't have wings like a bird, of course, but it can still fly away into the great unknown. Take it from someone who's lost enough data to fill an encyclopedia.

To close a file, you call upon the ever trusty `Close` statement, like this:

```
Close #1
```

You've probably already figured out that the number after the `Close` keyword is the same number the program gave the file when it opened it with the `Open` statement.

Entering the Buffer Zone

Closing files in a Visual Basic program (and most programs written in other languages, as well) is important because not all the data you've sent to the file has necessarily arrived there before you close the file. The reason for this anomaly is something called *buffering*. Because disk drives are so slow compared with computer memory, Visual Basic doesn't actually send data directly to the disk file. Instead, it saves up the data in your computer's memory until it has enough data to be worth taking the time to access the disk drive. The `Close` statement tells Visual Basic not only to close the file, but also to be sure to send all the data from the buffer first.

Automatic File Closing

Although it's important to close your files after accessing them, the truth is that if you don't, Visual Basic will. However, Visual Basic closes all open files only when the program ends normally. Leaving file closing up to Visual Basic is dangerous. If something should happen so that the program doesn't end normally, Visual Basic can't close the file for you, and you might lose data.

Trying It Out

It's time now to see all this file stuff put to work. To do this, start a new Visual Basic project (a Standard EXE), and place Label, Textbox, and Command Button controls on the form, as shown here:

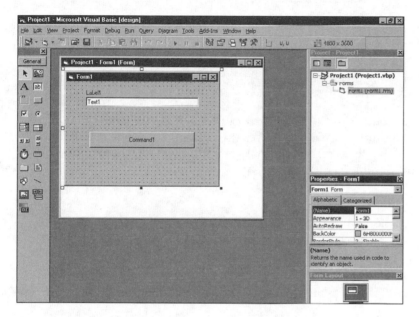

Position your controls as shown in this figure.

Now, double-click the Command Button control to bring up the code window, and type the following program lines (Visual Basic will have already started the Command1_Click procedure for you):

```
Private Sub Command1_Click()
    Dim data As String

    data = Text1.Text
    Open "c:\MyFile.dat" For Output As #1
    Print #1, data
    Close #1
    MsgBox "Text saved."
End Sub

Private Sub Form_Load()
    Label1.Caption = "Enter the text to file:"
    Text1.Text = "Default text"
    Command1.Caption = "Save Text"
End Sub
```

After typing the lines, save your work, and run the program. When you do, the application's main window appears, which looks like this:

This application saves the contents of the text box to a file.

Type whatever text you want into the text box (or just leave the default text as is), and click the Save Text button. Visual Basic saves the contents of the text box to a file named MyFile.dat. This happens in the Command1_Click procedure, the first line of which declares a string variable:

```
Dim data As String
```

After declaring the variable, the program sets the variable to the text in the Textbox control:

```
data = Text1.Text
```

Next comes the old familiar Open statement, which opens the file for output:

```
Open "c:\MyFile.dat" For Output As #1
```

With the file open, the program can save the contents of the variable data to the file:

```
Print #1, data
```

Finally, the program closes the file and displays a message box that informs the user that the text was saved:

```
Close #1
MsgBox "Text saved."
```

The thing to notice about this program is that rather than having the Print statement save a string literal as was done previously, this Print statement saves the contents of a string variable. Visual Basic can save a string to the file either way, without the slightest bit of whining.

Loading Data from a File

Your file now has data in it. What that data actually is depends on what you typed into the text box before clicking the Save Text button. Data in a file, however, is about as useful as a clock to a goldfish if you have no way of getting the data out again. That's where the Input statement comes in handy. Luckily, you're about to see how that works.

Go back to the program you just worked on and add another Command Button control, like this:

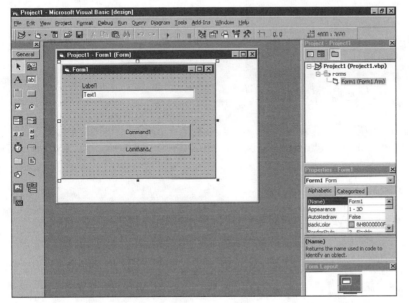

Add a button to the program's form.

Now add the following line to the Form_Load procedure (it can go anywhere in the procedure):

```
Command2.Caption = "Load Text"
```

Finally, double-click the new button to display the code window. Visual Basic will start the Command2_Click procedure for you. Add the lines needed to make the procedure look as follows:

```
Private Sub Command2_Click()
    Dim data As String

    Open "c:\MyFile.dat" For Input As #1
    Input #1, data
    Close #1
    Text1.Text = data
End Sub
```

You're now ready to try the program out again. Save your work and run the program. When the program's window appears, clear all the text from the text box, and click the Load Text button. When you do, the program gets the text you saved to the file and displays it in the text box. For example, if you previously saved the text line "You ain't nothin' but a hound dog", your program's window will look like the following figure after you click the Load Text button:

Now the program can load text, too.

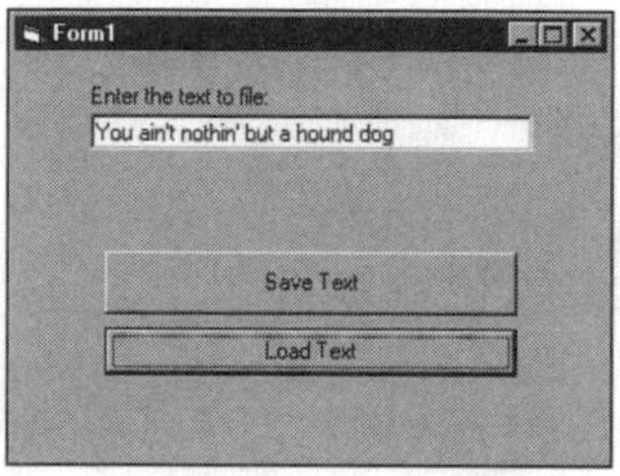

How does this program work? When you click the Load Text button, Visual Basic jumps to the Command2_Click procedure, the first line of which declares a string variable:

```
Dim data As String
```

After declaring the variable, the program opens the file for input:

```
Open "c:\MyFile.dat" For Input As #1
```

With the file open, the program can now load the text from the file and into the string variable data:

```
Input #1, data
```

Finally, the program closes the file and displays the loaded text in the text box:

```
Close #1
Text1.Text = data
```

Notice that the Input statement looks a lot like the Print statement. That is, the file number, a comma, and the variable name follow the Input keyword. In this case, though, the variable receives the data rather than holding the data that will go to the file.

Appending Data to a File

Every time you click the Save Text button, and the program opens the MyFile.dat file for output, the previous contents of the file get erased like a teacher's chalkboard at the end of the day. This is all fine and dandy if you want to start a new file, but what if you want to *add* something to the file? Easy! You open the file in Append mode.

To check this out, add yet another Command Button control to your program, so that the form looks like this:

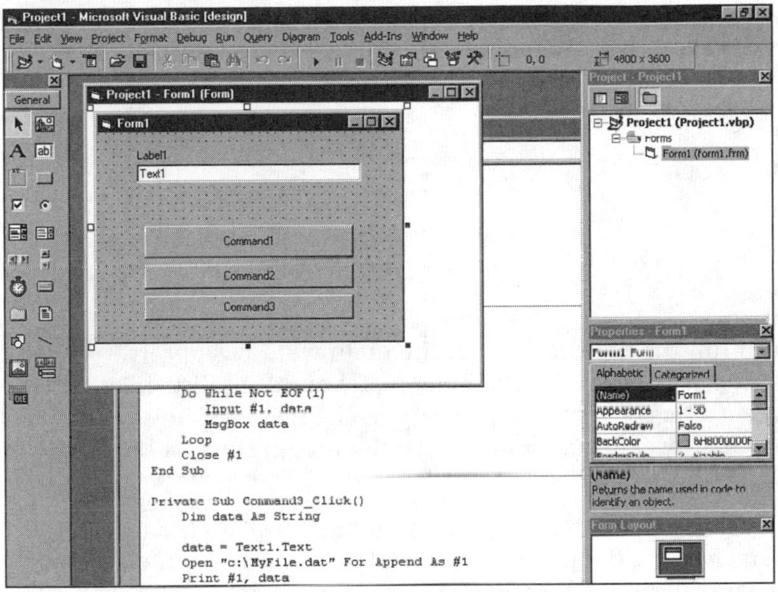

Add a third button to the program's form.

Now add the following line to the Form_Load procedure (it can go anywhere in the procedure):

```
Command3.Caption = "Append Text"
```

Finally, double-click the new button to display the code window. Visual Basic will start the Command3_Click procedure for you. Add the lines needed to make the procedure look as follows:

```
Private Sub Command3_Click()
    Dim data As String

    data = Text1.Text
    Open "c:\MyFile.dat" For Append As #1
    Print #1, data
    Close #1
    MsgBox "Text saved."
End Sub
```

This procedure is almost exactly like Command1_Click, except it opens the file in Append mode, rather than in Output mode.

Finally, because your file will have more than one line of text in it after the append, the program needs to change the way it inputs data from the file. Specifically, the program needs to keep loading text strings until it gets to the end of the file. To do this, replace the current Command2_Click procedure with the following revised procedure:

149

```
Private Sub Command2_Click()
    Dim data As String

    Open "c:\MyFile.dat" For Input As #1
    Do While Not EOF(1)
        Input #1, data
        MsgBox data
    Loop
    Close #1
End Sub
```

Now, save your work and run the program. When the main window appears, type some text into the text box, and then click the Append Text button. Visual Basic saves the text immediately after the text that's already in the file. You can save as many text strings as you like by continuing to change the text in the text box and clicking the Append Text button.

When you click the Load Text button, the program no longer displays the text in the text box, because there is more than one line of text in the file. Instead, the program loads a line of text, and displays it in a message box, as shown here:

The program now displays text in a text box.

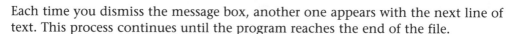

Each time you dismiss the message box, another one appears with the next line of text. This process continues until the program reaches the end of the file.

How does the program know when it's reached the end of the file? The secret to that little mystery lies in the revised Command2_Click procedure. The procedure opens the file for input as you would expect, but then it starts a Do While loop, the first line of which looks like this:

```
Do While Not EOF(1)
```

You already know what a Do While loop is, and you know what the Not operator does, but what's that EOF(1)? EOF is a function that equals the value True when the file is at the end and False if the file is not at its end. (Programmers say the function *returns* the value True or False.) The number in the parentheses is the number assigned to the file in the Open statement. Basically, the first line of the Do While loop can be translated into English as "Do while file #1 is not at the end of the file."

150

Inside the loop, the program loads and displays a line of text:

```
Input #1, data
MsgBox data
```

Then the `Loop` keyword sends Visual Basic back to the beginning of the loop, where the function `EOF` again checks for the end of the file. (Guess what EOF stands for?) If the program hasn't reached the end of the file yet, the loop loads another line of text; otherwise, the loops ends.

Strings, Integers, and More

In this chapter, you've used files only to save text data. However, you can use the file-handling techniques you've learned to save most kinds of data to a file, including integers and floating-point values. For example, if you have an integer variable called `myInt`, you can save it to an open file with a line like `Print #1, myInt`.

The Least You Need to Know

➤ Accessing a file requires three steps: Opening the file, saving or loading data to or from the file, and closing the file.

➤ The `Open` statement opens a file in one of five modes. Those modes are `Append`, `Binary`, `Input`, `Output`, and `Random`. Currently, you don't need to know about `Binary` and `Random` files; they're for more advanced programmers.

➤ The `Print #` statement stores data in an open file.

➤ The `Input #` statement loads data from an open file.

➤ When a program finishes with a file, it must close the file with the `Close` statement. Failure to close the file properly could result in lost data.

➤ The `Output` file mode creates the file if it doesn't exist or opens and erases the file if it does exist.

➤ The `Input` file mode enables a program to read data from an existing file.

➤ The `Append` file mode enables a program to add data to an already existing file.

➤ The `EOF` function returns `True` when the program has reached the end of a file and returns `False` if the program has not reached the end of the file.

Chapter 13

Procedures and Functions: Breaking Things Down

In This Chapter

➤ Organize programs into small parts

➤ Write your own procedures

➤ Learn to write functions

➤ Discover variable scope

➤ Find out how to pass arguments to procedures and functions

Until now, your programs have been pretty short, each designed to demonstrate a single programming technique. When you start writing real programs, however, you'll quickly discover that they can grow to many pages of code. When programs become long, they also become harder to organize and read. To overcome this problem, professional programmers developed something called modular programming, the topic you will study in this chapter.

The Top-Down Approach to Programming

As I said, long programs are hard to organize and read. A full-length program might contain twenty or more pages of code, and trying to find a specific part of the program in all that code can be tough. To solve this problem, you can use modular programming techniques. Using these techniques, you break a long program into individual subprograms, each of which performs a specific task.

To understand how modular programming works, consider how you might organize the cleaning of a house. (The only reasonable way to clean my house is to douse it with gasoline and throw in a lighted match, but I won't get into that now.) The main task might be called CLEAN HOUSE. Thinking about cleaning an entire house, however, can be overwhelming—just ask my wife. So, to make the task easier, you can break it down into a number of smaller steps. These steps might be

1. CLEAN LIVING ROOM
2. CLEAN BEDROOM
3. CLEAN KITCHEN
4. CLEAN BATHROOM

After breaking the housecleaning task down into room-by-room steps, you have a better idea of what to do. But cleaning a room is also a pretty big task—especially if it hasn't been done in a while or if you have cats coughing up fur balls all over the place. So why not break each room step down, too? For example, cleaning the living room could be broken down into

1. PICK UP ROOM
2. DUST AND POLISH
3. CLEAN FURNITURE
4. VACUUM RUG

After breaking each room's cleaning down into steps, your housecleaning job is organized much like a pyramid, with the general task on the top. As you work your way down the pyramid, from the main task to the room-by-room list, and finally to the tasks for each room, the tasks become more and more specific.

Of course, when cleaning a house, you don't usually write a list of steps. If you're an efficient housecleaner, the steps are organized in your mind. However, if you clean house like me, there are only two steps:

1. TURN ON TV
2. COLLAPSE ON COUCH

Getting back to writing a program, though, which is a more conceptual type of task, you might not have a clear idea of exactly what needs to be done. This can lead you to your being overwhelmed by the project. Overwhelmed programmers are easy to spot. They stare at their computer screens blankly and often break into bouts of weeping.

Breaking programming tasks down into steps is called *modular programming*. When you break your program's modules down into even smaller subprograms—as we did with the task of cleaning a house—you're using a *top-down* approach to program design. By using top-down programming techniques, you can write any program as a series of small, easy-to-handle tasks.

Visual Basic provides two types of subprograms you can use when writing programs. The first type, procedures, is covered in the next section. The second type, functions, is covered later in this chapter.

The Length of a Subprogram

You should break programs into small subprograms in order to make program code easier to understand. To this end, each subprogram in a program should perform only a single main task, so it stays short and to the point. When you try to cram too much functionality into a subprogram, it loses its identity. If you can't state a subprogram's purpose in two or three words, it's probably doing too much.

Using Procedures

One type of subprogram is a procedure. A procedure is like a small program within your main program. If you were writing a housecleaning program, the procedures in the main module might be called `CleanLivingRoom`, `CleanBedroom`, `CleanKitchen`, and `CleanBathroom`. The `CleanLivingRoom` procedure would contain all the steps needed to clean the living room, the `CleanBedroom` procedure would contain all the steps needed to clean a bedroom, and so on.

Of course, it takes an extremely talented programmer to get a computer to clean a house. If you manage that trick, contact me immediately. For now, we need a more computer-oriented example. Suppose you want to write a program that draws a moving arrow onscreen. (Don't ask why.) The following program shows how to do it.

First, start a new Visual Basic project (a Standard EXE), and place Label and Command Button controls on the form, as shown in the following figure:

Now, double-click the Command Button control to bring up Visual Basic's code window, and type the following program lines (Visual Basic will have already started the `Command1_Click` procedure for you):

```
Option Explicit

Private Sub Command1_Click()
    Dim x As Integer

    For x = 20 To 4000 Step 5
        Call Arrow(x)
```

```
        Next x
End Sub

Sub Arrow(x As Integer)
    Dim delay As Integer

    Label1.Left = x
    For delay = 1 To 10000
    Next delay
End Sub

Private Sub Form_Load()
    Label1.Caption = ">>--->"
    Command1.Caption = "Fire Arrow"
End Sub
```

Position your controls as
shown here.

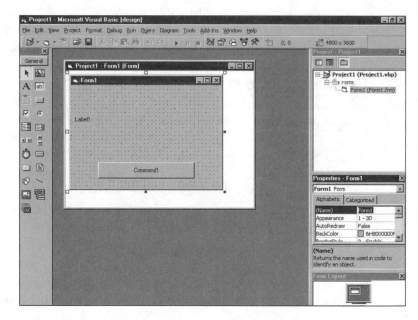

After you complete the typing, save your work and run the program. When you do, you see the window shown here:

Click the Fire Arrow button and then duck! Your new program fires the arrow across the application's window.

Now for the hundred-million-dollar question: How does this program work? The program is divided into three procedures. Two of these procedures, Form_Load and Command1_Click, are already good friends. The third procedure is named Arrow and is run (called) by the Command1_Click procedure. The For/Next loop in the Command1_Click calls the Arrow procedure each time through the loop.

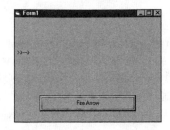

Your new application fires an arrow.

When the Command1_Click calls Arrow, the program lines in Arrow execute. In other words, the program branches to the first line of Arrow and executes all the statements until it gets to the End Sub line. When it reaches the End Sub line, the program branches back to Command1_Click, to the next line following the procedure call. Because the line following the procedure call is the end of the For/Next loop, the program goes back to the top of the loop, increments x by 5 (see the Step 5?), and calls Arrow yet again. This continues until the loop runs out, which is when x grows larger than 4,000. The following figure illustrates the process of calling the Arrow procedure in the For/Next loop:

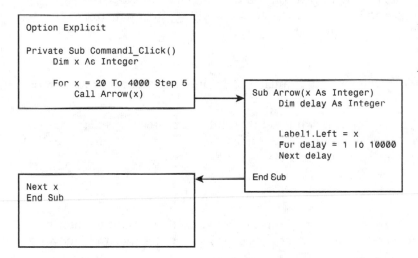

Program execution branches from the Command1_Click procedure to Arrow and back again.

Take a look at the call to the Arrow procedure, which looks like this:

```
Call Arrow(x)
```

See the x in the parentheses? That is a procedure argument. Arguments in procedures work just like the arguments you used when calling Visual Basic's built-in functions. You use arguments to pass into procedures the values those procedures need to do their job. For example, in Chapter 6, "String and Text: A Frank Textual Discussion," you learned to get a string's length by calling the Len function like this:

```
length = Len(str)
```

In this case, str is the function's argument, just as x in the call to Arrow is Arrow's argument. You need to give Arrow this argument because Arrow needs to know the current value of the loop-control variable. This value determines where the arrow is drawn, as you can see when you look at the program lines in the Arrow procedure.

The first line declares the procedure and its arguments:

```
Sub Arrow(x As Integer)
```

The Sub keyword stands for "subroutine" and is followed by the procedure's name. (The rules for naming procedures are the same as those for naming variables.) After the procedure's name come the procedure's arguments in parentheses. Notice that the argument's type is included, just as with a Dim statement.

The next line declares an integer variable called delay:

```
Dim delay As Integer
```

Because the arrow is just text in a Label control, the program can move the arrow by moving the label. It does this by setting the position of the label's left edge to the value passed into the procedure by Command1_Click:

```
Label1.Left = x
```

Setting the label's Left property causes Visual Basic to move the label to the new location.

Because computers process information faster than Bill Gates amasses dollars, a For/Next loop in the Arrow procedure forces the computer to count from 1 to 10,000 in order to slow down the speed of the arrow:

```
For delay = 1 To 10000
Next delay
```

You can change the 10000 in this loop to some other value if you want to change how fast the arrow moves. The smaller the loop's limit, the faster the arrow moves.

That wasn't too tough, was it? Unfortunately, using procedures is a little more complicated than it might appear from the above discussion. If you jump right in and try to write your own procedures at this point, you'll run into trouble faster than a dog catches fleas in the springtime. Before you can write good procedures, you must at least learn about something called variable scope. Coincidentally, variable scope is the next topic in this chapter.

The Number of Arguments

For all practical purposes, a procedure can have as many arguments as you like. But you must be sure the arguments you specify in the procedure's call exactly match the type and order of the arguments in the procedure's Sub line.

To use more than one argument in a procedure, separate the arguments with commas. For example, to add the argument y to the Arrow call, you would type Call Arrow(x, y). Then, so the arguments match, you must change the first line of Arrow to Sub Arrow (x As Integer, y As Integer).

You can use different variable names in the Sub line, as long as they are the same type. In other words, using the arrow example, you can also type Sub Arrow(col As Integer, length As Integer). In the procedure, you would then use the variable names col and length, rather than the original x and y.

Procedures don't have to have arguments. To call a procedure that has no arguments, you wouldn't need the parentheses. For example: Call Arrow.

The Order of Arguments

You can pass one or more arguments to a procedure. However, keep in mind that the arguments are passed to the procedure in the order in which they appear in the procedure call. The procedure's Sub line should list the arguments in the same order they are listed in the procedure call.

Variable Scope

Now that you know a little about procedures, you should know how Visual Basic organizes variables between procedures. You might wonder, for example, why x must be an argument in the call to Arrow. Why couldn't you just use the variable x in the procedure? After all, they're part of the same program, right?

You need arguments in your procedures because of something called *variable scope*, which determines whether program procedures can "see" a specific variable. For example, if you were to change the program so Command1_Click did not pass x as an argument to Arrow, you would get a Variable Not Defined error when the program tried to execute Arrow. (This assumes that you have the line Option Explicit in the program.)

Here's why: A variable in one procedure is not accessible in another. When you don't explicitly pass x as an argument, the Arrow procedure can't access it. When the procedure tries to access the variable anyway, Visual Basic doesn't recognize it and generates an error.

In Arrow's case, the x is *local* to Arrow. Just as Command1_Click's x cannot be seen in any other procedure (it's local to Command1_Click), Arrow's x cannot be seen in any procedure except Arrow. This might seem at first like a crazy way to do things, but when you think about it, it makes a lot of sense.

By not allowing a variable to be seen outside of the procedure in which it's declared, you never have to worry about some other procedure accidentally changing that variable's value. Moreover, local variables make procedures self-contained, as if everything the procedure needs were put together in a little box. If the value of a variable used in a procedure is giving your program trouble, you know exactly which module to check. You don't need to search your entire program to find the problem any more than you need to search your entire house to find a quart of milk. The following figure illustrates the concept of global and local variables:

Global variables, represented here by GlobalA and GlobalB, are available in any procedure.

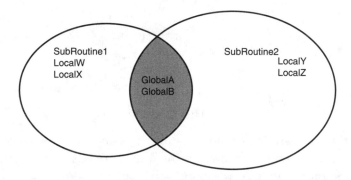

The opposite of a local variable is a *global* variable. You can use global variables in any procedure anywhere in your program. Here is a new version of your arrow program, which makes x a global variable. Because x is now a global variable, it need not be passed as an argument to the Arrow procedure.

More About Undeclared Variables

As you know, if you include the Option Explicit statement in your program, Visual Basic will present you with an error when it comes across a variable it doesn't recognize. In the Arrow procedure, this keeps you from forgetting to pass x as an argument. However, if you left off the Option Explicit, Visual Basic will no longer insist on all variables being declared before they're used. So, when Visual Basic sees the undeclared x in Arrow, it will just assume that x is a new variable and will assign it the default value of 0. That will make your arrow label move to position 0 and stay there. Talk about a sluggish arrow!

```
Option Explicit
Dim x As Integer

Private Sub Command1_Click()
    For x = 20 To 4000 Step 5
        Call Arrow
    Next x
End Sub

Sub Arrow()
    Dim delay As Integer

    Label1.Left = x
    For delay = 1 To 10000
    Next delay
End Sub

Private Sub Form_Load()
    Label1.Caption = ">>--->"
    Command1.Caption = "Fire Arrow"
End Sub
```

Near the top of the program, the line

```
Dim x As Integer
```

is the statement that makes x a global variable. This variable becomes global because the program declares the variable outside of all the other procedures.

A Big No-No

As a novice programmer, you might think using global variables is a great programming shortcut. After all, if you make all your variables global, you'll never have to worry about passing arguments to procedures. However, a program with a lot of global variables is a poorly designed program—hard to read and hard to debug. You should write your programs to include as few global variables as possible.

Using Functions

Functions are another way you can break up your programs into small parts. But unlike procedures, functions return a value to the procedure that calls them. You've used Visual Basic functions before in this book; the Len function, for example. The value it returns is the number of characters in a string.

You write functions much like procedures. However, function calls must assign the function's return value to a variable. Suppose you have a function named GetNum that gets a number from the user and returns it to your program. A call to the function might look something like num = GetNum().

To get some experience with functions, start a new Visual Basic project (a Standard EXE), and place Label, Textbox, and Command Button controls on the form, as shown in the following figure:

Now, double-click the Command Button control to bring up Visual Basic's code window, and type the following program lines (Visual Basic will have already started the Command1_Click procedure for you):

```
Option Explicit

Private Sub Command1_Click()
    Dim msg As String
    msg = GetResponse()
    MsgBox msg
End Sub

Function GetResponse() As String
    GetResponse = Text1.Text
End Function
```

```
Private Sub Form_Load()
    Label1.Caption = "Type a response:"
    Text1.Text = "Default response"
    Command1.Caption = "Get Response"
End Sub
```

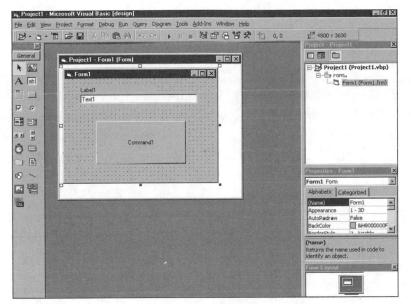

Position your controls as shown here.

After you complete the typing, save your work and run the program. When you do, you will see the window shown here:

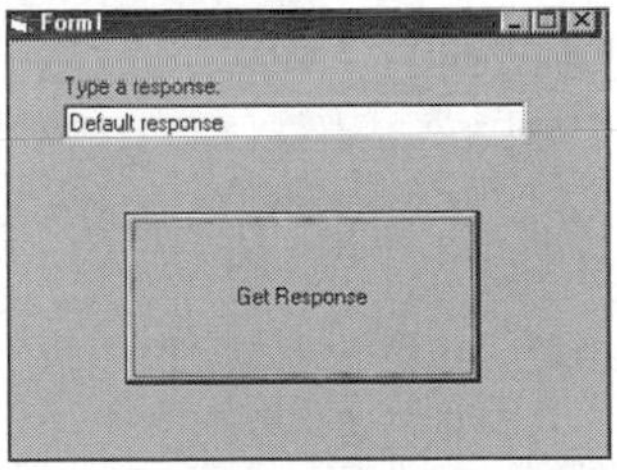

This program calls a function when you click the button.

Type something into the text box, and then click the Get Response button. The program displays a message box that contains the text from the text box. This wouldn't be such a big deal all by itself, except for the fact that the program is using your own function GetResponse to get the text from the text box.

The first line of the function declares the function and its return-value type:

```
Function GetResponse() As String
```

163

The keyword `Function`, of course, tells Visual Basic that you're declaring a function. The name of the function and a set of parentheses follow the `Function` keyword. If this function required arguments, you would have to declare them in the parentheses, just as you did with a procedure. The `As String` part of the line tells Visual Basic that this function returns a string value to the calling procedure.

The next line of the function is the line that tells Visual Basic what value to return from the function:

```
GetResponse = Text1.Text
```

In this case, the function returns the string the user entered into the `Text1` text box. Notice that to return a value from a function, you assign the function's name a value, the same way you assign values to a variable.

Finally, the function's last line tells Visual Basic it has reached the end of the function:

```
End Function
```

The Least You Need to Know

➤ *Modular programming* means breaking a program up into a series of simple tasks.

➤ *Top-down programming* means organizing procedures in a hierarchy, with general-purpose procedures at the top that call specific-purpose procedures lower in the hierarchy.

➤ Procedures and functions are the two types of subprograms you can use when writing a Visual Basic program. Functions must return values, whereas procedures do not.

➤ A function declaration includes not only the keyword `Function` and the function name, but also the clause `As` *type*, which tells Visual Basic the type of value the function returns. In this case, *type* is a data type such as `Integer` or `String`.

➤ A program returns a value from a function by assigning a value to the function's name.

➤ Procedures and functions might or might not receive values called arguments, which are sent to the subprogram by the calling procedure.

➤ *Local* variables are accessible only within the subprogram in which they appear. *Global* variables, which are declared outside of any subprogram, are accessible anywhere in a program.

Chapter 14

Printing: Your Own Edition of Hard Copy

In This Chapter

➤ Discover Visual Basic's Printer object

➤ Print text on a page

➤ Print multiple pages of text

➤ Position text on the page

Since you started studying Visual Basic, you've learned quite a lot about I/O. You now know how to get data from the user, how to give information back to the user, and even how to save and load data to and from a hard disk. There's only one more trick you need to know: How to get your data from the computer onto a piece of paper. That's where Visual Basic's Printer object comes in. Using the Printer object is a heck of a lot easier than copying data off the screen with a pencil and pad!

The Printer Object

Visual Basic provides a special object, called Printer, that gives a program access to the current system printer. Using the Printer object, you can do all sort of printing tasks like printing text and images. Using the Printer object is a snap. In fact, it takes only one Visual Basic program line to print a line of text on the printer. For example, the following line prints the text Yep, the printer's working! on the current default printer:

```
Printer.Print "Yep, the printer's working!"
```

Objects, Properties, and Methods

As you'll learn in Chapter 16, "Controls and Objects: There's a Difference?" Visual Basic provides a set of standard objects that enable programs to access system peripherals such as the screen and the printer. The Printer object is one of those objects, and like most objects and controls, Printer features a number of methods and properties that enable a program to control the object in various ways. In this chapter, you'll explore a few of the Printer object's methods and properties.

A Collection of Printers

Many computer systems—maybe even yours—have more than one printer connected simultaneously. One of those printers is the default printer, which is the printer that the Printer object represents. However, you can get at the other printers by accessing the application's Printers collection, which, apropos of its name, represents the collection of printers currently on the system. Manipulating the Printers collection is not especially difficult, but is beyond the scope of this book. If you're interested in learning more, though, look up the Printers collection in your Visual Basic online documentation.

To try printing yourself (well, you won't be printing yourself; threading yourself through the printer's rollers can be a nasty business), start a new Visual Basic project (a Standard EXE), and place Label, Textbox, and Command Button controls on the form, as shown here:

After placing the controls, double-click the Command Button control to bring up the code window. Type the following lines into the code window (Visual Basic will have already started the Command1_Click procedure for you):

```
Private Sub Command1_Click()
    Dim line1 As String
```

```
        line1 = Text1.Text
        Printer.Print line1
        Printer.EndDoc
    End Sub

    Private Sub Form_Load()
        Label1.Caption = "Line #1:"
        Text1.Text = "Default line #1"
        Command1.Caption = "Print Text"
    End Sub
```

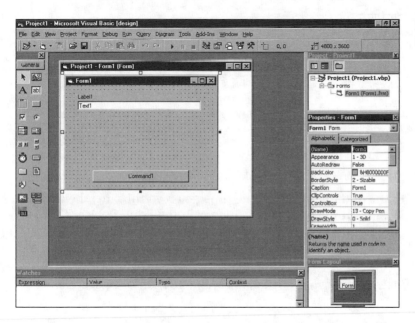

Position the controls as shown in this figure.

When you're done typing, save your work, and run the program. When you do, you'll see the following window:

This program sends the contents of a text box to a printer.

Type some text into the text box (or stick with the default text) and click the Print Text button. The program then grabs the text from the text box and sends it to your printer. When your newly printed page drops into your printer's hopper, whoop with delight and then quickly assure the rest of the family that you're really just fine. (Spouses and children often become alarmed when Mom or Dad starts yelling "Whoop, whoop, whooooop!" for no apparent reason.)

Now that you've gotten all that whooping out of your system, take a look at the program's source-code lines. When you clicked the Print Text button, Visual Basic jumped to the `Command1_Click` procedure, where the first line declares a string variable:

```
Dim line1 As String
```

Next, the program assigns the contents of the text box to the newly declared string variable:

```
line1 = Text1.Text
```

With the text in hand (Visual Basic programs have hands?), the program can send the text to the printer, which it does by calling the Printer object's `Print` method, like this:

```
Printer.Print line1
```

Now your text is off to the printer. In fact, by the time you read this line, the text is already printed. The last line in the procedure, which calls the Printer object's `EndDoc` method, ensures that the printer ejects the printed page:

```
Printer.EndDoc
```

That was easy, eh? What? You say your documents are more than one page? No problem. Read on.

Multiple Lines of Text

Although the previous sample program printed only a single line of text, printing multiple lines is a simple matter of calling the Printer object's `Print` method once for each line you want to print. Just don't call the `EndDoc` method until you've printed all the text you want on the current page.

Printing Multiple Pages

In the previous section, you learned about the Printer object's `EndDoc` method, which ends the current document. The Printer object also has a method, called `NewPage`, that enables a program to start a new page in a document. By using both the `EndDoc` and `NewPage` methods, you can print a complete document, no matter how many pages it is.

To try this out, add a Label control and a Textbox control to the previous program, as shown here:

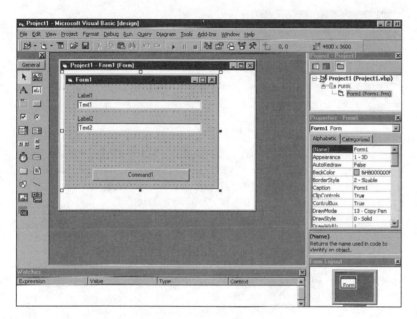

Position the new label and text box as shown in this figure.

After placing the controls, double-click the form to bring up the code window. Modify the existing `Command1_Click` and `Form_Load` procedures so that they look like this:

```
Private Sub Command1_Click()
    Dim line1 As String

    line1 = Text1.Text
    Printer.Print line1
    Printer.NewPage
    line1 = Text2.Text
    Printer.Print line1
    Printer.EndDoc
End Sub


Private Sub Form_Load()
```

```
        Label1.Caption = "Line #1:"
        Text1.Text = "Default line #1"
        Command1.Caption = "Print Text"
        Label2.Caption = "Line #2:"
        Text2.Text = "Default line #2"
    End Sub
```

When you're done typing, save your work, and run the program. When you do, you'll see the following window:

This program prints two pages of text.

Type some text into both text boxes (or stick with the default text), and click the Print Text button. The program then prints the first line on page one of the document and the second line on page two of the document. Go ahead now and frighten your family again with those ghastly whoop sounds. You've earned it!

Headers and Footers

After you get thehang of the NewPage method, printing headers and footers on a page is pretty easy. Print your header text right after the call to NewPage. Print the footer text right before the next call to NewPage. In the following section of this chapter, you'll see how to position text anywhere you want on the page, which will help you get your headers and footer in the right places.

Positioning Text

It takes a lot of work to print out a sophisticated document like Microsoft Word prints. You'll have to do some serious studying to get that far with your printing skills. However, another pretty easy trick you can use to flex your printing muscles is to position text or images on the page. By setting the values of the Printer object's

CurrentX and CurrentY properties, you can determine where on a page data gets printed. Moreover, you can determine the size of a page by getting the values of the Printer object's Width and Height properties.

Ready to try this trick out? Start a new Visual Basic project (a Standard EXE), and place Label, Textbox, and Command Button controls on the form, as shown here:

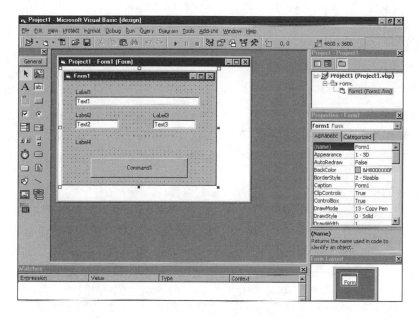

Position the controls as shown in this figure.

After placing the controls, double-click the Command Button control to bring up the code window. Type the following lines into the code window (Visual Basic will have already started the Command1_Click procedure for you):

```
Private Sub Command1_Click()
    Dim line As String
    Dim xPos As Integer
    Dim yPos As Integer

    line = Text1.Text
    xPos = Text2.Text
    yPos = Text3.Text
    Printer.CurrentX = xPos
    Printer.CurrentY = yPos
    Printer.Print line
    Printer.EndDoc
End Sub

Private Sub Form_Load()
    Label1.Caption = "Line to print:"
```

```
      Text1.Text = "Default line"
      Label2.Caption = "X position:"
      Text2.Text = "0"
      Label3.Caption = "Y position:"
      Text3.Text = "0"
      Label4.Caption = "Printer width: " & Printer.Width & _
           "            Printer height: " & Printer.Height
      Command1.Caption = "Print Text"
      Printer.FontSize = 24
   End Sub
```

When you're done typing, save your work, and run the program. When you do, you'll see the following window:

This program can position text anywhere on the page.

This application's window gives you a place to type the text you want to print, as well as places to type the text's X (horizontal) and Y (vertical) positions on the page. To help you choose the correct X and Y values, the window also displays the current page's width and height (in twips, which are tiny units of measurement used in Visual Basic). The position 0,0 is the page's upper-left corner. When you use the highest X and Y values, you're positioning the start of the text in the page's lower-right corner.

Type some text into the first text box, type the horizontal and vertical positions for the text in the remaining text boxes, and then click the Print Text button. The program then retrieves the text from the text box and sends it to your printer, right at the location you specified. Whoop!

The Form_Load procedure is the first place in this program you'll stumble across unfamiliar programming stuff. Most of the lines in this procedure should be no mystery, but the lines

```
      Label4.Caption = "Printer width: " & Printer.Width & _
           "            Printer height: " & Printer.Height
```

might be slightly perplexing. This line does a lot of work, as described here:

1. Gets the page's width and height from the Printer object's Width and Height properties.

2. Builds a text string from string literals and the width and height values.

3. Assigns the text string to the Label4 control's Caption property, which makes the printer's width and height appear in the application's window when you run the program.

Another strange line is

```
Printer.FontSize = 24
```

which does nothing more than set the current text size for the Printer object to 24 points. Thanks to this line, when you print your text, it won't be as tiny as it was in previous versions of the program.

A Little Something to Point Out

If the term *points* sounds unfamiliar, you probably haven't done much on your computer with text applications. Simply, points are a measurement of a font's size. Specifically, a point equals 1/72 of an inch. Therefore, a 72-point font is one-inch high, a 36-point font is 1/2-inch high, and so on.

The next place to look is the Command1_Click procedure, the first lines of which declare the variables needed in the procedure:

```
Dim line As String
Dim xPos As Integer
Dim yPos As Integer
```

The procedure then gets the text to print and the position at which to print it:

```
line = Text1.Text
xPos = Text2.Text
yPos = Text3.Text
```

Setting the Printer object's CurrentX and CurrentY properties to the specified values positions the text printing position on the page:

```
Printer.CurrentX = xPos
Printer.CurrentY = yPos
```

Finally, the program prints the line of text, and ends the document:

```
Printer.Print line
Printer.EndDoc
```

173

The Least You Need to Know

➤ Visual Basic's Printer object provides a program with quick and easy access to the current default printer on a system.

➤ The Printer object's `Print` method sends text to the printer.

➤ The Printer object's `EndDoc` method ends a document and ejects the page from the printer.

➤ To print multiple-page documents, call the Printer object's `NewPage` method to start each new page.

➤ The Printer object's `CurrentX` and `CurrentY` properties determine the position at which the next call to `Print` will print data.

➤ The Printer object's `Width` and `Height` properties hold the width and height of a page (in twips).

Chapter 15

The Art of Bug Extermination: Raid for the New Millennium

In This Chapter

➤ Examine the Debug menu

➤ Step through a program line by line

➤ Toggle breakpoints on and off

➤ Peek at the values of variables while a program runs

A problem you'll discover when writing full-length programs is finding and fixing programming errors. When a program is only a few lines long, you can easily examine each line of code and locate problems. But when a program grows to hundreds or even thousands of lines, you won't want to look at every line in the program (unless you're the type of person who likes to read phone books from cover to cover). Instead, you'll want to isolate the problem to a specific part of the program so you can find your error more quickly. Visual Basic's built-in debugger, which you study in this chapter, can help you find these errors.

Program Debugging

As your programs get longer, you'll discover finding errors can be difficult and confusing. Often, something will go wrong with your program, and you'll have no idea where to look for the problem. This can lead to sleepless nights, a bad disposition, and the inability to eat pizza for breakfast. Luckily, Visual Basic includes a simple debugger that can help you find programming errors. The commands that control the debugger are found in the Debug menu, shown here:

The Debug menu will help you find program-ming errors.

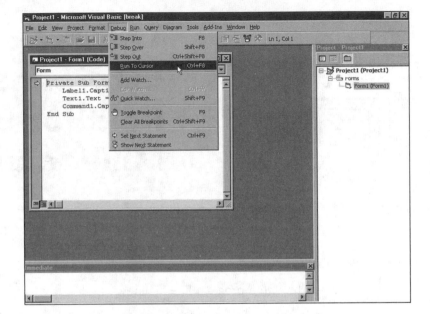

Types of Program Bugs

Two types of programming errors might crop up in your programs. The first is a *runtime error*, which usually causes the program to crash and display an error message. The other type of error, a *logic error*, is much more insidious and hard to find. A logic error occurs when you think you've written the program to do one thing, but it's really doing something else entirely. Such errors cause programmers to scream, "Don't do what I say; do what I want!"

Stepping Through a Program

The first command in the Debug menu is Step Into, which allows you to step through your program a line at a time. Each time you select this command (the easiest way is to press F8), your program executes a single line of code and then pauses for your next command.

To see how this works, start a new Visual Basic project (a Standard EXE) and place Label, Textbox, and Command Button controls on the form, as shown here:

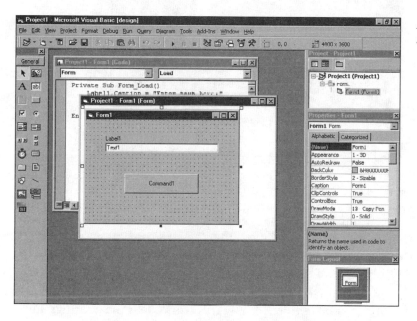

Position the controls as shown in this figure.

After placing the controls, double-click the form to bring up the code window, and type the following program lines (Visual Basic will have already started the Form_Load procedure for you):

```
Private Sub Form_Load()
    Label1.Caption = "Enter text here:"
    Text1.Text = "Default text"
    Command1.Caption = "Click Me"
End Sub
```

After typing the code, you can run the program, but this time rather than starting the program with the Start command, use the Step Into command. To do this, select the Step Into command from the Debug menu, or just press F8 on your keyboard. When you do, Visual Basic starts running the program, but pauses on the first program line, as shown here:

The Step Into command pauses the program on each line.

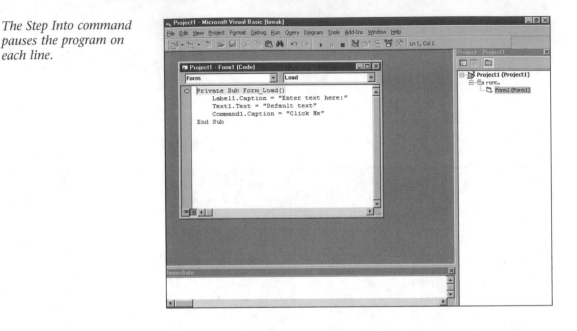

The highlighted line is the next line the computer will execute. Press F8 and the program enters the `Form_Load` procedure, and the next line in your program is highlighted. Go ahead and press F8 again. Visual Basic executes the highlighted line, sets the `Label1` control's caption, and highlights the next line. Press F8 three more times, watching as Visual Basic steps through your program. When there are no more lines to execute, the program's window appears on the screen.

As you can see, the Step Into command enables you to watch how Visual Basic executes each program line. To get a better idea of how this works, let's make things a little more complicated. Replace your current `Form_Load` procedure with the following two procedures:

```
Private Sub Form_Load()
    Call InitControls
End Sub

Sub InitControls()
    Label1.Caption = "Enter text here:"
    Text1.Text = "Default text"
    Command1.Caption = "Click Me"
End Sub
```

In this version of the program, `Form_Load` calls the `InitControls` procedure, which handles the task of setting the controls' captions and text. This little change will dramatically affect the way the Step Into command works. To see how, run the new version of the program by pressing F8 to select the Step Into command. Visual Basic runs the program and stops on the Form_Load line. Press F8 once more, and Visual Basic enters the Form_Load procedure and stops on the Call line, as shown here:

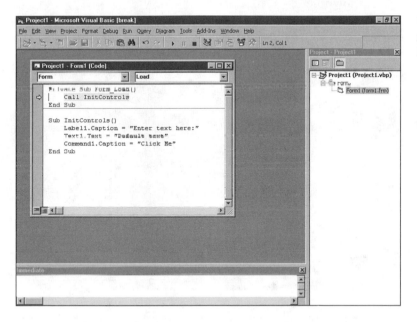

Visual Basic is about ready to step into the InitControls procedure.

Now, you're about to see why Visual Basic names this command Step Into, rather than just Step. Press F8, and Visual Basic "steps into" the InitControls procedure, as shown in the following figure:

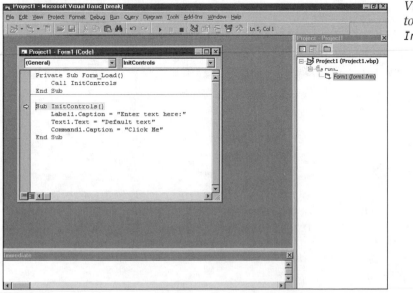

Visual Basic is now ready to execute the InitControls procedure.

Press F8 five times, and watch Visual Basic execute each of the lines in the InitControls procedure. The program returns to the Form_Load procedure right after the call to InitControls, as shown here:

Visual Basic is now back to the Form_Load procedure.

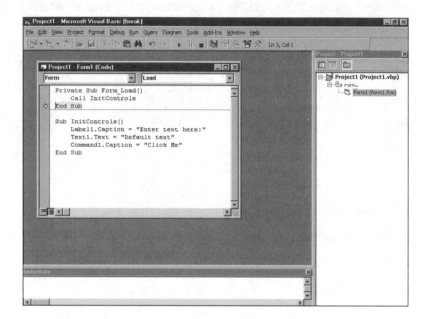

Another handy Visual Basic debugging command is Step Over, which you can select from the Debug menu or by pressing Shift+F8. The Step Over command enables you to skip over procedure and function calls, without stepping through them line by line. The skipped-over procedure or function still executes normally; you just don't see it.

To see the Step Over command in action, restart the program by pressing F8. Then press F8 a second time to highlight the Call InitControls line. Instead of pressing F8 this time, press Shift+F8. Visual Basic executes the InitControls procedure without stepping through it line by line.

The Step Over command can save you a lot of time when you don't care about what's happening inside a procedure.

Watching Variables

When you're stepping through a program, you can do more than just watch the program flow. You can also check the values of variables. (You can even check your socks for holes, but this is unlikely to help with your programming.) For example, double-click the Command Button control to bring up Visual Basic's code window. Then complete the Command1_Click procedure so it looks like this:

Major League Debuggers

Visual Basic's debugger is actually very easy to use, especially when compared with the powerhouse debuggers that come with languages like Visual C++. Most C++ debuggers enable the programmer to do wild and crazy things like look at the contents of the computer's memory, view the program's instructions as assembly language, and even examine special memory areas called *registers* that hold all kinds of insanely important technical information about the currently running program. If you saw one of these debuggers up on your screen, you would probably faint or start speaking in tongues.

```
Private Sub Command1_Click()
    Dim txt As String

    txt = Text1.Text
    MsgBox txt
End Sub
```

After saving your work, place the text cursor in the code window on the line

```
txt = Text1.Text
```

Now, press F9, and Visual Basic highlights the program line in red, as shown here:

This newly highlighted line is called a *breakpoint*. As your program runs, when Visual Basic gets to a breakpoint, it performs the following actions:

➤ Jumps into debug mode

➤ Displays the code window

➤ Highlights the next line to execute

➤ Waits for your next command

Go ahead and run the program normally, using the Start command. Then click the Click Me button. When you do, Visual Basic starts executing the `Command1_Click` procedure, but before it gets too far, it hits the breakpoint and stops.

Visual Basic can set breakpoints.

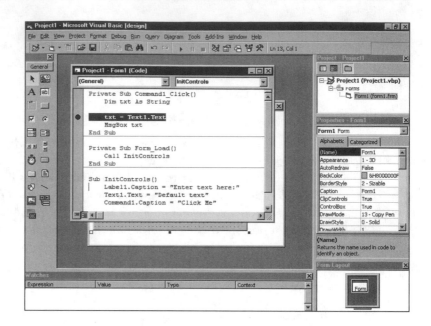

Breakpoints, Breakpoints, Everywhere Breakpoints

You can have more than one breakpoint set at a time. In fact, you can pretty much have as many breakpoints set as you want. For example, you might set breakpoints at the beginning of several functions so you can step through those functions when they're called. If you have a lot of breakpoints, you can turn them off all at once with the Clear All Breakpoints command. You can select this command from the Debug menu or by pressing Ctrl+Shift+F9 on your keyboard.

Now, put your mouse pointer over the variable txt in the highlighted line. (You don't need to click the variable; just place the pointer over it.) Visual Basic displays a small box with the message txt="", as shown here:

You're now looking at the current value of the txt variable. Talk about handy! To prove Visual Basic is showing the actual value of the variable txt, press F8 to execute the highlighted line, which assigns the text in the text box to the txt variable. Place your mouse cursor over txt again, and this time Visual Basic tells you txt="Default text", as the following figure shows:

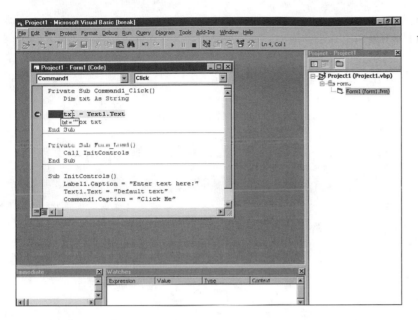

Visual Basic displays the values of variables.

To turn off the breakpoint, place your mouse cursor on the breakpoint line, and press F9 to select the Toggle Breakpoint command. You can also select this command from the Debug menu.

Now that you can trace through your programs and sneak a peek at the values of your variables as the program executes, you have no excuse for not hunting down those program bugs and squashing them like...well...like *bugs*!

Visual Basic displays the correct value even after the value has changed.

The Least You Need to Know

➤ The Step Into command enables you to watch program execution line by line, jumping into any procedures or functions the program calls.

➤ The Step Over command also enables you to watch program execution line by line, but it executes procedure and function calls without tracing through them line by line.

➤ By setting a breakpoint, you can force Visual Basic to stop on a specific line and wait for your instructions.

➤ You can turn off all the breakpoints in a program by selecting the Clear All Breakpoints command.

➤ When Visual Basic is running a program in debug mode, you can view the value of a variable by placing the mouse cursor over the variable's name in the code window.

Part 3

Elements of Visual Basic Windows Programs

Windows is a graphical operating system, which means virtually everything the user needs to see or know about is represented graphically on the screen. In order for your Visual Basic applications to accommodate Windows graphical requirements, Visual Basic supplies a set of objects and controls with which you build your application's graphical user interface (also known as a GUI, or "gooey"). In this part of the book, you'll discover the many graphical elements you use to create your own Visual Basic applications.

Chapter 16

Controls and Objects: There's a Difference?

In This Chapter

➤ Learn the many meanings of "object"

➤ Discover Visual Basic objects

➤ Compare Visual Basic objects with Visual Basic controls

Throughout the book so far, you've been reading a lot about controls and objects. You probably have a fuzzy idea of what these things are, but you can't quite bring it into focus. Don't worry, you're not the only one. Unfortunately, although the word "control" has a clear definition in Visual Basic, the word "object" in Visual Basic (and many other languages) tends to mean different things at different times. It's all a matter of context, you know?

Thinking About Objects

So what exactly is a Visual Basic object? Technically, an object is any piece of data in a program. An integer is an object, a string is an object, the Printer object is (of course) an object, and a Textbox control is an object. Some objects are much more sophisticated than others. For example, whereas an integer is only a few bytes of memory, a Textbox control is a whole collection of properties, methods, and event handlers, and usually (though not always) features some sort of graphical user interface.

Object-Oriented Programming and Objects

The concept of objects started with something called *object-oriented programming* (OOP). With OOP, programmers create something called a *class*, which is a set of functions and variables that represents some sort of...well...object. For example, the programmer might create a class that represents a vampire in a game, an automobile in a simulation, or even something more abstract such as an array of strings. After writing the class, the programmer writes the source code needed to create an *instance* of the class. An instance of a class is called an object.

In Visual Basic programming, though, an object usually has a more specific definition. Usually, an object is something more abstract than a control and something more complex than an integer or a string. For example, you learned about the Printer object in Chapter 14, "Printing: Your Own Edition of Hard Copy." The Printer object is a Visual Basic object, in the strict sense of the word "object." You can't see a Printer object. It doesn't appear on the screen and the user can interact with it only indirectly through your program. Yet it represents a set of methods and properties a program can access to control the object and, indirectly, control the actual printer associated with the object.

Visual Basic provides many of these types of objects, including not only the Printer object, but also the Font, Drive, File, Folder, Screen, Clipboard, and Picture objects. You can tell by the objects' names what type of real-world objects they represent. For example, the Drive object comprises the properties and methods a program needs to manipulate a disk drive, whereas the Screen object comprises the properties and methods a program needs to manipulate the computer's screen. The main thing these objects have in common is that none is interactive. The user can't manipulate them directly; only your program can.

Thinking About Controls

Unlike Visual Basic objects such as Font, Screen, and Printer, controls are interactive. Most (though not all) can be manipulated directly by the user, most (though not all) have a graphical user interface, and all respond to events, enabling them to interact not only with the user, but also with the program and the operating system.

Take a Textbox control, for example, which boasts the following attributes:

➤ Has a graphical user interface, which is the box into which the user can type text

➤ Is interactive because the user can change its contents

➤ Responds to events the user generates when he changes the contents of the control

If you still have a hard time telling the difference between controls and objects, just remember that controls always appear in your Visual Basic toolbox, whereas objects appear only in your program's source code, as shown in the following figure:

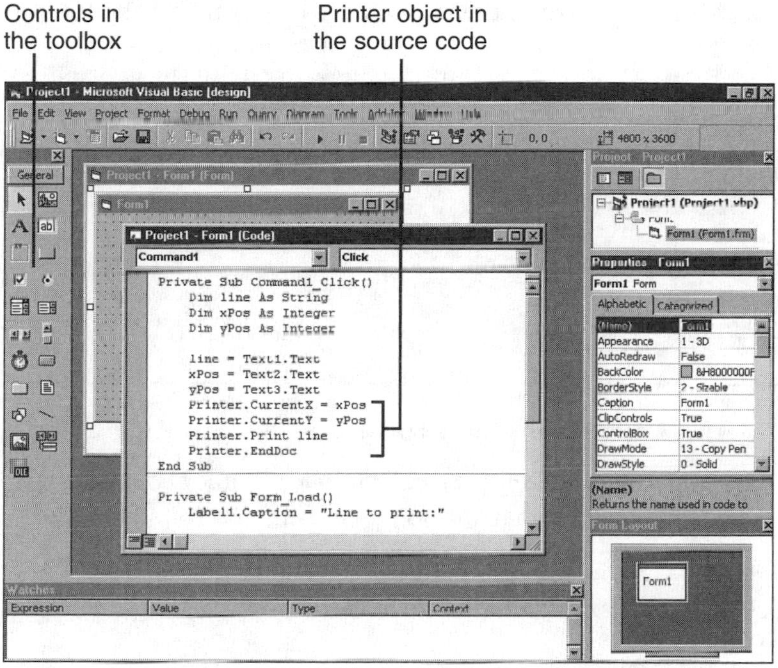

Controls in
the toolbox

Printer object in
the source code

Controls and objects show up in different places.

Third-Party Controls

Visual Basic comes with many of its own controls, often called *intrinsic controls*. However, many companies and even hobbyist programmers have created many, many other controls you can add to your Visual Basic toolbox. You might even already have some installed on your system that you don't know about. To see the control packages installed on your machine, select the Project menu's Components command, or just press Ctrl+T on your keyboard. When you do, the Components dialog box appears, listing all the available controls on your machine. Just select the controls you want, and click OK. Visual Basic then adds the selected controls to your toolbox. Note that some controls require that you purchase a license to use them.

To Put It Simply

Both controls and objects have properties and methods, but only controls can respond to events. If you can keep that one point in your head, you'll always be able to tell the difference between the two.

Of course, you can refer to a control by its name in your program's source code. In that way, a control also appears in your program's source code. However, a control always starts out in the toolbox. An object (using the strict definition) never appears in the toolbox. (But...ahem...if you want to use the general definition of "object," a control *is* an object; therefore, objects appear in the toolbox. Confused yet?)

The Least You Need to Know

➤ When used in a general way, the term "object" can refer to just about any piece of data or code in your program, including integers, controls, and more.

➤ In Visual Basic, an object usually comprises properties and methods that enable the program to access and control a real-world object such as a disk drive, the screen, or a printer.

➤ Controls differ from Visual Basic objects in that controls respond to events. Moreover, controls usually (but not always) are interactive with a graphical interface.

➤ Controls appear in your Visual Basic toolbox, whereas objects appear only in your program lines.

Chapter 17

Methods, Properties, and Events: An Object's Inner Workings

In This Chapter

➤ Learn about properties and how to manage them

➤ Discover how to call methods

➤ Learn how Visual Basic enables your program to respond to events

➤ See how Visual Basic helps you with properties, methods, and event procedures

In the previous chapter, you learned to tell the difference between a control and an object. Along the way, you read about properties, methods, and events. In fact, you've seen a little about properties, methods, and events scattered throughout this whole book. Up until now, though, you might have been a little fuzzy on what these important elements of a control or object actually are. In this chapter, you get the inside scoop.

Introducing Properties

Most objects and controls have properties, which you can think of as nothing more complicated than attributes. For example, as you've already learned, a Command

Button control has a property called Caption, which determines the text that appears in the button. Lots of other controls, such as the familiar Label control, also have a Caption property. Some properties are common in Visual Basic, whereas others are associated with only a single control or object.

The Name property is an example of a property that every control has. Without a control's name, your program would have no way to refer to the control. Most visible controls also have Left, Top, Width, and Height properties, which determine the location and size of the control. However, the MaxButton property, which determines whether a window has a maximize button in its title bar, is unique to forms. You wouldn't, after all, want a maximize button on something like a button. One wrong click, and suddenly you would have a button the size of the full screen! Such a button would sure be hard to miss with the mouse!

Setting Properties

Both controls and objects can have properties. However, the ways you set a property for a control and an object are different. You can set a control's properties in the Properties window, like this:

You can access most properties in a control's Properties window.

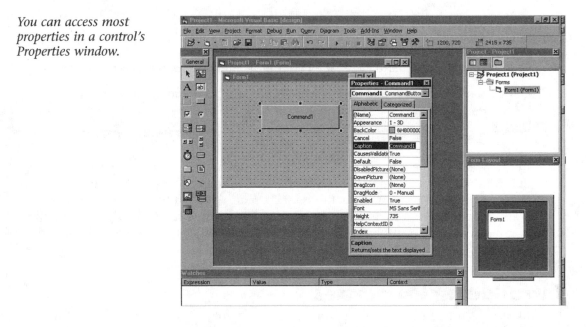

Or you can set a control's properties in your program's source code, like this:

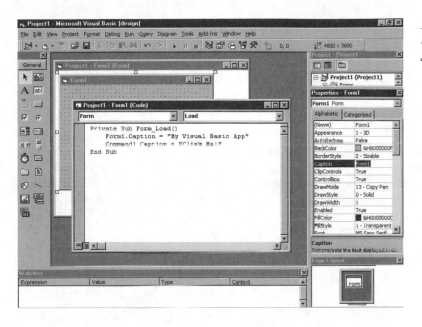

Many properties can be set from within the program.

Which way you set a control's properties depends on the property and your preference.

On the other hand, you must set an object's properties in your program because an object doesn't display a Properties window the way a control does. In fact, with the exception of the Form object (which, if you ask me, is really a control), objects don't even exist until you run your program.

To complicate matters, some properties work differently depending on whether the program is in *design time* (when you're writing the program) or *runtime* (when the program is actually running). For example, you can set a form's `MaxButton` property in the Properties window when you're designing the form, but you can't set the `MaxButton` property in the program because that particular property is read-only at runtime. *Read-only* means you can check the value of the property, like this:

```
Dim hasMaxButton As Boolean
hasMaxButton = Form1.MaxButton
```

Reading, Writing, but No Arithmetic

In programming, you run across the terms *read* and *write* a lot. For example, when a program sends data to a disk file, it's writing to the file. Conversely, when a program retrieves data from a file, it's reading the file. The same is true of properties. When a program changes the value of a property, it's writing to the property, and when a program retrieves the value of a property, it's reading the property.

193

But you can't change the property's value in the program, like this:

```
Form1.MaxButton = False
```

Some properties are read and write at both design time and runtime, whereas others are read-only at runtime. Some properties don't exist at design time and can be accessed only at runtime. Which all goes to show you that the ways you can access a property depend on the property itself.

One cool thing about Visual Basic is its ability to help you find the right property as you're writing a program. When you type the name of a control or an object and then type the dot that separates the name from the property or method, Visual Basic displays a list box containing all the available properties and methods, as shown in the following figure:

Visual Basic displays a form's properties and methods.

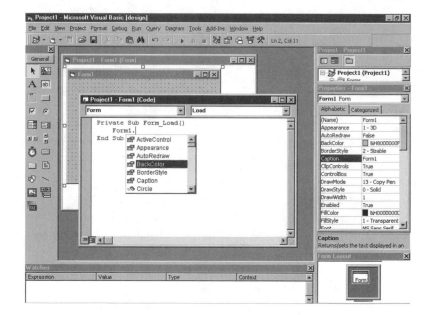

All you have to do is find the name of the property or method you want and press Enter on your keyboard. No more digging through hundreds of pages of documentation looking for the name of a property or method. More importantly, no more paper cuts from the edges of the pages!

Introducing Methods

If properties represent a control's or object's attributes, methods represent the control's or object's abilities. For example, many controls have a Move method, which moves and sizes the control. Similarly, as you learned in Chapter 14, "Printing: Your Own Edition of Hard Copy," the Printer object has a Print method that sends data to the printer.

Although a small set of methods (such as `Drag`, `Move`, `Refresh`, and `ZOrder`) is common to many controls, most controls and objects feature methods unique to that particular control or object. No other control or object other than the Printer object has the `NewPage` method. Similarly, no other control or object other than the Clipboard object has a `SetText` method.

Calling Methods

Methods are similar to procedures and functions in that your program not only calls them, but also often needs to call them with a set of arguments. The Printer object's `Print` function, for example, requires as an argument the data you want to print.

To call a control or object's method, you just type the name of the control or object followed by a dot and then the name of the method. Just as with properties, Visual Basic will help you—when it can—to figure out the correct arguments to include in the method call. The following figure, for example, shows a programmer about to enter the arguments for a call to a button's `Move` method:

OOP, Properties, and Methods

You learned in a previous chapter's Techno Talk that the idea of objects comes from object-oriented programming (OOP). You also learned that OOP programmers create classes, which are like templates for an object. Classes have properties and methods, too, but they are called different things in different languages. If you were programming a class in Visual C++, for example, you would call properties *data members* or *member variables*, and you would call methods *member functions*.

Visual Basic displays the types of arguments needed for a method call.

Stacking 'Em Up

There might be times when an object or control contains another object for which you want to access a property or method. In cases like this, you use the object names and the dots to create a kind of map to the property, like this: Object1.Object2.Property. For example, every Form object has a Picture property, which holds a reference to a Picture object that can be displayed in the form. In turn, the Picture object has a property called Height, which is the height of the picture. If your program needs the height of the picture, you could write something like picHeight = Form1.Picture.Height.

Introducing Events

Events are kind of like methods in that they are called like procedures and functions. The big difference between methods and events, though, is that whereas your program calls a method, Visual Basic calls event procedures on its own, in response to events generated by the user or the operating system. In your program, you supply the event procedure, which tells Visual Basic what to do when a particular event occurs, and then Visual Basic does the rest.

Take the Command Button control (please!). As you've noticed in previous chapters, the Command Button control responds to an event called Click. This means that when the user clicks the button, Visual Basic calls the button's Click procedure and performs whatever the program instructs it to do in the procedure. If the program has no Click event procedure, when the user clicks the button, nothing happens. (As you'll soon discover, sometimes a button does nothing even when there is a Click event procedure. This usually means you fell asleep while writing the procedure or, when you glanced away, your cat walked across the keyboard, filling the procedure with strange feline words Visual Basic can't possibly understand.)

Writing Event Procedures

As mentioned previously, the program lines Visual Basic executes when an event occurs are called an event procedure. An event procedure is not unlike other procedures you might write, except for the fact that Visual Basic itself calls the event procedure. (Your program can also call an event procedure, but this would be an uncommon thing to do.)

Event procedures are another place where Visual Basic is as smart as Bart Simpson's mouth. First, Visual Basic can list all the events for any control in your program. Just select the control's name in the code window's left list box, and all the available events appear in the second list box, as shown here:

Select the control here   The events appear here

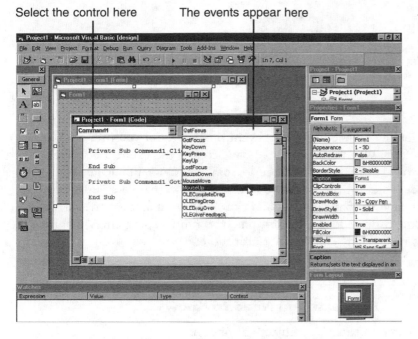

Here, Visual Basic lists the events for a Command Button control called Command1.

Once you find the event you want, just press Enter with the event highlighted. In the code window, Visual Basic automatically starts the event procedure for you. All you have to do is complete the procedure, adding the program lines you want executed when the event occurs. The following figure shows the event procedure Visual Basic starts for a button's MouseDown event:

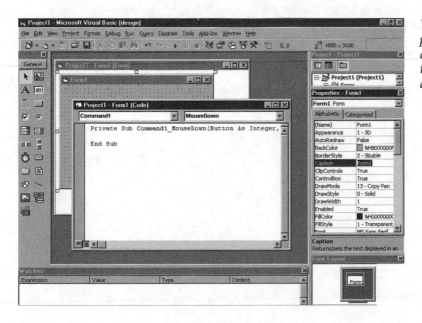

Visual Basic starts event procedures for you, so you don't have to remember the syntax and all the arguments.

More Automatic Code

Another way to get Visual Basic to start an event procedure for you is to double-click a control or form. When you do, Visual Basic creates the event procedure you'll most likely need at that time. Of course, sometimes Visual Basic guesses wrong and provides an event procedure you don't want. In that case, just ignore the event procedure Visual Basic created and choose the event you want from the event list box in the code window. The first time you run the program, Visual Basic will automatically remove any empty event procedures.

The Least You Need to Know

➤ Properties represent a control's or object's attributes.

➤ Some properties can be set in the program's source code at runtime, whereas other properties must be set in the Properties window at design time. Some properties can be set either way.

➤ Methods represent a control or object's abilities, the things it can do.

➤ Calling a method is much like calling procedures. Often, you need to supply one or more arguments.

➤ An event procedure holds the program lines Visual Basic should execute when a specific event occurs.

Chapter 18

Forms and Containers: Places to Put Controls

In This Chapter

➤ Explore the Form object's properties

➤ Learn to call a Form object's methods

➤ Discover how Form events enable a program to respond to user and system actions

---

You've finally got all the rudimentary programming stuff behind you. Now, you can start digging deeper into Visual Basic, learning about what makes Visual Basic Windows applications tick. The first step toward this goal is to have a close look at Visual Basic containers, which are nothing more than objects that can hold other objects. The most important container is the Form object, which you'll explore in this chapter.

The Form Object

Whether you've given it much thought or not, you already know that a Form object is a container. How do you know that? Because all throughout this book, you've been placing controls on your forms, and only a container object can hold other controls. The Form object, in fact, is the most common container object because it represents your Visual Basic application's main window. The following figure shows an empty Form object in Visual Basic's Project window:

A Form object looks like a window because it represents your application's main window.

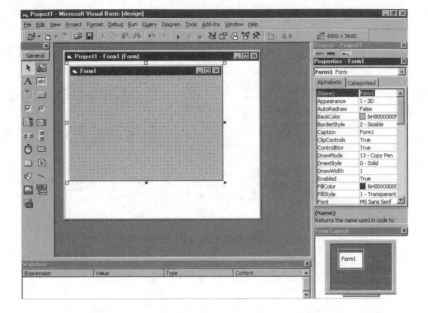

Previously in this book, you've been using a form for little more than holding the few controls needed to run sample programs. But a form is a powerful object, featuring many properties and methods your programs can use to control the way the form looks and acts. Moreover, the form responds to a whole host of events. By responding to those events, a program can tap into the interaction going on between the application, the user, and the operating system.

Form Properties

Okay, I'm going to scare you a little bit now: The Form object features over 60 properties! Stop screaming; things aren't as bad as they seem. Luckily, until you become a full-fledged Visual Basic geek (you'll know when that happens; you'll have a constant craving for gummy bears and Diet Coke), you don't need to know all 60 properties and what they do. The following list shows the 12 properties of the Form object that are easiest to use and understand, and, for someone just starting out, are also the most useful:

A Container of Another Kind

A PictureBox control is another object that can be used as a container. To use a PictureBox as a container, you must first place the PictureBox on the form. Then you can put other controls inside the PictureBox control. The form ends up as the container for the PictureBox, and the PictureBox ends up as the container for the controls you place in it. Containers within containers—what a concept!

➤ AutoRedraw—Determines whether the form will automatically redraw itself as needed

➤ BackColor—Determines the form's background color

➤ Caption—Determines the text that appears in the form's title bar

➤ CurrentX—Determines the horizontal position at which the next drawing operation will take place

➤ CurrentY—Determines the vertical position at which the next drawing operation will take place

➤ DrawWidth—Determines the width of lines drawn in the form

➤ FillColor—Determines the color used to fill shapes

➤ ForeColor—Determines the color used to draw text and lines in the form

➤ Height—Determines the height of the form

➤ Left—Determines the position of the form's left edge

➤ Top—Determines the position of the form's top edge

➤ Width—Determines the width of the form

Some of these properties—including BackColor, Caption, CurrentX, and CurrentY—you've already had experience with in previous chapters. Others (okay, most of them) are new to you. The good news is you can set many of these properties in the Properties window when you're designing your program. This is the easiest way to handle the properties because Visual Basic lists all a property's possible settings for you. All you have to do is choose one, as shown in the following figure:

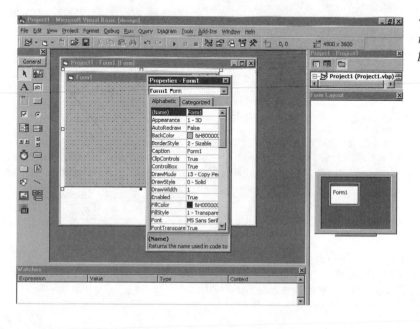

The Properties window makes it easy to set a property's value.

Not all properties are available in the Properties window, however. Some are only available when your program is running. The CurrentX and CurrentY properties are examples. You can set this type of property only with a program line.

Using Form Properties

There's not enough room in this chapter to cover all the Form properties, even just the easy ones. However, this section will give you some experience with a few of the properties. You can experiment with the others on your own.

The AutoRedraw Property

Whenever you hide one window under another, the buried window loses its contents, so that when you again uncover the window, its contents must be redrawn. You can do this redrawing in your program, but it's a lot more convenient to let Visual Basic handle the task for you. That's what the AutoRedraw property does.

To see AutoRedraw in action, start a new Visual Basic project (a Standard EXE), and position two Command Button controls on the form, as shown in the following figure:

Position the buttons as shown here.

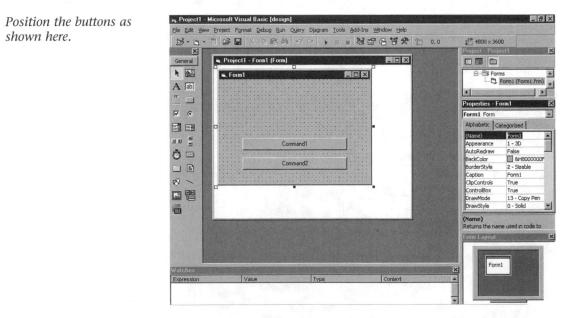

After placing the controls on the form, double-click the Command1 button to bring up the code window, and type the following program lines (Visual Basic will have already started the Command1_Click procedure for you):

```
Private Sub Command1_Click()
    Form1.CurrentX = 1700
    Form1.CurrentY = 800
    Form1.Print "THIS IS A TEST"
End Sub

Private Sub Command2_Click()
    If Form1.AutoRedraw = False Then
        Form1.AutoRedraw = True
        Command2.Caption = "Turn Off AutoRedraw"
    Else
        Form1.AutoRedraw = False
        Command2.Caption = "Turn On AutoRedraw"
    End If
End Sub

Private Sub Form_Load()
    Command1.Caption = "Draw Text"
    Command2.Caption = "Turn On AutoRedraw"
    Form1.AutoRedraw = False
End Sub
```

After typing the source code, save your work and run the program. When the window appears, click the Draw Text button. The text THIS IS A TEST appears in the window, as shown here:

The line of text shown in the window may or may not redraw depending on the setting of the form's AutoRedraw property.

Now, click the window's Minimize button to reduce the application to an icon on the taskbar. Select the icon in the taskbar to restore the window, and...whoops!...the window's text has vanished like a drop of rain in a brook.

That's what happens when the AutoRedraw property is set to False. Click the Turn On AutoRedraw button, and try the same experiment again. This time, Visual Basic redraws the text in the window when you restore the application to its original size. Handy, to say the least.

The ForeColor *Property*

Usually, when you display data in the form, it's drawn using the default foreground color, which is black. However, your program can control this color setting in order to display data in different colors. To see how this works, start a new Visual Basic project, double-click the form to display the code window, and type the following program lines. (Note that this time, Visual Basic won't automatically start the event procedure you want because you're not creating the Load procedure):

```
Private Sub Form_Click()
    Form1.FontSize = 18
    Form1.CurrentX = 500
    Form1.CurrentY = 500
    Form1.Print "This is black"
    Form1.ForeColor = RGB(255, 0, 0)
    Form1.CurrentX = 500
    Form1.CurrentY = 900
    Form1.Print "This is red"
    Form1.ForeColor = RGB(0, 255, 0)
    Form1.CurrentX = 500
    Form1.CurrentY = 1300
    Form1.Print "This is green"
    Form1.ForeColor = RGB(0, 0, 255)
    Form1.CurrentX = 500
    Form1.CurrentY = 1700
    Form1.Print "This is blue"
End Sub
```

After typing the source code, save your work, and run the program. When the program's window appears, click inside the form. Four lines of text appear, each a different color, as shown here:

This program prints multicolor text.

How this program works should be pretty obvious, except for the way the procedure sets the ForeColor property. The RGB function returns a color based on the given values for the red, green, and blue components, respectively. The value 0 is the darkest color and 255 is the lightest color. Therefore RGB(0,0,0) returns black and

RGB(255,255,255) returns white. Other colors are formed by varying the values of the red, green, and blue color components—just like mixing paints when you were a kid, something a lot of us did right after eating the paste.

Form Methods

The Form object also provides a set of methods, 22 of them to be exact. Just as with the properties, though, you don't have to know all the methods to get started with Visual Basic forms. The following list of five will get you going:

➤ Circle—Draws a circle or oval

➤ Cls—Erases the form

➤ Hide—Hides the form

➤ Line—Draws a line

➤ Show—Shows the form

To see how the Circle, Line, and Cls methods work, start a new Visual Basic project, and position three Command Button controls in the form, as shown in the following figure:

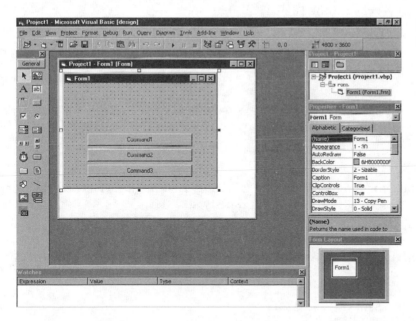

Position the buttons as shown here.

After positioning the controls, double-click the Command1 button to bring up Visual Basic's code window. Type the following text into the window (Visual Basic will have already started the Command1_Click procedure for you):

```
Private Sub Command1_Click()
    Form1.DrawWidth = 3
    Form1.Line (500, 500)-(4000, 500)
End Sub

Private Sub Command2_Click()
    Form1.Circle (2400, 800), 500
End Sub

Private Sub Command3_Click()
    Form1.Cls
End Sub

Private Sub Form_Load()
    Command1.Caption = "Draw Line"
    Command2.Caption = "Draw Circle"
    Command3.Caption = "Clear Window"
End Sub
```

After typing the source code, save your work, and run the program. Click a button to call the `Line`, `Circle`, or `Cls` method. For example, the following figure shows the window after the user has clicked the Draw Circle button:

The `Circle` method draws circles, of course.

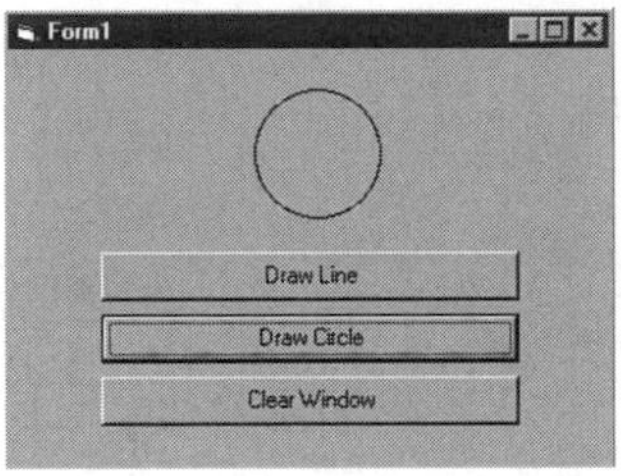

Three methods in this program require some explaining. First, the program sets the thickness of the line by setting the `DrawWidth` property, like this:

```
Form1.DrawWidth = 3
```

The larger the width, the thicker the line.

The following source-code line draws a line on the screen:

```
Form1.Line (500, 500)-(4000, 500)
```

The two numbers in the first set of parentheses are the coordinates of the line's starting point, and the two numbers in the second set of parentheses are the coordinates of the line's ending point. Simple.

Finally, the source-code line

```
Form1.Circle (2400, 800), 500
```

draws a circle. The two numbers in the parentheses are the coordinates of the center of the circle, and the last number is the circle's radius. When you use these methods, make sure you get all the commas and parentheses in the right places. Failure to do so will result in a visit from the Visual Basic police who will fine you $200 per infraction, as well as whack your knuckles with a keyboard. (OK, so there's no Visual Basic police. If you want your program to run right, though, you still have to get everything just right.)

Form Events

The Form object responds to many kinds of events, 17 in all. The more you know about these events, the more control you have over the interactions between your program, the user, and the operating system. Still, some events are more important than others are. The following list shows the events most important to a new Visual Basic programmer:

➤ Click—Called when the user clicks the form

➤ DblClick—Called when the user double-clicks the form

➤ Load—Called when Visual Basic first loads the form

➤ Unload—Called when Visual Basic unloads the form

The following program demonstrates how form events cause Visual Basic to call the associated event procedures.

Start a new Visual Basic project, and double-click the form to bring up the code window. Type the following source-code lines (Visual Basic will have already started the Form_Load procedure for you):

```
Private Sub Form_Click()
    MsgBox "Click Event"
End Sub

Private Sub Form_Load()
    MsgBox "Load Event"
End Sub

Private Sub Form_Unload(Cancel As Integer)
    MsgBox "Unload Event"
End Sub
```

Two Sides of the Same Coin

Just as you use the Form_Load procedure to set up controls and other values in your program, so you can use its counterpart, Form_Unload, to do what needs to be done before the application closes. An example is warning the user if he hasn't yet saved whatever data he's been editing, or displaying a message box that says something like "Do You Really Want to Quit?"

After typing the source-code lines, save your work and run the program. When you do, a message box appears that tells you the Load event has occurred. The Load event, which is handled by the Form_Load event procedure, occurs when Visual Basic first loads the form but has not yet displayed the form.

Dismiss the message box and the application's window appears. Click in the window, and a message box appears that tells you a Click event just occurred. Dismiss the message box, and terminate the application by clicking its Close button. Before Visual Basic removes the window from the screen, it calls the Form_Unload event procedure, as you can tell by the message box that appears.

The Least You Need to Know

➤ The Form object is Visual Basic's most important container. A container is an object that can hold other objects.

➤ The Form object's properties include AutoRedraw, BackColor, Caption, CurrentX, CurrentY, and others.

➤ The Form object's Circle, Cls, Hide, Line, and Show methods are the most useful to a new Visual Basic programmer.

➤ The Load and Unload events enable a program to initialize and shut down a program elegantly.

Part 4

Writing Windows Applications

In the previous p[...] [...]ed to forms, controls, objects, and other concepts that are essential to [...] [...]ional Windows applications. Now that you have a gene[...] [...] ready to put them to work. In this pa[...] [...]f Visual Basic's many controls and le[...] [...]ons.

Chapter 19

Button Controls: Clicking Your Way to Success

In This Chapter

➤ Learn more about Command Button controls

➤ See how to use CheckBox controls to represent application options

➤ Discover how OptionButtons can be used as "radio buttons"

Button controls are nothing new to you. You've used one or more of them in almost every Visual Basic program so far. What you don't know is that there is a lot more to Command Button controls than just a Click event procedure. In fact, there are more kinds of buttons than just Command Button controls; there are also OptionButton and CheckBox controls, which are also considered buttons. In this chapter, you get a chance to go button crazy, so put on your party hat.

Command Button Controls

Command Button controls are the kind of button that you think of when you think of the word "button." That is, just like buttons in the real world, you press these onscreen buttons to issue commands to the device. However, because it's very difficult to get flesh and bone into a computer's memory, you have to use a magical device called a mouse to click an onscreen button. Of course, you already know all this—unless you're one of those folks who always has sore fingers from poking at onscreen buttons.

In your previous Visual Basic programs, you've learned to respond to button clicks in the Command Button control's Click event procedure. This is the most common way to handle buttons. There's a lot more you can do with a button, however, considering that it has over 40 properties, seven methods, and responds to 17 events. All this power in that little rectangle. What a bargain!

I won't force you to use all those properties, methods, and events (you're welcome!). However, in this chapter, you'll examine some of the more useful ones. Along the way, you'll see how versatile a button can really be.

Command Button Properties

You'll probably use a button's properties more than its methods and events. In fact, that's likely to be the case with most controls. Some of the Command Button control's more useful properties are listed below:

➤ BackColor—Represents the button's background color. For this property to have an effect, the button's Style property must be set to Graphical.

➤ Caption—Represents the button's text.

➤ DisabledPicture—Represents the image that's displayed on a graphical button when the button is disabled. For this property to have an effect, the button's Style property must be set to Graphical.

➤ DownPicture—Represents the image that's displayed on a graphical button when the button is pressed. For this property to have an effect, the button's Style property must be set to Graphical.

➤ Enabled—Represents whether the user can interact with the button.

➤ Height—Represents the button's height.

➤ Left—Represents the position of the button's left edge.

➤ Picture—Represents the image that's displayed in the button. For this property to have an effect, the button's Style property must be set to Graphical.

➤ Style—Represents whether the button is standard or graphical.

➤ Top—Represents the position of the button's top edge.

➤ Width—Represents the button's width.

The following program demonstrates a few of the Command Button control's properties. To build the program, start a new Visual Basic project (a Standard EXE), and then place four Command Button controls on the form, as shown here:

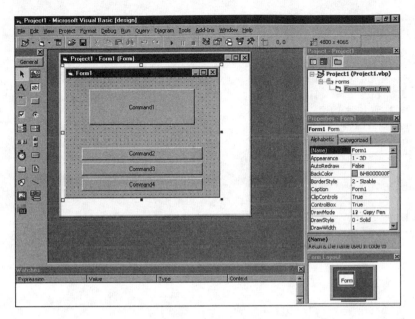

Position the buttons as shown in this figure.

Then, double-click the Command1 Command Button to display the code window, and type the following lines (Visual Basic will have already started the Command1_Click event procedure for you):

```
Option Explicit

Private Sub Command1_Click()
    MsgBox "Yep, the button works."
End Sub

Private Sub Command2_Click()
    If Command1.Enabled = True Then
        Command1.Enabled = False
        Command2.Caption = "Enable Button"
    Else
        Command1.Enabled = True
        Command2.Caption = "Disable Button"
    End If
End Sub

Private Sub Command3_Click()
    If Command1.BackColor = RGB(255, 0, 0) Then
        Command1.BackColor = RGB(192, 192, 192)
    Else
```

```
        Command1.BackColor = RGB(255, 0, 0)
    End If
End Sub

Private Sub Command4_Click()
    If Command1.Top = 100 Then
        Command1.Top = 360
        Command1.Left = 720
        Command1.Width = 3255
        Command1.Height = 1095
    Else
        Command1.Top = 100
        Command1.Left = 100
        Command1.Width = 4450
        Command1.Height = 1800
    End If
End Sub

Private Sub Form_Load()
    Command1.Caption = "TEST BUTTON"
    Command2.Caption = "Disable Button"
    Command3.Caption = "Change Button Color"
    Command4.Caption = "Change Button Size"
End Sub
```

When you're done typing, click the Command1 button to select it, and then, in the button's Properties window, set the Style property to 1-Graphical, as shown here:

You must set the Style *property in the Properties window.*

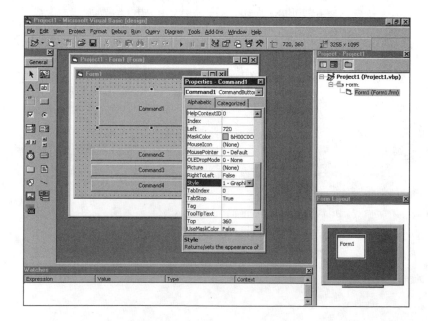

Now, save your work, and run the program. When you do, the main window appears. To prove that the Command1 button is working normally, give it a click. A message box appears. Dismiss the message box and click Disable Button. Visual Basic disables the Command1 button; if you click it, nothing will happen.

Next, click Enable Button (it used to be Disable Button; fancy trickery, eh?) to re-enable the Command1 button. Now the button will work normally. Click the Change Color button to toggle the button's background color between red and gray. Click the Change Button Size button to toggle between two button sizes. The following figure shows the application when the Command1 button is set to its large size with a red background:

Runtime Read-only Properties

You have to set the Style property in the Properties window because it is a read-only property at runtime, which means you can't change its value when the program is running. You'll run into more properties like this as you learn more about Visual Basic, although most properties can be set at both design time and runtime.

Here's the button sample program in action.

Command Button Methods

The Command Button control features seven methods, but only one is of interest to a Visual Basic novice. That method is Move, which positions and resizes the button. To see Move in action, replace your program's Command4_Click event procedure with the following:

```
Private Sub Command4_Click()
    If Command1.Top = 100 Then
        Command1.Move 720, 360, 3255, 1095
    Else
        Command1.Move 100, 100, 4450, 1800
    End If
End Sub
```

When you run the program, it will act exactly as before. However, now the program is changing the button's position and size all at once, with a single method call, rather than having to set four different properties. (Of course, someone has to do the work; in the case of the Move method, Visual Basic sets the Left, Top, Height, and Width properties for you. What a buddy!)

The four numbers following the call to the Move method are its arguments, which are the control's left position, top position, width, and height, respectively. The only other way I know of to move a button control when the program is running is to use a glass cutter to cut the button off the screen and then glue the button back on in its new location. The problem with this method is that it works only once, and then you have to buy a new monitor. Also, the rest of the family is likely to whine and bicker about the smoke and flames.

Command Button Events

The Command Button control responds to 17 different events. However, none except Click is likely to be useful to you for a while. After you become a Visual Basic guru, you might want to check into some of the other events. Even then, however, Click will be the one you use 99 percent of the time.

CheckBox Controls

If you've been using Windows for any time at all, you've seen almost as many CheckBox controls as Command Button controls in windows, dialog boxes, and property sheets. CheckBox controls are usually used to represent program options. When you click the control, a check mark appears in its box, indicating that the associated option is active. A second click removes the check mark and turns off the option. The following figure shows several CheckBox controls in a window:

CheckBox controls enable a user to select options.

CheckBox controls have 48 properties, seven methods, and respond to 18 events. As with Command Button controls, however, you'll only need to master a few of these, which you do in the following sections, so get cranked up.

CheckBox Properties

The CheckBox control has even more properties than the Command Button, 48 instead of only (only?) 43. Some of the more useful CheckBox control properties are listed below:

➤ Alignment—Represents whether the check box's text is on the left or the right.

➤ BackColor—Represents the check box's background color.

➤ Caption—Represents the check box's text.

➤ Enabled—Represents whether the user can interact with the check box.

➤ ForeColor—Represents the color of the check box's text.

➤ Height—Represents the check box's height.

➤ Left—Represents the position of the check box's left edge.

➤ Picture—Represents the image that's displayed in the check box. For this property to have an effect, the button's Style property must be set to Graphical.

➤ Style—represents whether the check box is standard or is a two-position, graphical push button.

➤ Top—Represents the position of the check box's top edge.

➤ Value—Represents whether the check box is unchecked or checked.

➤ Width—Represents the check box's width.

The CheckBox properties that have the same name as Command Button properties work about the same way, so there's no point in demonstrating them here. One point of interest, however, is the difference between a standard check box and a graphical check box. Specifically, when you set a CheckBox control's property to Graphical, it no longer looks like a check box, but more like a regular button. What's special about this button is that when it's clicked, the button stays pressed to indicate the checked state, rather than showing a check mark. The following figure shows the CheckBox control's four different looks:

The CheckBox control doesn't always look like a check box.

In this figure, the first control is a standard check box in its unchecked state, the second control is a standard check box in its checked state, the third control is a graphical check box in its unchecked state, and the fourth control is a graphical check box in its checked state.

The following program demonstrates a few of the CheckBox control's properties. To build the program, start a new Visual Basic project (a Standard EXE), and then place one Command Button and three CheckBox controls on the form, as shown here:

Position the buttons as shown in this figure.

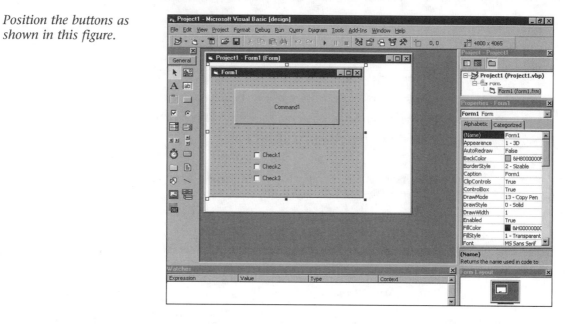

Then, double-click the Command Button to display the code window, and type the following lines (Visual Basic will have already started the Command1_Click event procedure for you):

```
Option Explicit

Private Sub Command1_Click()
    MsgBox "Yep, the button works."
End Sub

Private Sub Check1_Click()
    If Check1.Value = vbChecked Then
        Command1.Enabled = False
    Else
        Command1.Enabled = True
    End If
End Sub

Private Sub Check2_Click()
    If Check2.Value = vbUnchecked Then
        Command1.BackColor = RGB(192, 192, 192)
    Else
```

```
                Command1.BackColor = RGB(255, 0, 0)
        End If
    End Sub


    Private Sub Check3_Click()
        If Check3.Value = vbUnchecked Then
            Command1.Move 720, 360, 3255, 1095
        Else
            Command1.Move 100, 100, 4450, 1800
        End If
    End Sub


    Private Sub Form_Load()
        Command1.Caption = "TEST BUTTON"
        Check1.Caption = "Disable Button"
        Check2.Caption = "Change Button Color"
        Check3.Caption = "Change Button Size"
    End Sub
```

When you're done typing, click the Command1
button to select it, and then, in the button's
Properties window, set the Style property to
1-Graphical.

Now, save your work, and run the program.
When you do, the main window appears. To
prove that the Command1 button is working
normally, give it a click. A message box appears.
Dismiss the message box, and click the Disable
Button check box. Visual Basic checks the box
and disables the Command1 button; if you
click the Command1 button, nothing will happen.

Next, click the Disable Button check box a second time to remove the check mark and to re-
enable the Command1 button. Click the
Change Color check box to toggle the
Command1 button's background color between
red and gray. Click the Change Button Size
check box to toggle between two button sizes.
The following figure shows the application
when the Command1 button is disabled and
set to its large size:

In a Check Box State of Mind

Notice in the source code how the
program compares the value of a
CheckBox control's Value property
to two values named vbChecked
and vbUnchecked. Visual Basic provides the vbChecked and
vbUnchecked values to make it
easier to manage check boxes.
Thanks to these predefined values
(called *constants*), you don't have
to remember that the value of an
unchecked check box is 0 and the
value of a checked check box is 1.

219

The check boxes take over the task formally handled by regular Command Button controls.

CheckBox Methods and Events

In the previous program, you can see that the `Click` event is every bit as important to a CheckBox control as it is to a Command Button. The added bonus is that Visual Basic automatically shows or hides the control's check mark for you. Send all thank-yous to Microsoft's Visual Basic programming team. Send all money to your humble author (that's me).

Other than the `Move` method, which you already learned about in the section on Command Button controls, and the `Click` event procedure, you can pretty much ignore the rest of the CheckBox stuff. Someday, when you're really bored, you might want to look over the other methods and events, just to see what's there. On the other hand, if you ever get that bored, I'd seriously consider taking up a hobby.

Just Like a Radio

Because only one OptionButton in a group of OptionButton controls can be selected at a time, OptionButton controls are sometimes called *radio buttons*. The name comes from the car radio buttons that enable you to select a station. Even though you have two ears, you can listen to only one station at a time, right? If you have more than two ears, you better be carrying your intergalactic green card.

OptionButton Controls

Like CheckBoxes, you've undoubtedly seen plenty of OptionButton controls before. OptionButton controls, again like CheckBoxes, are usually used to represent program options. However, OptionButton controls represent a set of options in which only one can be selected simultaneously. When you click the control, a dark circle appears in its box, indicating that the associated option is active. Unlike a check box, a second click does not remove the circle or turn off the option. To change the option, you must click another OptionButton control in the group.

OptionButton controls also boast over 40 properties, as well as seven methods, and they respond to 19 events. You are introduced to the most important of these in the following sections.

OptionButton Properties

The OptionButton control has about the same number of properties as a Command Button control, through for most you'll have little need. Some of the more useful OptionButton control properties are listed below:

➤ Alignment—Represents whether the option button's text is on the left or the right.

➤ BackColor—Represents the option button's background color.

➤ Caption—Represents the option button's text.

➤ Enabled—Represents whether the user can interact with the option button.

➤ ForeColor—Represents the color of the option button's text.

➤ Height—Represents the option button's height.

➤ Left—Represents the position of the option button's left edge.

➤ Picture—Represents the image that's displayed in the option button. For this property to have an effect, the button's Style property must be set to Graphical.

➤ Style—Represents whether the option button is standard or is a two-position, graphical push button.

➤ Top—Represents the position of the option button's top edge.

➤ Value—Represents whether the option button is unselected or selected.

➤ Width—Represents the option button's width.

As you can see, the OptionButton control's properties are much like the CheckBox control's properties. The two controls are closely related. Like a check box, when you set an OptionButton control's Style property to Graphical, it no longer looks like an option button, but more like a regular button. This button stays pressed to indicate the selected state. The following figure shows the OptionButton control's four different looks:

The OptionButton control has four different looks, not counting its disabled look.

In this figure, the first control is a standard option button in its unselected state, the second control is a standard option button in its selected state, the third control is a graphical option button in its unselected state, and the fourth control is a graphical option button in its checked state.

The following program demonstrates how to use OptionButton controls. To build the program, start a new Visual Basic project (a Standard EXE), and then place one Command Button, one Frame, and three OptionButton controls on the form, as shown here:

Position the controls as shown in this figure.

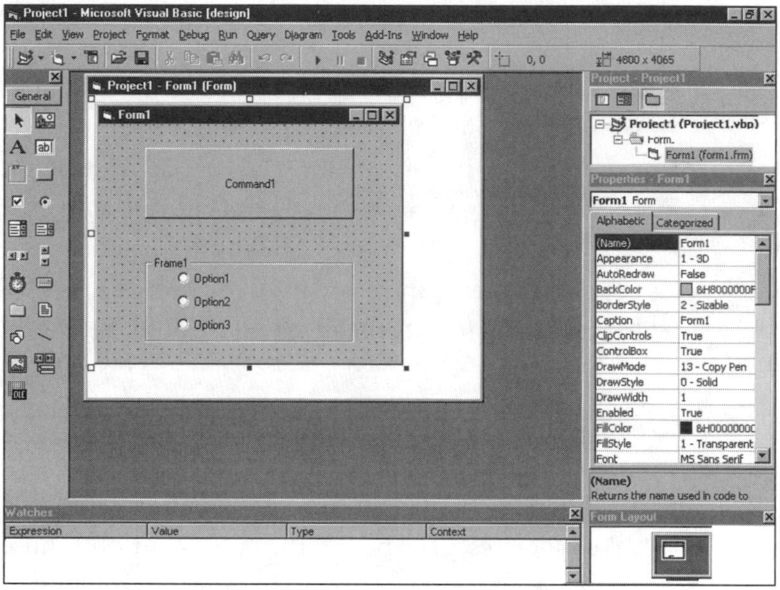

Double-click the Command Button to display the code window, and type the following lines (Visual Basic will have already started the Command1_Click event procedure for you):

```
Option Explicit

Private Sub Command1_Click()
    MsgBox "Yep, the button works."
End Sub

Private Sub Option1_Click()
    Command1.BackColor = RGB(192, 192, 192)
End Sub

Private Sub Option2_Click()
    Command1.BackColor = RGB(255, 0, 0)
End Sub
```

```
Private Sub Option3_Click()
    Command1.BackColor = RGB(0, 255, 0)
End Sub

Private Sub Form_Load()
    Command1.Caption = "TEST BUTTON"
    Frame1.Caption = "Button Color"
    Option1.Caption = "Gray Button"
    Option2.Caption = "Red Button"
    Option3.Caption = "Green Button"
    Option1.Value = vbChecked
End Sub
```

When you're done typing, click the Command1 button to select it, and then, in the button's Properties window, set the `Style` property to `1-Graphical`.

Now, save your work, and run the program. When you do, the main window appears. To prove that the Command1 button is working normally, give it a click. A message box appears. Dismiss the message box, and click the Red Button option button. Visual Basic selects the button, deselects the previously selected button, and changes the Command1 button's background color to red. Click the Green Button option button to change the Command1 control to green. As you can see, you can select only one color at a time. The following figure shows the application when the Command1 button is set to green:

Suitable for Framing

As you've noticed in the sample program, Frame controls are great for grouping together controls that have similar functions. In the next chapter, you'll use frames again to group sets of OptionButton controls that are being used as radio buttons.

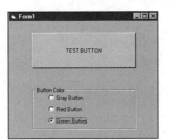

The option buttons enable the user to choose a color for the Command1 button.

CheckBox Methods and Events

In the previous program, you can see that the `Click` event is important to an OptionButton control, as it is to a CheckBox or Command Button control. Outside of

223

the Move method and the Click event procedure, there's only one other event that you might find interesting. That's the DblClick event, whose event procedure looks almost exactly like the Click event procedure. The only difference is that Visual Basic jumps to the DblClick event procedure when the user double-clicks the option button, rather than just single-clicking it.

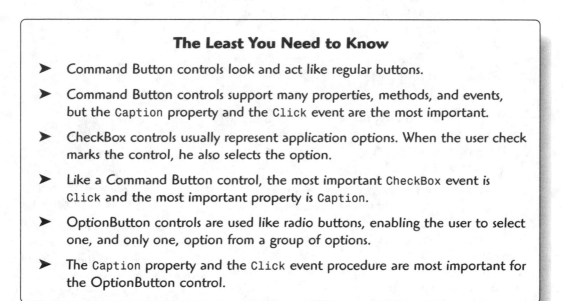

The Least You Need to Know

➤ Command Button controls look and act like regular buttons.

➤ Command Button controls support many properties, methods, and events, but the Caption property and the Click event are the most important.

➤ CheckBox controls usually represent application options. When the user check marks the control, he also selects the option.

➤ Like a Command Button control, the most important CheckBox event is Click and the most important property is Caption.

➤ OptionButton controls are used like radio buttons, enabling the user to select one, and only one, option from a group of options.

➤ The Caption property and the Click event procedure are most important for the OptionButton control.

Chapter 20

Text Controls: Computers and the English Language

In This Chapter

➤ Learn about the Label control's many properties, methods, and events

➤ Set the appearance of Label controls

➤ Discover new Textbox programming techniques

➤ Find out which Textbox properties, methods, and events can do the most for your programs

---

Just like button controls, you've been using a lot of Label and Textbox controls in the programs you've explored so far in this book. Although you're pretty familiar by now with their basic use, these handy controls have a few tricks up their sleeves that you might not know about. This chapter will fix that.

Label Controls

Label controls are sometimes called *static text* controls because they hold text that the user cannot edit. As such, Label controls are great for, as their name hints, creating labels. Labels are important on your application's user interface, so that the user knows what different controls do and what's expected of him. If you present your application's user with a screen full of unlabeled controls, he'll make a voodoo doll in your image and poke at it with floppy disks. Ouch!

Although the user cannot edit the text in a Label control, it can be changed easily by your program. For this reason, Label controls are also a great way to put a line of text in a window, a line of text that your program can change as needed. For example, you could use a Label control to hold the name of the currently loaded file or the name of the directory to which the file will be saved.

Using Controls as Guinea Pigs

One of the best ways to learn about a control's properties, methods, and events is to start Visual Basic and experiment with the control, changing things to see what happens. In fact, you can use the sample programs provided in this book as your starting point. When you get a program working properly, save your work, and then see what else you can do with the controls in the program. Nothing you can do with Visual Basic will hurt your computer. (Although you could end up having to restart the computer.) Dig in and have fun!

Label Properties

The Label control features more than 40 properties that enable a program to do everything from align the text in the label to change the colors used to display the control. The following list presents the most useful label properties:

➤ Alignment—Represents whether the label's text is left justified, right justified, or centered

➤ AutoSize—Represents whether the label will automatically size itself to fit its contents

➤ BackColor—Represents the label's background color. This property has an effect only if the label's BackStyle property is set to Opaque

➤ BackStyle—Represents whether the label's background is transparent or opaque

➤ BorderStyle—Represents the type of border used to display the label

➤ Caption—Represents the label's text

➤ Enabled—Represents whether the label is displayed grayed out

➤ ForeColor—Represents the color of the label's text

➤ Height—Represents the label's height

➤ Left—Represents the position of the label's left edge

➤ Top—Represents the position of the label's top edge

➤ Width—Represents the label's width

Although reading a list of properties can be informative (do I hear snoring?), nothing beats seeing the properties in action—except maybe a huge bowl of mint chocolate chip ice cream. The following program gives you a chance to experiment with many of the Label control's properties.

First, start a new Visual Basic project (a Standard EXE), and then position one Label control, four Frame controls, and thirteen OptionButton controls, as shown here:

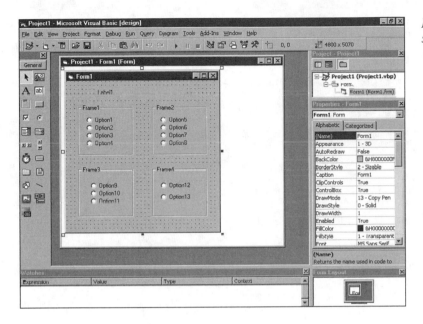

Position the buttons as shown in this figure.

Sure, that's a lot of controls, but you need some experience building larger programs. And I'm just the guy to give it to you (evil chuckle).

Now, double-click the form to display the code window, and type the following lines (Visual Basic will have already started the Form_Load event procedure for you):

Easy Procedure Typing

Don't forget that you can have Visual Basic start a control's event procedures for you. All you have to do is double-click the control on the form. For example, to start the Option1_Click event procedure, double-click the Option1 control on the form. This technique can save you a lot of time and a lot of typing.

```
Private Sub Form_Load()
    Label1.Caption = "THIS IS A _
TEST LABEL"
    Label1.Alignment = vbCenter
    Frame1.Caption = "BackColor"
    Frame2.Caption = "ForeColor"
    Frame3.Caption = "Alignment"
    Frame4.Caption = "Border"
    Option1.Caption = "Red"
    Option2.Caption = "Green"
    Option3.Caption = "Blue"
    Option4.Caption = "Transparent"
    Option5.Caption = "Red"
```

```
      Option6.Caption = "Green"
      Option7.Caption = "Blue"
      Option8.Caption = "Black"
      Option9.Caption = "Left"
      Option10.Caption = "Right"
      Option11.Caption = "Center"
      Option12.Caption = "None"
      Option13.Caption = "Fixed Single"
      Option4.Value = vbChecked
      Option8.Value = vbChecked
      Option11.Value = vbChecked
      Option12.Value = vbChecked
End Sub

Private Sub Option1_Click()
      Label1.BackStyle = 1
      Label1.BackColor = RGB(255, 0, 0)
End Sub

Private Sub Option2_Click()
      Label1.BackStyle = 1
      Label1.BackColor = RGB(0, 255, 0)
End Sub

Private Sub Option3_Click()
     Label1.BackStyle = 1
      Label1.BackColor = RGB(0, 0, 255)
End Sub

Private Sub Option4_Click()
      Label1.BackStyle = 0
End Sub

Private Sub Option5_Click()
      Label1.ForeColor = RGB(255, 0, 0)
End Sub

Private Sub Option6_Click()
      Label1.ForeColor = RGB(0, 255, 0)
End Sub

Private Sub Option7_Click()
      Label1.ForeColor = RGB(0, 0, 255)
End Sub
```

```
Private Sub Option8_Click()
    Label1.ForeColor = RGB(0, 0, 0)
End Sub

Private Sub Option9_Click()
    Label1.Alignment = vbLeftJustify
End Sub

Private Sub Option10_Click()
    Label1.Alignment = vbRightJustify
End Sub

Private Sub Option11_Click()
    Label1.Alignment = vbCenter
End Sub

Private Sub Option12_Click()
    Label1.BorderStyle = 0
End Sub

Private Sub Option13_Click()
    Label1.BorderStyle = 1
End Sub
```

Now, save your program. When you do, the main window appears. Click the appropriate option buttons to set the Label control's BackColor, ForeColor, Alignment, and BorderStyle properties. Have you ever had so much fun?

The following figure shows the application with the Label control's BackColor property set to Green, the ForeColor property set to Red, the Alignment property set to Center, and the BorderStyle property set to Fixed Single:

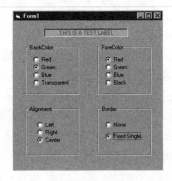

This application enables you to set a Label control's properties and immediately see the results.

The only label meathod you need to know at this point is Move, which does the same thing for a Label control that it does for any other control. (In case you've forgotten, the Move method repositions and resizes a control.)

Because the Label control isn't usually used in an interactive way, your programs probably won't need to handle Label events. However, even though the Label control represents static text, it does respond to 18 events. Of those 18 events, only Click and DblClick are likely to be useful to you until you learn more about Visual Basic. As you've already learned, the Click event occurs when the user clicks a control, and the DblClick event occurs when the user double-clicks a control

Textbox Controls

The Textbox is the last of the controls with which you've had previous experience. For example, you know that you can use a Textbox control to retrieve input from the user. You can also give information back to the user by setting the Textbox control's text, but that would be an unusual way of providing output. In the following sections, you'll stumble upon some other cool ways to use a Textbox control.

Textbox Properties

The Textbox control features more than 50 properties, more properties than any other control you've looked at so far. The following list presents the most useful Label properties:

➤ Alignment—Represents whether the text box's text is left justified, right justified, or centered

➤ BackColor—Represents the text box's background color

➤ BorderStyle—Represents the type of border used to display the text box

➤ Enabled—Represents whether the text box can accept input from the user

➤ ForeColor—Represents the color of the text box's text

➤ Height—Represents the text box's height

➤ Left—Represents the position of the text box's left edge

➤ Locked—Represents whether the text box's contents are locked from editing

➤ MaxLength—Represents the number of characters the text box can hold

➤ MultiLine—Represents whether the text box can display multiple lines of text

➤ Top—Represents the position of the text box's top edge

➤ Text—Represents the text box's contents

➤ Width—Represents the text box's width

In the next section, you'll experiment with a program that puts Textbox properties to the test. But first, read on to learn a little about this control's methods and events.

Textbox Methods and Events

The Textbox control features several methods and events you might find useful. One of the methods, Move, and two of the events, Click and DblClick, you already learned about with other controls. They work the same for the Textbox control. However, the SetFocus method and the Change event, which are new to you, are handy to know when you're working with Textbox controls.

A Matter of Focus

Clicking a control with your mouse is only one way to give the control the focus. You can also move the focus around from one control to the next by pressing your keyboard's Tab key.

The SetFocus method gives the input focus to the Textbox control. *Input focus* means a control can accept input from the user. Visual Basic sends the Change event every time a Textbox control's content changes. In the following program, you'll see how to use the SetFocus method and the Change event, as well as experiment with a few Textbox properties.

First, start a new Visual Basic project (a Standard EXE), and then position two Textbox controls and one CheckBox control, as shown here:

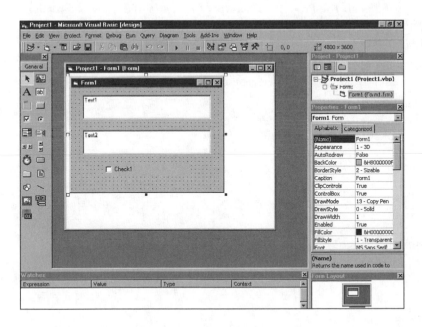

Position the controls as shown in this figure.

Select the first Textbox control on the form (click it with your mouse), and change its MultiLine property in the Properties window to True, as shown here:

The MultiLine property enables a Textbox to display more than one line of text.

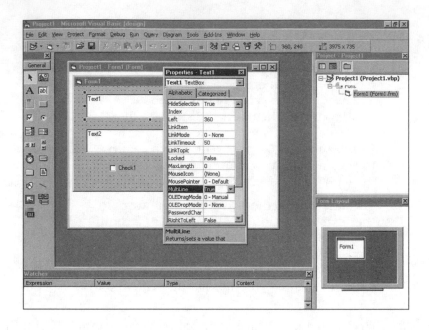

Set the MultiLine property for the second Textbox control in the same way. You have to set the MultiLine property in the Properties window because MultiLine is a read-only property at runtime. If you try to set it in your program, Visual Basic will annoy you with an error message.

Now double-click the form to display the code window, and type the following lines (Visual Basic will have already started the Form_Load event procedure for you):

```
Private Sub Check1_Click()
    If Check1.Value = vbChecked Then
        Text1.Locked = True
    Else
        Text1.Locked = False
    End If
    Text1.SetFocus
End Sub

Private Sub Text1_Change()
    Text2.Text = Text1.Text
End Sub

Private Sub Form_Load()
    Dim str As String

    str = "This is a test of a TextBox "
    str = str & "control's Locked, Enabled, "
```

232

```
        str = str & " and MultiLine properties. "
        str = str & "As long as the check box "
        str = str & "below is not checked "
        str = str & "you can edit this text."
        Text1.Text = str
        Text2.Text = str
        Text2.Enabled = False
        Check1.Caption = "Lock Text"
    End Sub
```

Save your work, and run the program. When you do, the main window appears, which looks like this:

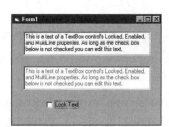

This application demonstrates handy things you can do with a text box.

Try deleting or adding text to the first Textbox control. The second Textbox control mirrors all your changes, thanks to the Change event. If you look at the Change event procedure in the source code, you'll see that the procedure assigns the first Textbox control's text to the second Textbox control. This happens every time you change even a single character in the first text box.

Now, click the Lock Text check box to turn on its check mark. You've now locked the text in the first Textbox so that it cannot be edited. Go ahead and try. Can't change the text, can you? If you do manage to change the text, you've either mistyped the program, or you've been transported to a parallel universe where Visual Basic works differently.

The text is locked in the Check1_Click event procedure, to which Visual Basic jumps when you click the check box. In that procedure, the program sets the Textbox control's Locked property to True or False, depending on the state (checked or unchecked) of the check box.

Getting and Losing the Focus

As you now know, the SetFocus method gives the input focus to a control. Most Visual Basic controls feature two event procedures that are related to the input focus. When the control receives the input focus, the control generates a GotFocus event to which your program can respond in the GotFocus event procedure. When a control loses the focus, it generates a LostFocus event.

The Check1_Click event procedure also calls the Textbox control's SetFocus method. Here's why: The input focus automatically goes to the last control you selected. So, when you click the check box, it gets the input focus. Worse, it *keeps* the input focus, which means that before you can type more text in the text box, you first have to click the text box with your mouse. By calling SetFocus on behalf of the text box, you can keep typing right after clicking the check box.

The Least You Need to Know

➤ Programmers usually use Label controls to label controls on the application's user interface and to display lines of text in a window.

➤ The user cannot edit the text in a Label control, which is often called a *static text* control. (The term "static" means unchanging.)

➤ Of all the Label control's properties, Alignment, BorderStyle, and Caption are the most important.

➤ Textbox controls enable a user to input text to an application. A program can also use a text box to present text to the user.

➤ The most important Textbox properties are Enabled, Locked, MultiLine, and Text.

➤ When the user changes the text in a text box, the control generates a Change event, which the program can handle in the Change event procedure.

➤ The SetFocus method enables a program to return the input focus to a text box after the user has made a selection from another control.

Chapter 21

List Controls: It's the User's Choice

Often in your Visual Basic programs, you need to enable the user to select an item from a list of possibilities. Although you can use check boxes and option buttons for presenting limited choices, ListBox and ComboBox controls can hold a list of many more choices that takes up little screen real estate. In this chapter, you'll see how these handy controls work.

ListBox Controls

A ListBox control is little more than a box that contains a list of selections. The user can use his mouse to select a choice from the list, and the program can respond to the choice through the control's event procedures. You might use a ListBox control to present a list of choices that is too long to accommodate with check boxes or option buttons, but still short enough not to take up too much screen space.

ListBox Properties

The ListBox control features more than 50 properties. The following list presents the most useful:

- ➤ `BackColor`—Represents the list box's background color
- ➤ `Enabled`—Represents whether the user can interact with the list box
- ➤ `ForeColor`—Represents the color of the list box's text
- ➤ `Height`—Represents the list box's height
- ➤ `Left`—Represents the position of the list box's left edge
- ➤ `List`—Represents a string array that contains the items in the control's list
- ➤ `ListCount`—Represents the number of items in the control's list
- ➤ `ListIndex`—Represents the index of the currently selected item in the control
- ➤ `MultiSelect`—Represents whether the control supports multiple selection of items
- ➤ `Sorted`—Represents whether the items in the control's list are sorted
- ➤ `Text`—Represents the currently selected item in the list
- ➤ `Top`—Represents the position of the control's top edge
- ➤ `Width`—Represents the control's width

Later in this chapter, you'll build a program that shows how many of these properties work. In the next section, however, you'll first look over the control's most important methods and events.

ListBox Methods and Events

The ListBox control features 10 methods, several of which you might find especially useful. The lucky winners are listed below:

- ➤ `AddItem`—Adds an item to the control's list
- ➤ `Clear`—Clears all items from the control's list
- ➤ `Move`—Positions and sizes the control
- ➤ `RemoveItem`—Removes a single item from the control's list

Besides its properties and methods, the ListBox control responds to 21 events, two of which are particularly useful to you at this time. Those events are `Click` and

DblClick, both of which you've run into before in this book. In case you've forgotten, the Click event occurs when the user clicks the control, and the DblClick event occurs when the user double-clicks the control. (The triple-click event occurs when the user accidentally sits on the mouse.)

Because you've probably sensed a pattern to these chapters, you know that a sample program is next. If you don't know that a sample program is next, consider yourself warned. To build the sample program, first, start a new Visual Basic project (a Standard EXE), and then position one ListBox control, one Label control, one TextBox control, and three Command Button controls as shown here:

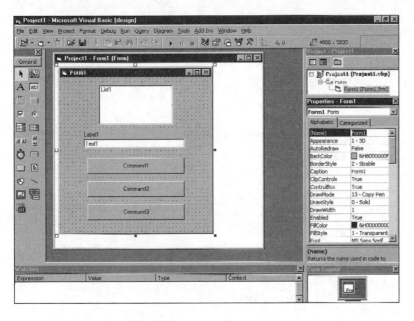

Position the controls as shown in this figure.

Now, double-click the form to display the code window, and type the following lines (Visual Basic will have already started the Form_Load event procedure for you):

```
Private Sub Command1_Click()
    Dim newItem As String

    newItem = Text1.Text
    If newItem <> "" Then List1.AddItem newItem
End Sub

Private Sub Command2_Click()
    List1.Clear
End Sub
```

```
Private Sub Command3_Click()
    Dim selItemIndex As Integer

    selItemIndex = List1.ListIndex
    If selItemIndex = -1 Then
        MsgBox "No item selected."
    Else
        List1.RemoveItem selItemIndex
    End If
End Sub

Private Sub List1_DblClick()
    Dim selItem As String

    selItem = List1.Text
    MsgBox "You selected: " & selItem
End Sub

Private Sub Form_Load()
    List1.AddItem "Elephant"
    List1.AddItem "Cheetah"
    List1.AddItem "Lion"
    List1.AddItem "Giraffe"
    List1.AddItem "Monkey"
    List1.AddItem "Boa Constrictor"
    List1.AddItem "Antelope"
    List1.AddItem "Water Buffalo"
    List1.BackColor = RGB(255, 255, 0)
    List1.ForeColor = RGB(0, 0, 255)
    Label1.Caption = "Enter a new item:"
    Command1.Caption = "Add New Item"
    Command2.Caption = "Remove All Items"
    Command3.Caption = "Remove Selected Item"
    Text1.Text = "Default Item"
End Sub
```

After typing the source code, select the list box in the form by clicking it with your mouse. (Actually, you should probably use the computer's mouse and leave your own mouse in its cage. Clicking with a real mouse gums up your keyboard with fur and droppings, which can be nasty to clean.) In the Properties window, set the list box's Sorted property to True, as shown here:

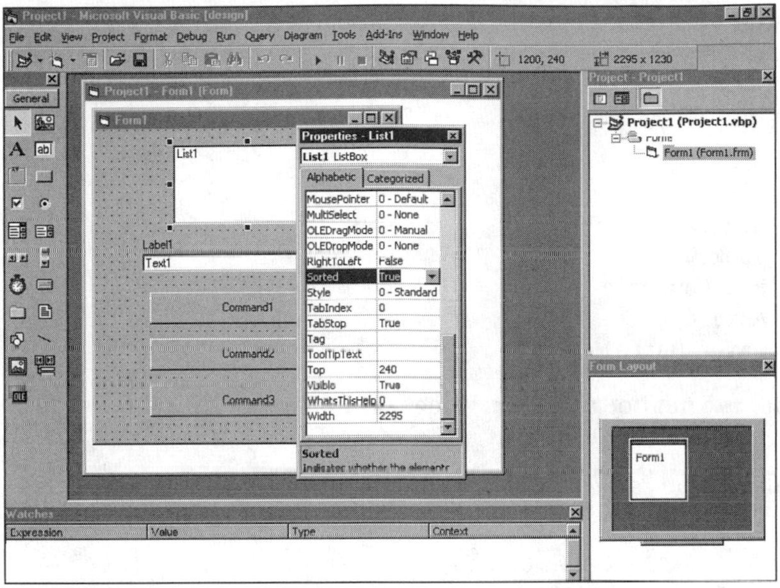

You have to set the Sorted property in the Properties window because this property is read-only at runtime.

Finally, save your work, and run the program. When you do, the main window appears, as shown in the following figure:

This program puts a ListBox control through its paces.

Double-click an item in the list box, and a message box appears showing the item you picked. You can add your own items to the list box by typing the item into the text box and clicking the Add New Item button. You can clear all items from the list box by clicking the Remove All Items button. Finally, you can remove any single item from the list box by selecting the item in the list and clicking the Remove Selected Item button.

This program demonstrates how to use many ListBox properties, methods, and events. Let's take a look. First, the Form_Load procedure calls the AddItem method to load items into the list box:

```
List1.AddItem "Elephant"
List1.AddItem "Cheetah"
List1.AddItem "Lion"
List1.AddItem "Giraffe"
List1.AddItem "Monkey"
List1.AddItem "Boa Constrictor"
List1.AddItem "Antelope"
List1.AddItem "Water Buffalo"
```

As you can see, the AddItem method's single argument is the text of the item to add to the list. Couldn't get much easier than that, eh?

Next, Form_Load sets the list box's BackColor and ForeColor properties to yellow and blue, respectively:

```
List1.BackColor = RGB(255, 255, 0)
List1.ForeColor = RGB(0, 0, 255)
```

It's the DblClick event procedure that displays the user's selection:

```
Private Sub List1_DblClick()
    Dim selItem As String

    selItem = List1.Text
    MsgBox "You selected: " & selItem
End Sub
```

In this procedure, the program gets the selected item from the list box's Text property, which holds the text of the selected item. The program then displays the text in a message box. Nothing tricky going on here.

The Command1_Click procedure adds new items to the list:

```
Private Sub Command1_Click()
    Dim newItem As String

    newItem = Text1.Text
    If newItem <> "" Then List1.AddItem newItem
End Sub
```

First, this procedure gets the text from the text box. The If statement ensures that the text box actually contains text before it adds the item to the list box. If the text box contains no text, the Text property returns an empty string, which you represent in a program by two double quotes with nothing between them, which is kind of like what my wife says is between my ears.

The `Command2_Click` event procedure gets the job of removing all items from the list box, which it does by calling the list box's `Clear` method, as shown here:

```
Private Sub Command2_Click()
    List1.Clear
End Sub
```

Finally, the `Command3_Click` event procedure removes the selected item from the list box:

```
Private Sub Command3_Click()
    Dim selItemIndex As Integer

    selItemIndex = List1.ListIndex
    If selItemIndex = -1 Then
        MsgBox "No item selected."
    Else
        List1.RemoveItem selItemIndex
    End If
End Sub
```

This procedure gets the index of the selected item from the list box's `ListIndex` property. If this index is `-1`, the list box has no selected item, and the procedure shows a message box that presents the user with an error message. Otherwise, the procedure calls the list box's `RemoveItem` method to remove the selected item from the list. This method's single argument is the index of the item to remove.

ComboBox Controls

A ComboBox control is like a ListBox control combined with a Textbox control. I've long suspected that that's where the name "ComboBox" came from. (Duh!) The user can select items from the combo box's list or can type a selection into the control's text box. If the user selects an item from the list, the selected item automatically appears in the text box. Because the ComboBox control's items appear in a drop-down list that doesn't appear until the user clicks an onscreen arrow, a ComboBox control is great for especially long lists.

ComboBox Properties

Like the ListBox, the ComboBox control features more than 50 properties. The following list presents the most useful ComboBox properties, which are pretty much the same as the ListBox's handiest properties:

➤ `BackColor`—Represents the combo box's background color

➤ `Enabled`—Represents whether the user can interact with the combo box

➤ ForeColor—Represents the color of the combo box's text

➤ Height—Represents the combo box's height

➤ Left—Represents the position of the combo box's left edge

➤ List—Represents a string array that contains the items in the control's list

➤ ListCount—Represents the number of items in the control's list

➤ ListIndex—Represents the index of the currently selected item in the control

➤ Locked—Represents whether the user can type in the control's text box

➤ Sorted—Represents whether the items in the control's list are sorted

➤ Style—Determines how the ComboBox control looks and how items can be selected from the control's list

➤ Text—Represents the currently selected item in the list

➤ Top—Represents the position of the control's top edge

➤ Width—Represents the control's width

The Many Faces of a ComboBox Control

By setting a ComboBox control's Style property, you can create several different kinds of combo boxes. For example, set the Style property to vbComboDropDown (which is the default), and you get the standard ComboBox with a drop-down list and a text box. However, set the Style property to vbComboSimple, and you get a combo box whose list is always visible (it doesn't drop down). Finally, the vbComboDropdownList style yields a combo box in which the user must select items only from the list and can't type selections into the control's text box.

ComboBox Methods and Events

Again, like the ListBox, the ComboBox control features 10 methods, several of which you might find especially useful. The more useful methods, which should look familiar, introduce themselves in the following list:

➤ AddItem—Adds an item to the control's list

➤ Clear—Clears all items from the control's list

➤ Move—Positions and sizes the control

➤ RemoveItem—Removes a single item from the control's list

Besides its properties and methods, the ListBox control responds to 21 events, three of which are particularly useful to a Visual Basic novice. Those events are Change, Click, and DblClick. You reviewed the Click and DblClick events in the section on the ListBox control. You should also recognize the Change event from your work with the Textbox control. The Change event occurs when the user changes the text in the control's text box. (I know, tell you something you don't already know.)

Time for the inevitable sample program. Please face the front of the class, throw away your gum, and stop passing notes. To build the program, first start a new Visual Basic project (a Standard EXE), and then position one ComboBox control, one Label control, one Textbox control, and four Command Button controls, as shown here:

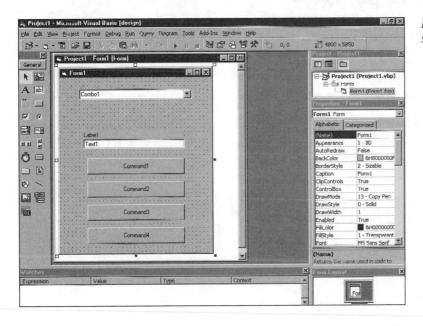

Position the controls as shown in this figure.

Now, double-click the form to display the code window, and type the following lines (Visual Basic will have already started the Form_Load event procedure for you):

```
Private Sub Command1_Click()
    Dim newItem As String

    newItem = Text1.Text
    If newItem <> "" Then Combo1.AddItem newItem
End Sub

Private Sub Command2_Click()
    Combo1.Clear
End Sub
```

243

```
Private Sub Command3_Click()
    Dim selItemIndex As Integer

    selItemIndex = Combo1.ListIndex
    If selItemIndex = -1 Then
        MsgBox "No item selected."
    Else
        Combo1.RemoveItem selItemIndex
    End If
End Sub

Private Sub Command4_Click()
    If Combo1.Locked = True Then
        Combo1.Locked = False
        Command4.Caption = "Lock ComboBox"
    Else
        Combo1.Locked = True
        Command4.Caption = "Unlock ComboBox"
    End If
End Sub

Private Sub Combo1_Click()
    Dim selItem As String

    selItem = Combo1.Text
    MsgBox "You selected: " & selItem
End Sub

Private Sub Form_Load()
    Combo1.AddItem "Elephant"
    Combo1.AddItem "Cheetah"
    Combo1.AddItem "Lion"
    Combo1.AddItem "Giraffe"
    Combo1.AddItem "Monkey"
    Combo1.AddItem "Boa Constrictor"
    Combo1.AddItem "Antelope"
    Combo1.AddItem "Water Buffalo"
    Combo1.BackColor = RGB(255, 255, 0)
    Combo1.ForeColor = RGB(0, 0, 255)
    Combo1.Text = ""
    Label1.Caption = "Enter a new item:"
    Command1.Caption = "Add New Item"
    Command2.Caption = "Remove All Items"
    Command3.Caption = "Remove Selected Item"
    Command4.Caption = "Lock ComboBox"
    Text1.Text = "Default Item"
End Sub
```

After typing the source code, select the ComboBox in the form by clicking it with your mouse. In the Properties window, set the combo box's Sorted property to True. Finally, save your work, and run the program. When you do, the main window appears, as shown in the following figure:

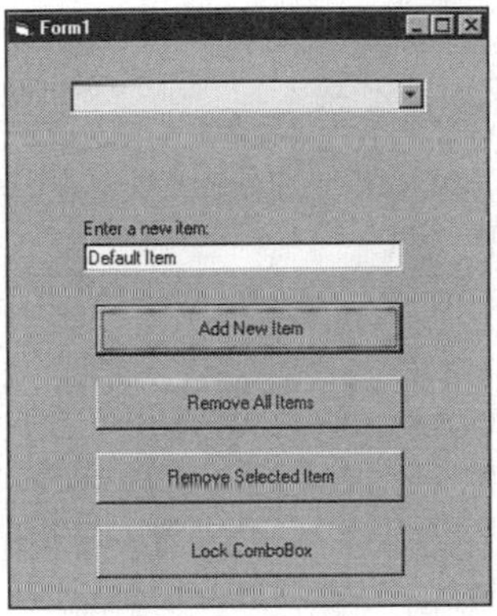

This program demonstrates the ComboBox control.

Because a ComboBox works much like a ListBox, this program is very similar to the ListBox demo program. Click the combo box's arrow to display its drop-down list, which looks like this:

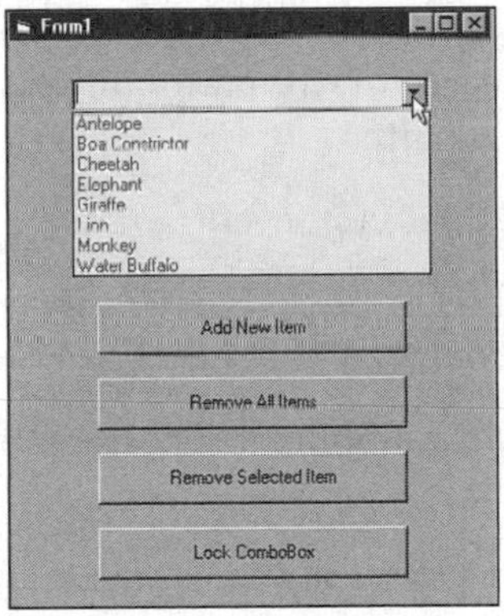

Unlike a ListBox control, a ComboBox control has a drop-down list.

Click an item in the list, and a message box appears showing the item you picked. Add your own items to the list box by typing the item into the text box and clicking the Add New Item button. Clear all items from the list box by clicking the Remove All Items button. Remove any single item from the list box by selecting the item in the list and clicking the Remove Selected Item button. Finally, click the Lock ComboBox button to prevent the user from making any changes in the ComboBox. A second click unlocks the control.

Most of this program's source code should be familiar territory, thanks to your previous experience with the ListBox control. The Command4_Click event procedure, however, is new:

```
Private Sub Command4_Click()
    If Combo1.Locked = True Then
        Combo1.Locked = False
        Command4.Caption = "Lock ComboBox"
    Else
        Combo1.Locked = True
        Command4.Caption = "Unlock ComboBox"
    End If
End Sub
```

This procedure locks or unlocks the ComboBox control. When the control is locked, the user cannot change the contents of the ComboBox control's text box. As you can see, this procedure also changes the Command4 button's caption, depending on the state of the Locked property.

The Least You Need to Know

➤ A ListBox control is a small box that contains a list of selectable items.

➤ The most useful ListBox properties are ListIndex, Sorted, and Text.

➤ Of the ListBox control's 10 methods, you'll probably use AddItem, Clear, and RemoveItem most often.

➤ The Click and DblClick events enable a program to respond to a user's selection in a ListBox control.

➤ A ComboBox control is like a ListBox combined with a Textbox.

➤ The most useful ComboBox properties are ListIndex, Locked, Sorted, and Text.

➤ As with a ListBox control, you'll probably use a ComboBox control's AddItem, Clear, and RemoveItem methods most often.

➤ The Change, Click, and DblClick events enable a program to respond to a user's interactions with a ComboBox control.

Chapter 22

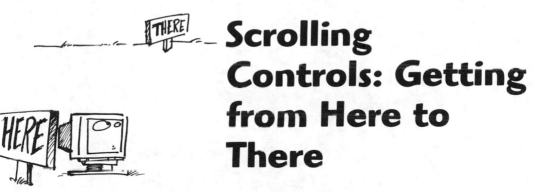

Scrolling Controls: Getting from Here to There

In This Chapter

- Learn to use scrollbars in a program
- Get the scrollbar's current setting
- Discover how to set a scrollbar's properties
- Explore a scrollbar control's methods and events

A program can get a value from the user in several ways. The most obvious way is to have the user enter the value into a text box. However, your programs can have greater control over the values entered by the user by incorporating a scrollbar control into the application's user interface. In this chapter, you'll see how.

Scrollbar Controls

Scrollbars are everywhere in Windows. Usually, applications have scrollbars that enable the user to change the view of data in a window, displaying data that doesn't currently appear on the screen, as shown here:

In many applications, scrollbars enable the user to manipulate the application's view of the data.

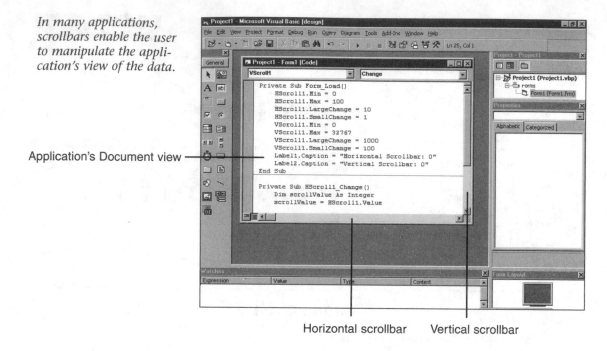

Application's Document view

Horizontal scrollbar   Vertical scrollbar

However, scrollbars have many other uses. In a Visual Basic application, for example, you might use a scrollbar to get a value from the user. Because a scrollbar forces the user to select the value from a predetermined, limited range, the program is guaranteed to get a valid value. On the other hand, if you tried to use a text box to get a value from the user, you could get anything from –9847 to an order for a pizza without anchovies.

Visual Basic's toolbox offers two types of scrollbars. The first is the HScrollBar control, which represents a horizontal scrollbar. The second type is the VScrollBar control, which is a vertical scrollbar. Because both of these controls work virtually identically, the following sections show you how to use both.

Scrollbar Properties

As with most controls, a scrollbar's properties determine, for the most part, the way the control looks and acts. Some of the scrollbar control's properties are for advanced users. (You know, the folks who wear Spock ears and say "May the force be with you" whenever they leave a room.) In fact, the scrollbar controls feature nearly 30 properties, all told, only 10 of which will interest you at this time. The following list introduces those interesting properties:

➤ Enabled—Represents whether the user can interact with the scrollbar

➤ Height—Represents the scrollbar's height

➤ LargeChange—Represents how much the scrollbar's value changes when the user clicks inside the scrollbar

➤ Left—Represents the position of the scrollbar's left edge

➤ Max—Represents the scrollbar's maximum value

➤ Min—Represents the scrollbar's minimum value

➤ SmallChange—Represents how much the scrollbar's value changes when the user clicks the scrollbar's arrow buttons

➤ Top—Represents the position of the control's top edge

➤ Value—Represents the scrollbar's current value

➤ Width—Represents the control's width

Later in this chapter, you'll build a program that shows how many of these properties work. In the next section, though, you'll look over the scrollbar's most important methods and events.

Up and Down or Left and Right

In Windows applications, a horizontal scrollbar usually scrolls that application's display from left to right, whereas a vertical scrollbar scrolls the display up and down. However, because both controls work almost identically, which one you choose to use in your program's interface depends on taste and a little bit of common sense.

For example, if a program needed a scrollbar to move an object on the screen left and right, the horizontal scrollbar would be the logical choice. If the program only needs to get a value from 1 to 100, though, either the horizontal or vertical scrollbar will work just fine. Which one you use depends mostly on your user interface's layout.

Scrollbar Methods and Events

The scrollbar controls feature six methods, only one of which, Move, might be especially useful to you at this point in your Visual Basic programming career. As luck would have it, you already know about the Move method from previous controls in this book, so you might as well dive right into the control's events.

Besides its properties and methods, the scrollbar controls respond to 10 events, one of which is particularly useful to you at this time. This event is Change, which occurs whenever the user changes the value of the scrollbar. As you can guess by now, a program responds to the Change event in the Change event procedure, which you'll see in the following sample program. And speaking of sample programs…

The Promised Sample Program

First start a new Visual Basic project (a standard EXE), and then position one HScrollBar bar control, one VScrollBar bar control, and two Label controls, as shown here:

Position the controls as shown in this figure.

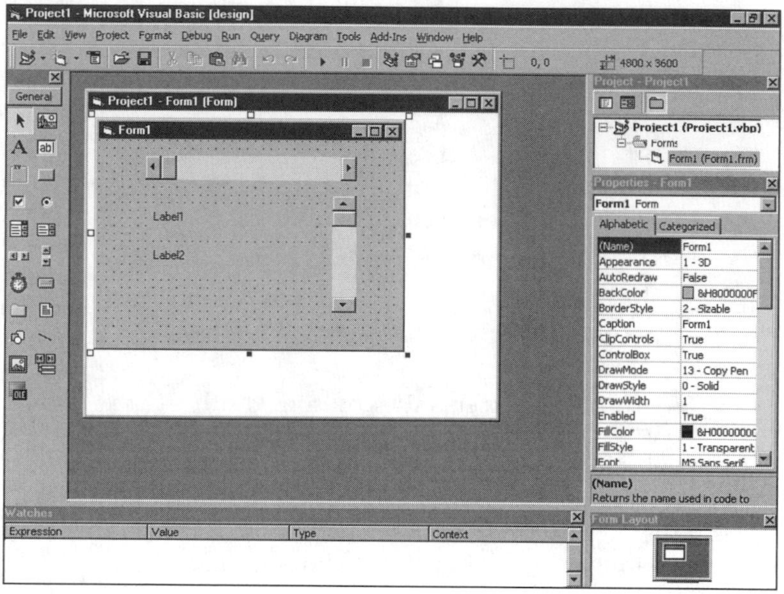

Now double-click the form to display the code window, and type the following lines (Visual Basic will have already started the Form_Load event procedure for you):

```
Private Sub Form_Load()
    HScroll1.Min = 0
    HScroll1.Max = 100
    HScroll1.LargeChange = 10
    HScroll1.SmallChange = 1
    VScroll1.Min = 0
    VScroll1.Max = 32767
    VScroll1.LargeChange = 1000
    VScroll1.SmallChange = 100
    Label1.Caption = "Horizontal Scroll bar: 0"
    Label2.Caption = "Vertical Scroll bar: 0"
End Sub

Private Sub HScroll1_Change()
    Dim scrollValue As Integer
    scrollValue = HScroll1.Value
    Label1.Caption = "Horizontal Scroll bar: " & scrollValue
End Sub
```

```
Private Sub VScroll1_Change()
    Dim scrollValue As Integer
    scrollValue = VScroll1.Value
    Label2.Caption = "Vertical Scroll bar: " & scrollValue
End Sub
```

Finally, save your work and run the program. When you do, the main window appears. Manipulate either of the scrollbar controls by clicking inside the scrollbar, dragging the small box (called the *scroll thumb*) in the scrollbar, or clicking a scrollbar's arrow buttons. The application's Label controls keep you up to date with the scrollbar's current settings. For example, the following figure shows the application after the user has set the scrollbars to the values 23 and 10,100:

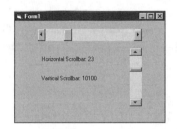

This program demonstrates scrollbar controls.

This program demonstrates how to use many scrollbar properties and events. For example, turn your attention from that bag of potato chips you sneaked from the kitchen (caught you!) to the Form_Load event procedure. First, the Form_Load procedure sets the horizontal scrollbar's minimum and maximum values:

```
HScroll1.Min = 0
HScroll1.Max = 100
```

A horizontal scrollbar's minimum value is the value when the scrollbar's thumb is set fully to the left. Conversely, a horizontal scrollbar's maximum value is the value when the scrollbar's thumb is fully to the right. In the case of a vertical scrollbar, the minimum value is at the top of the scrollbar and the maximum value is at the bottom.

The Least and the Most

A scrollbar's Min and Max properties can be set to a wide range of values, enabling the control to handle just about any scrolling situation a program might run into. However, the Min property must be 0 or greater and the Max property can be no larger than 32,767.

The Significance of 32,767

You just learned that a scrollbar's maximum value can be no more than 32,767. Who picks these numbers, anyway? Wouldn't a good round 32,000 or 33,000 be more logical? To your human mind, such numbers might make more sense, but to a computer the number 32,767 has special significance. It's the number of times the computer has seen a GIF image of Cindy Crawford... No, wait! (I really need to take down that swimsuit calendar.) It turns out that 32,767 is the maximum value that can be stored as a normal integer. (To Cindy Crawford, the number 32,767 is either the number after 32,766 or the amount she gets paid for ten minutes in front of a camera.)

After setting the scrollbar's `Min` and `Max` properties, the `Form_Load` procedure sets the `LargeChange` and `SmallChange` properties:

```
HScroll1.LargeChange = 10
HScroll1.SmallChange = 1
```

The first of the preceding lines sets the scrollbar so that when the user clicks inside the scrollbar, the control's `Value` property goes up or down 10. Which way the value goes depends on whether the user clicks to the left of the scrollbar's thumb (`Value` goes down) or to the right (`Value` goes up). The second line sets the scrollbar so that when the user clicks one of the scrollbar's arrow buttons, the `Value` property changes by only 1. Whether `Value` goes up or down 1 depends on whether the user clicks the left arrow button or the right arrow button.

After setting the horizontal scrollbar's properties, the procedure sets the vertical scrollbar's properties:

```
VScroll1.Min = 0
VScroll1.Max = 32767
VScroll1.LargeChange = 1000
VScroll1.SmallChange = 100
```

These property settings have an effect on the vertical scrollbar similar to the one they have on the horizontal scrollbar. The difference (besides the different values being used for the properties) is that the `VScroll1` control is oriented up and down rather than left to right.

Finally, Form_Load sets the Label controls to their starting text:

```
Label1.Caption = "Horizontal Scroll bar: 0"
Label2.Caption = "Vertical Scroll bar: 0"
```

Whenever the user changes the value of a scrollbar, Visual Basic jumps to the scrollbar's Change event procedure. For example, in the case of this program's horizontal scrollbar, the Change event procedure looks like this:

```
Private Sub HScroll1_Change()
    Dim scrollValue As Integer
    scrollValue = HScroll1.Value
    Label1.Caption = "Horizontal Scroll bar: " & scrollValue
End Sub
```

Here, the program gets the value of the scrollbar's Value property, which is the scrollbar's current setting. The program does nothing more than display this value in the first Label control.

The vertical scrollbar's Change event procedure is very similar to the horizontal scrollbar's:

```
Private Sub VScroll1_Change()
    Dim scrollValue As Integer
    scrollValue = VScroll1.Value
    Label2.Caption = "Vertical Scroll bar: " & scrollValue
End Sub
```

Amazingly, you've already reached the point in this chapter when you get to prove how smart you are. Put on your thinking cap and follow me.

The Least You Need to Know

➤ A scrollbar control enables a user to select a value from a range of acceptable values.

➤ There are two types of scrollbars: horizontal (represented by the HScrollBar control) and vertical (represented by the VScrollBar control).

➤ Horizontal and vertical scrollbars work almost identically. Their only real difference is their onscreen orientation.

➤ A scrollbar's most useful properties are Min, Max, LargeChange, SmallChange, and Value.

➤ To respond to changes in a scrollbar's value, a program needs to supply a Change event procedure for the scrollbar.

Chapter 23

Graphical Controls: Get the Picture, Dude?

In This Chapter

➤ Draw various types of lines in a form

➤ Display several kinds of shapes in a form

➤ Display photographic-quality pictures in your application's window

Visual Basic offers several ways to display graphics in a form. The easiest way to draw lines and shapes is with the Line and Shape controls. However, Visual Basic also enables your application to display photographic-quality images. In this chapter, you'll discover Visual Basic's graphical secrets. (Well, some of them, anyway.)

Line Controls

If you want to display a line as part of your application's user interface, you need look no further than the Line control. The Line control enables a program to not only display a line, but also to choose various styles for the line, including dotted and dashed lines, as well as different line thicknesses. The following sections give you the skinny on this handy control.

Line Properties

The Line control features 14 properties, seven of which are of particular interest. Those seven properties are described as follows:

➤ BorderColor—Represents the color of the line.

➤ BorderStyle—Represents whether the line is solid or is drawn with a pattern. This property has an effect only when the BorderWidth property is set to 1.

➤ BorderWidth—Represents the thickness of the line.

➤ X1—Represents the horizontal position of the line's left end.

➤ X2—Represents the horizontal position of the line's right end.

➤ Y1—Represents the vertical position of the line's left end.

➤ Y2—Represents the vertical position of the line's right end.

Seeing these properties in action is easier than beating a fish in a road race. Just place a Line control on a form and then change the control's properties in its Properties window, which is shown in the following figure:

You can experiment with the Line control by setting its properties in the Properties window.

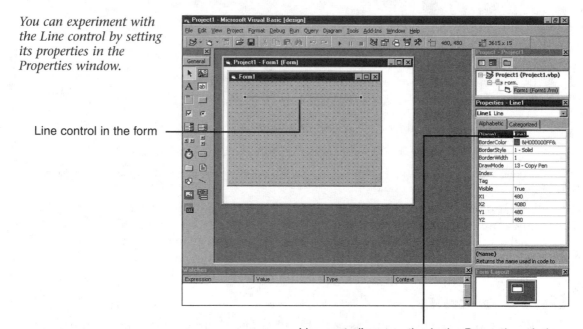

Line control in the form

Line control's properties in the Properties window

For example, suppose you want to see a red line that's 10 dots thick. In the Properties window, set the Line control's BorderColor property to Red, and set the BorderWidth property to 10. You'll then have a form with a line like this:

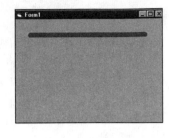

This red line is 10 dots (pixels) thick.

Displaying a Control's Properties

The easiest way to get a control's properties to appear in the Properties window is to select the control on the form (click it with the mouse). You can also select the control in the Properties window's drop-down list. Just click the small arrow near the top left of the window, and select the control you want from the list that appears.

Setting Colors in the Properties Window

When you select a color property, such as BackColor, in the Properties window, a box appears with Palette and System tabs. To select a color from Visual Basic's color palette, click on the Palette tab and then select the color. To select a system color, use the colors displayed when you click the System tab.

To see how the X1, X2, Y1, and Y2 properties work, change their values in the Properties window. For example, suppose you want Visual Basic to draw the line from the coordinates 500,700 to the coordinates 3000,1800. Set the X1, X2, Y1, and Y2 properties to 500, 3000, 700, and 1800, respectively. You'll then get the line shown in the following figure:

The line moves to the coordinates you select.

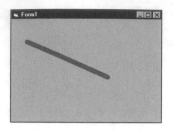

Of course, you can set the Line control's properties in your program, as well, just as you've been doing with controls in previous programs in this book. For example, the following `Form_Load` event procedure sets a Line control to the same settings illustrated in the previous figure:

```
Private Sub Form_Load()
    Line1.BorderColor = RGB(255, 0, 0)
    Line1.BorderWidth = 10
    Line1.X1 = 500
    Line1.X2 = 3000
    Line1.Y1 = 700
    Line1.Y2 = 1800
End Sub
```

Setting Properties Your Way

Throughout much of this book, you've set control properties in the `Form_Load` procedure of your program. This method of property setting is great for a book like this because it avoids having to explain property setting step-by-step. However, most Visual Basic programmers (the ones who aren't writing books, anyway, and a lot who are) prefer to set a control's initial property values in the Properties window, if for no other reason than because all the settings are listed there for you to see.

Go ahead and fiddle with some other Line properties and see what happens.

Line Methods and Events

The Line control features two methods, neither of which will be particularly useful to you until you know a lot more about Visual Basic. Moreover, because a line is just a visual decoration for your application's window, the control responds to no events. This unusual situation makes it particularly easy for your humble author to discuss the Line control's methods and events. In fact, that portion of our class is already over!

Shape Controls

If you want to display something a little snazzier than a line, you can step up to the Shape control, which can draw a rectangle, a square, an oval, a circle, a rounded rectangle, and a rounded square. The control can draw these shapes as outlines or filled with a color and pattern the program specifies. Moreover, the control can draw the shape's border with various types of lines, including solid, dotted, or dashed lines.

Shape Properties

The Shape control has nearly 20 properties, all told, seven of which are of particular interest. Those seven properties are described as follows:

➤ BackColor—Represents the Shape control's background color. This property has an effect only if the BackStyle property is set to Opaque and the FillStyle property is set to something other than solid.

➤ BackStyle—Represents whether the shape's background is transparent or opaque.

➤ BorderColor—Represents the color of the shape's border.

➤ BorderStyle—Represents whether the shape's border is solid or is drawn with a pattern.

➤ BorderWidth—Represents the thickness of the shape's border.

➤ FillColor—Represents the color used to fill the shape.

➤ FillStyle—Represents the pattern used to fill the shape.

➤ Height—Represents the shape's height.

➤ Left—Represents the position of the shape's left edge.

➤ Shape—Represents the shape the control displays.

➤ Top—Represents the position of the shape's top edge.

➤ Width—Represents the shape's width.

Just as with the Line control, seeing how the Shape properties affect the control is as easy as placing a Shape control on a form and changing the control's properties in its Properties window.

Let's say, for example, you want to see a rounded square with a 10-pixel blue border. Moreover, you want this square to have a yellow background color, a red fill color, and horizontal-line fill pattern. In the Properties window, set the Shape control's properties as follows:

➤ BackColor—Yellow

➤ BackStyle—Opaque

➤ BorderColor—Blue

➤ BorderWidth—10

➤ FillColor—Red

➤ FillStyle—Horizontal Line

➤ Shape—Rounded Square

When you're done setting the properties, you'll have a form with a shape control that looks like this:

Here's the result of all your Shape property settings.

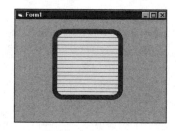

You can set the Shape control's properties in your program, as well. For example, the following Form_Load event procedure sets a Shape control to the same settings illustrated in the previous figure:

```
Private Sub Form_Load()
    Shape1.BackColor = RGB(255, 255, 0)
    Shape1.BackStyle = 1
    Shape1.BorderColor = RGB(0, 0, 255)
    Shape1.BorderWidth = 10
    Shape1.FillColor = RGB(255, 0, 0)
    Shape1.FillStyle = 2
    Shape1.Shape = 5
End Sub
```

Shape Methods and Events

The Shape control features three methods, only one of which, Move, is particularly useful to you until you know a lot more about Visual Basic. Moreover, because like a Line control, a shape is just a visual decoration for your application's window, the control responds to no events.

PictureBox Controls

Now you're getting to the real fancy stuff. A PictureBox control enables a program to display photographic-quality images such as those stored in GIF and BMP (bitmap) files. To add to the fun, the PictureBox control can act as a container, which means it can hold other controls in the same way a Form object holds other controls. You probably won't need to use a PictureBox as a container very often. However, just like doing 25 sit-ups, it's just nice to know that you can.

PictureBox Properties

The PictureBox control is a sophisticated object, boasting nearly 70 properties, 11 of which are especially handy. Those 11 properties are described as follows:

➤ AutoRedraw—Determines whether the control will automatically redraw itself as needed

➤ AutoSize—Represents whether the control will automatically size itself to fit a picture

➤ BackColor—Represents the control's background color

➤ CurrentX—Determines the horizontal position at which the next drawing operation will take place

➤ CurrentY—Determines the vertical position at which the next drawing operation will take place

➤ ForeColor—Represents the color used to draw lines and text inside the control

➤ Height—Represents the control's height

➤ Left—Represents the position of the control's left edge

➤ Picture—Represents the picture currently displayed in the control

➤ Top—Represents the position of the control's top edge

➤ Width—Represents the control's width

A Certain Similarity

Notice how the PictureBox control shares many properties with a Form object. This is because a Form object and a PictureBox control are both containers, and so can perform many of the same functions. For example, you can draw lines, circles, and text in a PictureBox control just as you can in a Form object. Just thought you would like to know.

Because one of the main purposes of a PictureBox control is to display a picture, you might want to try that out right now. First, place a PictureBox control on a form. Then, click the `Picture` property in the Properties window. When you do, an ellipsis button appears. Click this button to bring up a Load Picture dialog box, from which you can select a picture to display in the control. In the following figure, the programmer has selected the Stilllife.gif picture:

You can load a picture into a PictureBox control using the Load Picture dialog box.

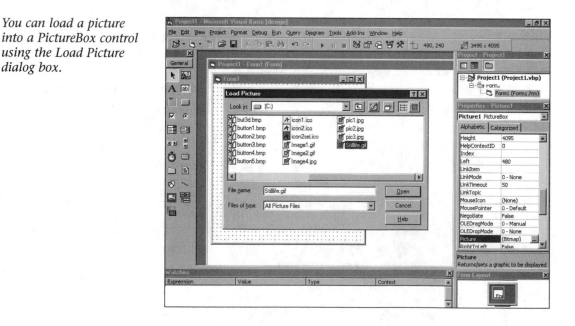

How your PictureBox control looks after you load a picture depends, of course, on the picture you load.

If you want to load a picture into a PictureBox control at runtime, you'll need to learn about the LoadPicture function. Luckily, you're about to do just that. The following line shows how to use the LoadPicture function:

```
Picture1.Picture = LoadPicture("c:\Stilllife.gif")
```

All you need to do is give the LoadPicture function the location of the image you want to load and you're golden. For example, in the previous example, the location of the image is c:\Stilllife.jpg.

A Picture's Home

If you provide the LoadPicture function only with the name of the image file you want and don't include a drive letter or directory (for example, LoadPicture("Stilllife.jpg")), the function assumes the picture is in the current directory. In most cases, when the user first runs a program, the current directory is the directory from which the program was run.

PictureBox Methods and Events

The PictureBox control also provides over 20 methods. Just as with the properties, though, you don't have to know all the methods to get started. The following list of four, all of which you've stumbled over before, will get you going:

➤ Circle—Draws a circle or oval

➤ Cls—Erases the form

➤ Line—Draws a line

➤ Move—Positions and sizes the control

As for PictureBox events, the two most useful are Click and DblClick. You might recall that the Click event occurs when the user clicks a control, and the DblClick event occurs when the user double-clicks the control.

The Simpler Image Control

Visual Basic actually provides two controls for displaying pictures. You've already learned about the PictureBox control. The other is the Image control, which is much less sophisticated than the PictureBox control. When you don't need a lot of power over the image being displayed, you might want to use the Image control instead of the PictureBox control. However, keep in mind that an Image control can't act as a container.

The Least You Need to Know

➤ The Line control can draw various types of lines on a form. These lines can be solid or patterned and can be drawn in a variety of colors and thicknesses.

➤ The Line control has no methods that are useful to a Visual Basic novice and responds to no events at all.

➤ A Shape control can display a rectangle, a square, an oval, a circle, a rounded rectangle, and a rounded square.

➤ The Shape control has only one method, Move, that is useful to a Visual Basic novice and responds to no events at all.

➤ A PictureBox control can display images that you have stored on your hard drive.

➤ A PictureBox control has many of the same properties as a Form object because both are containers.

➤ The LoadPicture function enables a program to load a picture into a PictureBox control at runtime.

Chapter 24

The Timer Control: Tick, Tick, Tick, Tick...

Some programs require that an action occur at a regular interval. For example, a program that displays an animation needs to time when to replace one image with another. A program might need to track elapsing time for many other reasons, as well. Luckily, Visual Basic features a special control, named Timer, that enables programs to keep track of time intervals.

The Timer Control

Managing a timer in your program might at first sound like a complicated task, but the truth is that Visual Basic's Timer control is easier to use than a squirt gun in a swimming pool. The Timer control does nothing more than send a Timer event to your program at whatever interval you set. Every time the Timer control sends a Timer event, Visual Basic jumps to the Timer control's Timer event procedure, where you place the program lines required to handle the event.

Your program might need to receive only a single Timer event. For example, you might want to give the user a limited time period in which to respond to some aspect of your program. On the other hand, you might need to have a steady stream of Timer events arriving at your program at an interval you specify. The Timer control can handle either of these eventualities, as you'll see in the sections that follow.

Timer Properties, Methods, and Events

Previously, you read that a Timer control is easy to use. The truth is that the Timer control is (at least from the programmer's point of view) one of the least-complicated controls you'll ever use. If you find this hard to believe, consider that the Timer control has only six properties, no methods, and responds to only one event.

Of the control's properties, only Enabled and Interval are useful to you at this time. The Enabled property determines whether the control is on or off. That is, when Enabled is set to True, the control is on and sends Timer events to the program at the interval specified by the Interval property. Conversely, when Enabled is set to False, the Timer control is turned off and does not generate Timer messages. When the Enabled property is set to Maybe, it's time to get a new copy of Visual Basic.

As hinted in the previous paragraph, the Interval property determines how often the Timer control sends Timer events to your program. This property is measured in milliseconds. (A millisecond is 1/1000 of a second.) So, if you want Timer messages to arrive at your program every second, you set the Interval property to 1000. If you want Timer messages every half-second, you set the Interval property to 500. Setting Interval to 0 turns off the Timer control, just as if you set the Timer control's Enabled property to False. Finally, setting the Timer control to a negative number (such as -100) causes time to run backwards, which is a great way to regain your lost youth.

The only event the Timer control responds to is Timer. (Aptly named, don't you think?) Visual Basic jumps to the Timer control's Timer event procedure each time a Timer event arrives. If you were to set a Timer control's Interval property to 1000, Visual Basic would jump to the Timer event procedure once a second.

A Single Timer Event

One way to use a Timer control is to determine when a specified period of time has elapsed. For example, you might want your program to display a prompt if the user doesn't react to some sort of request within a given period of time. The following sample program demonstrates how to use a Timer control in this way.

Start a new Visual Basic project (a standard EXE) and place one Label control, one Textbox control, two Command Button controls, and one Timer control, as shown here:

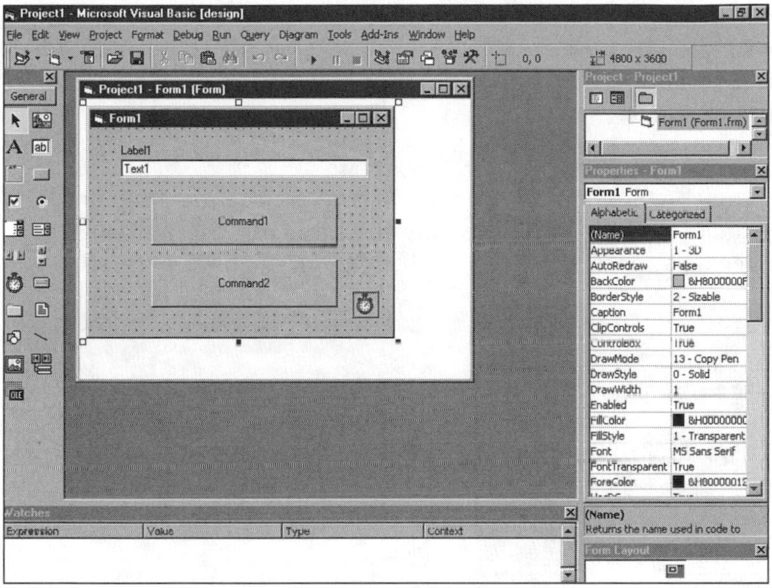

Position the controls as shown in this figure.

After placing the controls, double-click the form to bring up the code window, and type the following program lines (Visual Basic will have already started the `Form_Load` procedure for you):

```
Private Sub Command1_Click()
    Dim timeInterval As Integer
    Dim msg As String

    timeInterval = Text1.Text
    Timer1.Interval = timeInterval * 1000
    msg = "Timer interval set to " & timeInterval & " second"
    If timeInterval > 1 Then msg = msg & "s"
    MsgBox msg
End Sub

Private Sub Command2_Click()
    Timer1.Enabled = True
End Sub

Private Sub Form_Load()
    Label1.Caption = "Enter Timer Interval:"
    Text1.Text = "5"
    Command1.Caption = "Set Timer Interval"
    Command2.Caption = "Start Timer"
    Timer1.Enabled = False
End Sub
```

```
Private Sub Timer1_Timer()
    MsgBox "Time is up."
    Timer1.Enabled = False
End Sub
```

After saving your work, run the program. When you do, you see the main window. Type the number of seconds you want to set the timer to, and click the Set Timer Interval button. A message box appears telling you that the interval has been set, as shown here:

The message box verifies the timer interval setting.

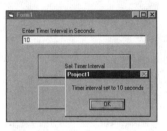

Now that you've set the timer's interval, you can start the timer by clicking the Start Timer button. After the number of seconds you requested, a message box appears, informing you that the time is up, as shown in the following figure:

The message box notifies you that the requested time has elapsed.

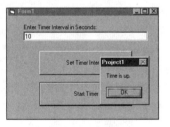

Invisible Controls

When you ran the previous sample program, you probably noticed that the Timer control, which you could see just fine on your form at design time, suddenly vanished at runtime. This is because the Timer control has no user interface and operates behind the scenes. The Timer control is the only invisible control in the standard Visual Basic toolbox. However, you're likely to run into other invisible controls as you add third-party controls to your Visual Basic toolbox.

Digging In

There's a lot of stuff going on in this program. First, in the Form_Load event procedure, the program sets the Label, Text, and Command Button controls' Caption and
Text properties:

```
Label1.Caption = "Enter Timer Interval:"
Text1.Text = "5"
Command1.Caption = "Set Timer Interval"
Command2.Caption = "Start Timer"
```

Also in the Form_Load procedure, the program turns off the Timer control:

```
Timer1.Enabled = False
```

Turning off the Timer control ensures that the timer won't start running until the
user clicks the Start Timer button.

To set the Timer's interval, the user must type a value into the text box and click the
Set Timer Interval button. When the user clicks the button, Visual Basic jumps to the
Command1_Click procedure, which first declares integer and string variables:

```
Dim timeInterval As Integer
Dim msg As String
```

Then the procedure gets the user's entry from the text box and multiplies the requested value by 1000 in order to set the Timer control's Interval property correctly:

```
timeInterval = Text1.Text
Timer1.Interval = timeInterval * 1000
```

Why multiply the value from the text box by 1000? Remember that the Timer control
expects the time interval to be measured in 1/1000ths of a second. Multiplying the
user's entry by 1000 converts seconds to milliseconds.

Next, the program builds a message string to display in the message box:

```
msg = "Timer interval set to " & timeInterval & " second"
If timeInterval > 1 Then msg = msg & "s"
```

Notice that if the timer interval is larger than one second, the program tacks an "s"
on the end of the message, which makes the word "second" plural.

Finally, the Command1_Click procedure displays the message it just constructed:

```
MsgBox msg
```

To start the timer, the user must click the Start Timer button, which causes Visual
Basic to jump to the Command2_Click event procedure. That procedure, as shown fol-
lowing, does nothing more than turn on the timer by setting the Timer control's
Enabled property to True:

269

```
Private Sub Command2_Click()
    Timer1.Enabled = True
End Sub
```

Now, the timer starts keeping track of time. When the number of milliseconds specified in the `Interval` property has elapsed, the Timer goes off like an alarm clock and sends a Timer message to the program, which causes Visual Basic to jump to the `Timer1_Timer` event procedure. This procedure displays a message box and shuts off the timer:

```
Private Sub Timer1_Timer()
    MsgBox "Time is up."
    Timer1.Enabled = False
End Sub
```

Multiple Timer Events

Another way to use the Timer control is to send a constant stream of Timer messages to the program. You would do this when you want your program to repeatedly perform some action at a regular interval. The following sample program demonstrates how this programming technique works. It's also a complete, albeit simple, game that you just might find amusing.

For this program, you'll try something a little different. You'll set most control properties in the Properties window at design time, rather than setting them in the program source code. This is a more typical way to build a Visual Basic program than you've gotten used to in this book.

To get going, start a new Visual Basic project (a Standard EXE), and place two Command Button controls, one Timer control, one Line control, and one Label control on your form, as shown here:

Now, click the Command1 button on the form. The control's properties appear in the Properties window. Set the following Command Button properties in the Properties window:

- ➤ Name—btnTarget
- ➤ Caption—"Target"
- ➤ Height—1215
- ➤ Width—1215

Using a similar procedure, set the Line control's properties as shown here:

- ➤ BorderWidth—2
- ➤ X1—240
- ➤ X2—4440
- ➤ Y1—2520
- ➤ Y2—2520

Next, set the Label control's properties as shown here:

➤ Name—lblScore

➤ Caption—"SCORE:"

➤ Font—18-points

➤ Height—375

➤ Left—480

➤ Top—2640

➤ Width—3855

Finally, set the Command2 button's properties like this:

➤ Name—btnStart

➤ Caption—"Start Game"

➤ Height—375

➤ Left—3240

➤ Top—2640

➤ Width—1215

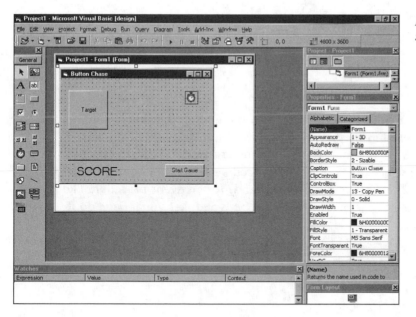

Position the controls as shown in this figure.

The Reason Is Obvious

Now that you've seen what a book has to go through to describe how to set properties in the Properties window, you know why this book usually sets properties in the program source code. Such program lines are, after all, self-explanatory. However, when you're done with this book and are creating your own Visual Basic program, you'll probably want to make more use of the Properties window, which is mucho handy for the programmer.

Now that you have your control's properties set, bring up the code window, and type the following program lines:

A Reminder

Remember that you don't need to actually type all the lines in the program listing. By double-clicking a control in the form, Visual Basic will start an event procedure for you. If VB (as Visual Basic is known to its close friends) doesn't start the procedure you want, you can select the control and procedure from the lists at the top of the code window. This technique is especially handy for an event procedure like MouseDown, which has several parameters that must be typed. Let Visual Basic do it for you!

```
Option Explicit
Dim score As Integer
Dim jumpCount As Integer

Private Sub btnStart_Click()
    score = 0
    jumpCount = 0
    Timer1.Interval = 750
    btnStart.Enabled = False
```

```
      btnTarget.Caption = "Target"
      lblScore.Caption = "SCORE: 0"
      Randomize
   End Sub

   Private Sub btnTarget_MouseDown(Button As Integer, _
      Shift As Integer, X As Single, Y As Single)
      If Timer1.Interval = 0 Then Exit Sub
      score = score + 1
      lblScore = "SCORE: " & score
      Beep
   End Sub

   Private Sub Timer1_Timer()
      Call MoveButton
      jumpCount = jumpCount + 1
      If jumpCount = 50 Then Call EndGame
   End Sub

   Private Sub MoveButton()
      Dim xPos As Integer
      Dim yPos As Integer
      Dim rndNumber As Single

      rndNumber = Rnd
      xPos = Int((3400) * rndNumber)
      rndNumber = Rnd
      yPos = Int((1200) * rndNumber)
      btnTarget.Left = xPos
      btnTarget.Top = yPos
   End Sub

   Private Sub EndGame()
      Timer1.Interval = 0
      btnStart.Enabled = True
      btnTarget.Caption = "Game Over"
   End Sub
```

Playing the Game

At last you're ready to have some fun. Save your work, and run the program. When the main window appears, click the Start Game button. When you do, the Target button starts jumping around the window. Try to click the button before it moves. Each time you manage to click the button, your score goes up by one. The button will jump 50 times, at which point its caption changes to Game Over and the game ends. To start a new game, click the Start Game button again. The following figure shows the Button Chase game after the user has played:

You need fast reflexes to get high scores in this game.

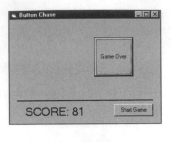

A Hint for High Scores

When you get the mouse pointer over the button, click as many times as you can. You can often get three, or even four, points before the button moves to its next location. With a little practice you should be able to get scores of 60 or more.

Digging In (Reprise)

If you've been putting your nose to the grindstone throughout this book, you should be able to figure out most of what this game program's source code does. You'll also probably have a flat nose. For those of you who still have nicely rounded nose ends, here's a program explanation.

First, the source code sets the Explicit option, which ensures that all variables are declared before they're used:

```
Option Explicit
```

The program then declares two global variables:

```
Dim score As Integer
Dim jumpCount As Integer
```

Because the program declares these variables outside of any procedure, the variables can be used anywhere in the program. This is important because if the variables were declared inside a procedure, they would lose their values every time the procedure ended.

The Mystery of the Missing Procedure

You might have noticed that this program doesn't have a Form_Load procedure. That's because you already set most control properties in the Properties window. Moreover, no variables need to have their values set at the very start of the program.

When the user clicks the Start Game button, Visual Basic jumps to the btnStart_Click procedure. That procedure first sets the score and jumpCount variables to their game-start values:

```
score = 0
jumpCount = 0
```

The score variable holds the player's score, of course, and the jumpCount variable counts how many times the button has jumped since the start of the game. You can see why it's important that these variables are set to 0 at the start of a game.

Next, the program sets the Timer control's interval to 750 milliseconds:

```
Timer1.Interval = 750
```

Tough as Nails

Changing the game's difficulty is easier than licking a stamp with a hose. If you want to make the game harder, set the Timer control's Interval property to a lower value. Similarly, if you want to make the game easier, set the Interval property to a higher value. If you set Interval to a high enough value, you can catch some TV and maybe a nap between button jumps.

After setting the timer's interval, the btnStart_Click procedure turns off the Start Game button, so that the user can't click it while the game is in progress:

```
btnStart.Enabled = False
```

Next, the procedure sets the Target button's and the label's captions:

```
btnTarget.Caption = "Target"
lblScore.Caption = "SCORE: 0"
```

Finally, the program calls the Randomize statement, which ensures that random numbers retrieved by the program in the MoveButton procedure are different for every game. This might not make a lot of sense to you at the moment. Just take it on faith that whenever you use random numbers in a program, you need to call the Randomize statement.

When the game begins, the Timer control starts sending Timer messages to the program every 750 milliseconds. Those Timer messages find their way to the Timer1_Timer event procedure:

```
Private Sub Timer1_Timer()
    Call MoveButton
    jumpCount = jumpCount + 1
    If jumpCount = 50 Then Call EndGame
End Sub
```

This procedure first calls another procedure, named MoveButton, that makes the button jump to its new location. The procedure then adds 1 to the jump count. If the jumpCount variable is 50, the procedure calls the EndGame procedure, which, in case you haven't guessed, ends the game.

The MoveButton procedure is a little tricky. First, the procedure declares the variables it needs to do its job:

```
Dim xPos As Integer
Dim yPos As Integer
Dim rndNumber As Single
```

The procedure then calls Visual Basic's Rnd function, which returns a random number between 0 and 1:

```
rndNumber = Rnd
```

If you think a number between 0 and 1 isn't all that useful, join the club. To fix this problem, the program performs a little math trickery to convert the random number to a number between 0 and 3400:

```
xPos = Int((3400) * rndNumber)
```

The number 3400 is the farthest to the right the Target button can move. (Any further and it would be off the window.) So the preceding statement takes the random number and converts it to a value between 0 and 3400. You don't need to know exactly how this works. Just know that the number in parentheses is the largest random number you need. For example, to get a random number between 0 and 10, you would write this:

```
rndNumber = Rnd
xPos = Int((10) * rndNumber)
```

You can combine these two statements in one statement, like this:

```
xPos = Int((10) * Rnd)
```

After getting a random horizontal position for the button, the procedure gets a random vertical position the same way:

```
rndNumber = Rnd
yPos = Int((1200) * rndNumber)
```

Having fun yet? Now that the procedure has random X and Y positions for the button, moving the button is as simple as setting the button's Left and Top properties:

```
btnTarget.Left = xPos
btnTarget.Top = yPos
```

Now you see how the program gets the button to jump around and make the player crazy. But what happens when the player manages to tag the button? You might think that the button's Click event procedure can fit the bill. The trouble is, if the button moves before the player releases the mouse button, the Click event never occurs, which cheats the user out of a point. So the Button Chase game uses the Target button's MouseDown event procedure instead. This event occurs the instant the user presses the mouse button over the Target button. Here's what the procedure looks like:

```
Private Sub btnTarget_MouseDown(Button As Integer, _
    Shift As Integer, X As Single, Y As Single)
    If Timer1.Interval = 0 Then Exit Sub
    score = score + 1
    lblScore = "SCORE: " & score
    Beep
End Sub
```

You don't need to pay any attention to the procedure's four parameters, Button, Shift, X, and Y. You won't be using them. However, notice that the first line inside the procedure checks to see whether the Timer control's Interval property is set to 0. If Interval is 0, the game is over, and the program shouldn't increase the player's score, even if she's clicking the button. No cheating allowed! In the case of a 0, the program immediately leaves the procedure thanks to the Exit Sub statement.

If the game isn't over yet, the procedure increases the player's score, displays the new score in the Label control, and beeps the computer's beeper.

The MouseDown **Parameters**

Although you don't need to know about the MouseDown event procedure's four parameters for this chapter's programs, you might find the parameters useful in the future. To put it briefly, the Button parameter represents the mouse button the user pressed; the Shift parameter represents the state of the Shift, Ctrl, and Alt keys at the time of the event; and the X and Y parameters represent the mouse's position at the time of the event. For more information, consult your Visual Basic documentation.

After the Target button has bounced around the window 50 times, which should be frustrating enough to make the player punch out the screen, the program calls the EndGame procedure:

```
Private Sub EndGame()
    Timer1.Interval = 0
    btnStart.Enabled = True
    btnTarget.Caption = "Game Over"
End Sub
```

This procedure turns off the Timer control by setting its Interval property to 0, turns on the Start Game button, and changes the Target button's caption to Game Over.

That was easy! (I know. Easy for me to say.)

The Least You Need to Know

➤ A Timer control enables a program to determine when a specified period of time has passed.

➤ The Timer control's `Interval` property determines how often `Timer` events arrive at the program.

➤ To turn the Timer control on and off, you set the control's `Enabled` property, setting it to `True` or `False`.

➤ By turning off the Timer control when the first `Timer` event arrives, you can use the timer to wait a specified period of time.

➤ Unless it's turned off, the Timer control sends a steady stream of Timer messages to the program.

➤ A control's `MouseDown` event occurs the instant the user presses a mouse button while the mouse cursor is over the control. The `MouseDown` event is a useful alternative to the `Click` event.

Chapter 25

Message Boxes and Dialog Boxes: Your Program Speaks Out!

In This Chapter

➤ Display system icons in your message boxes

➤ Choose between various combinations of message box buttons

➤ Add a title to your message box

➤ Respond to the user's message box button selection

In a Windows program, communicating with the user can be trickier than it was in the old days (you know, ten years ago). In most cases, when your program has something to tell the user, it will display a message box. Message boxes, however, can be much more useful than you might imagine at this point in your Visual Basic programming career. In this chapter, you'll learn to use a message box to its best advantage.

The Message Box

At this point in the book, message boxes are nothing new to you. You've already displayed message boxes in many of the sample programs you've explored. However, there's still a lot you don't know about message boxes. For example, a message box can display one of four system icons, depending upon the type of message being displayed. Moreover, a message box can contain not only the OK button you've gotten used to seeing, but also Yes, No, Cancel, Ignore, and Retry buttons. You can even change the message box's title.

Message Box Icons

As you just learned, a message box can display one of four system icons, depending on the type of message the message box will display and the message's urgency. The four types of message icons are as follows:

➤ Critical—Indicates that the message box displays information critical to the application's performance. This type of message and icon often appear to report fatal program errors. The following figure shows a message box with a Critical icon:

This message box displays a critical message.

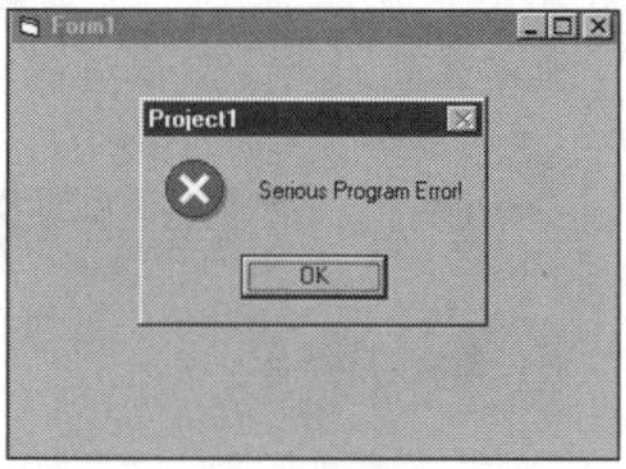

➤ Exclamation—Indicates that the message box displays important information that requires the user's attention. For example, a program might display this type of message box when a requested file could not be loaded. The following figure shows a message box with the Exclamation icon:

This message box displays an exclamatory message.

➤ Information—Indicates that the message box displays information that the user might find useful. For example, a program might display this type of message box to inform the user that a file has loaded successfully. The following figure shows a message box with the Information icon:

This message box displays an informational message.

➤ Question—Indicates that the message box displays a question that requires an answer from the user. For example, a program might display this type of message box to ask the user if he would like to save his work before exiting the program. The following figure shows a message box with the Question icon:

This message box asks a question.

Going with the Default

How come, you ask, you never had to bother with all this icon and button stuff with your message boxes before? All you did was supply a message and call it a day. When you leave the specifications for an icon and buttons out of the MsgBox statement, Visual Basic uses the defaults, which are an OK button and no icon. Having defaults makes the MsgBox statement easier to use when you don't care about all the extra stuff. It's just another way Visual Basic helps keep you from muttering under your breath and using the latest issue of *Visual Basic Guru World* as a dartboard.

To add one of these informative icons to your message box, you need only write a letter to Bill Gates begging his permission. When Mr. Gates receives your letter, he will (assuming he likes your penmanship and that your letter arrived on a Wednesday between 1:00 p.m. and 3:00 p.m.) chant a prayer to the Universal Binary Silicon Gods, who will enable your machine to use message box icons. *Ahem.* The truth is that adding an icon to a message box is as easy as tacking on a comma and the predefined value vbCritical, vbExclamation, vbInformation, or vbQuestion to your MsgBox line, like this:

```
MsgBox "Is anyone out there?", vbQuestion
```

This line results in the message box shown here:

*This message box displays
a Question icon.*

Message Box Buttons

In the previous example, you probably noticed how weird it is to ask a question in a message box and then have only an OK button. If you can answer a question with a single button, you're more clever than me. For a question message box to make sense, you need at least two buttons, probably of the Yes and No variety. (If you're working with that new technology called fuzzy logic, you could try a Maybe button, but I suspect you won't have much luck.)

Displaying different types of buttons in a message box is almost as easy as adding an icon. You need only add one of the following predefined values to your MsgBox line:

➤ vbAbortRetryIgnore—Displays Abort, Retry, and Ignore buttons in the message box.

➤ vbOKCancel—Displays OK and Cancel buttons in the message box, as shown here:

*A message box with the
vbOKCancel setting.*

➤ vbOKOnly—Displays only an OK button in the message box, as shown here:

*A message box with the
vbOKOnly setting.*

➤ vbRetryCancel—Displays Retry and Cancel buttons in the message box, as shown here:

A message box with the
vbRetryCancel setting.

➤ vbYesNo—Displays Yes and No buttons in the message box, as shown here:

A message box with the
vbYesNo setting.

➤ vbYesNoCancel—Displays Yes, No, and Cancel buttons in the message box, as shown here:

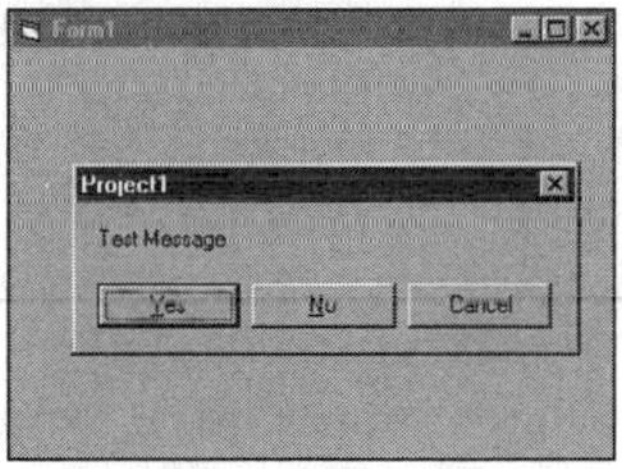

A message box with the
vbYesNoCancel setting.

So, now how about fixing up that question message box from the previous example? To do so, you might write something like this:

```
MsgBox "Is anyone out there?", vbQuestion + vbYesNo
```

Notice how the predefined value for the icon (vbQuestion) and the predefined value for the buttons (vbYesNo) are joined together with the + operator. The + operator is your way of telling Visual Basic that you want both the icon and the Yes/No buttons to appear. (How this actually works is way beyond the scope of this book. However, if you would like a hint, think of snow, sleighs, elves, and a guy named Santa Claus.) The result looks like this:

285

A question message box with sensible buttons.

Think you got it made now, eh? Okay, smart guy, how do you know whether the user clicked the Yes or No button? Lucky for you, the answer to that question is "Easy!" First, the MsgBox call is actually a function call, which means it returns a value. Guess what value MsgBox returns? Yep. It returns the value of the button the user clicked to dismiss the message box. To get the user's response, you might write program lines something like this:

```
Dim response As Integer
response = MsgBox("Is anyone out there?", vbQuestion + vbYesNo)
If response = vbYes Then
    MsgBox "You chose Yes."
ElseIf response = vbNo Then
    MsgBox "You chose No."
End If
```

First, notice that when you use MsgBox as a function call, you must enclose the call's arguments within parentheses. That is the standard difference between a Visual Basic statement and a Visual Basic function call. Next, notice that the program compares the value returned from MsgBox to the predefined values vbYes and vbNo. The other types of buttons have similar predefined values, which are vbOK, vbCancel, and vbRetry.

Message Box Titles

A message box, just like any other kind of window, can have a title in its title bar. The title Visual Basic automatically uses is the name of the project. However, you can put whatever title you like in a message box, even "Everything You Wanted to Know About Q-Tips but Were Afraid to Ask." All you have to do is add the title after the argument that selects the icon and buttons, like this:

```
response = MsgBox("Is anyone out there?", _
    vbQuestion Or vbYesNo, "Test Message")
```

This program line produces the message box shown in the following figure:

Your first complete box, with title, icon, buttons, and all.

Skipping the Icon and Buttons

Sooner or later, you're going to want to display a message box that displays a message (duh!) and has a title, but doesn't have an icon or any special buttons. Unfortunately, the argument for the icon and buttons is between the arguments for the message and the title. *Arrrggghhh!* What's an innocent VB programmer to do?

Visual Basic cleverness to the rescue. Often, when you don't want to include an argument, you can just plain ol' leave it out. However, you must be sure to put in the extra comma anyway so that Visual Basic doesn't confuse the third argument for the second argument. For example, to display a message box with a title but without a special icon or buttons, you might type something like this: `MsgBox "This is the message", , "This is the title"`. Notice the extra comma between the message and the title.

Putting It All Together

Got all this message box stuff down? In this section, you'll build a program that lets you experiment with message box options. To get started, create a new Visual Basic project (a Standard EXE), and place two Frame controls, nine OptionButton controls, two Label controls, two Textbox controls, and one Command Button control as shown here:

287

Position the controls as shown in this figure.

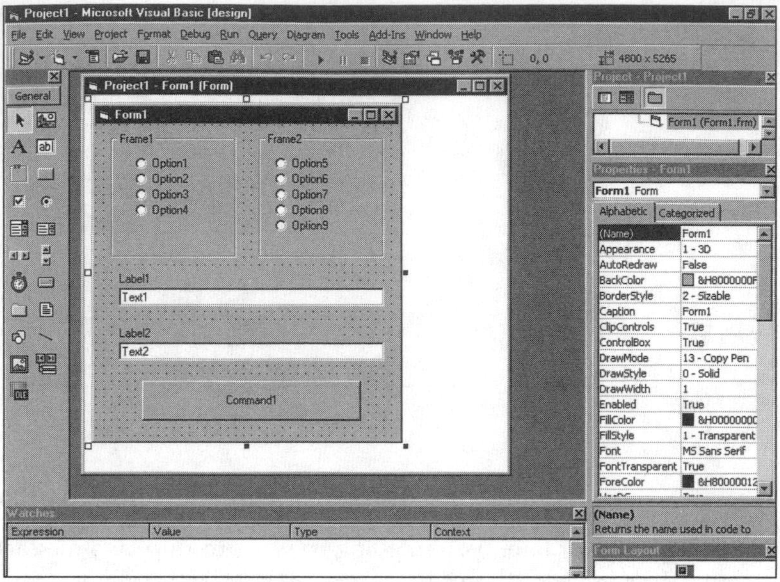

After positioning the controls, bring up the code window and add the following program lines to the project:

```
Option Explicit
Dim msgBoxIcon As Integer
Dim msgBoxButtons As Integer

Private Sub Command1_Click()
    Dim response As Integer
    Dim msgBoxTitle As String
    Dim msgBoxMessage As String

    msgBoxTitle = Text1.Text
    msgBoxMessage = Text2.Text
    response = MsgBox(msgBoxMessage, _
        msgBoxIcon Or msgBoxButtons, msgBoxTitle)
    If response = vbOK Then
        MsgBox "You chose OK.", vbInformation Or vbOKOnly
    ElseIf response = vbCancel Then
        MsgBox "You chose cancel.", vbInformation Or vbOKOnly
    ElseIf response = vbRetry Then
        MsgBox "You chose Retry.", vbInformation Or vbOKOnly
    ElseIf response = vbYes Then
        MsgBox "You chose Yes.", vbInformation Or vbOKOnly
    ElseIf response = vbNo Then
        MsgBox "You chose No.", vbInformation Or vbOKOnly
    End If
End Sub
```

```
Private Sub Form_Load()
    Frame1.Caption = "Icons"
    Frame2.Caption = "Buttons"
    Option1.Caption = "Critical"
    Option2.Caption = "Exclamation"
    Option3.Caption = "Information"
    Option4.Caption = "Question"
    Option5.Caption = "OK"
    Option6.Caption = "OK/Cancel"
    Option7.Caption = "Yes/No"
    Option8.Caption = "Retry/Cancel"
    Option9.Caption = "Yes/No/Cancel"
    Label1.Caption = "Enter Title:"
    Label2.Caption = "Enter Message:"
    Command1.Caption = "Show Message Box"
    Text1.Text = "Default Title"
    Text2.Text = "Default Message"
    Option1.Value = True
    Option5.Value = True
    msgBoxIcon = vbCritical
    msgBoxButtons = vbOKOnly
    Form1.Caption = "Message Box Demo"
End Sub

Private Sub Option1_Click()
    msgBoxIcon = vbCritical
End Sub

Private Sub Option2_Click()
    msgBoxIcon = vbExclamation
End Sub

Private Sub Option3_Click()
    msgBoxIcon = vbInformation
End Sub

Private Sub Option4_Click()
    msgBoxIcon = vbQuestion
End Sub

Private Sub Option5_Click()
    msgBoxButtons = vbOKOnly
End Sub

Private Sub Option6_Click()
```

```
        msgBoxButtons = vbOKCancel
    End Sub

    Private Sub Option7_Click()
        msgBoxButtons = vbYesNo
    End Sub

    Private Sub Option8_Click()
        msgBoxButtons = vbRetryCancel
    End Sub

    Private Sub Option9_Click()
        msgBoxButtons = vbYesNoCancel
    End Sub
```

When you've finished with the program lines, save your work, and run the program. When you do, you see the following window:

This program can display many types of message boxes.

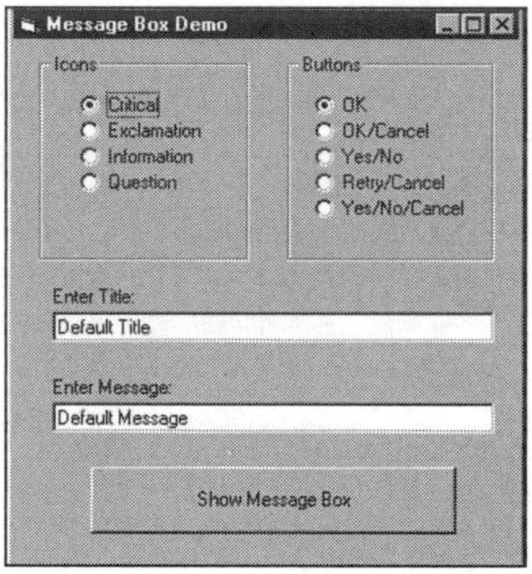

How you use the program should be fairly obvious. Just set the options that you want to appear in your message box, and then click the Show Message Box button. Your specified message box then appears. Click a button to dismiss the message box, and another message box pops up (startles you, doesn't it?) showing the button you clicked.

This program contains no tricky programming. There's nothing here you haven't seen before. Take a few moments to look over the program and figure it all out. Bet it won't take you more than ten minutes.

The Least You Need to Know

➤ A message box can display one of four different icons: Critical, Exclamation, Information, and Question.

➤ A program can display in a message box various combinations of OK, Cancel, Yes, No, and Retry buttons.

➤ The MsgBox function returns a value that represents the button the user selected to dismiss the dialog box.

➤ When you call the MsgBox function you can supply not only the message text, but also a title for the message box.

Chapter 26

Menus: Great Selections at a Great Price

In This Chapter

➤ Learn about standard types of menus

➤ Add a menu bar to your application's form

➤ Write event procedures for your menus' commands

Most Windows applications worth their weight in bits contain a menu bar that houses the commands needed to operate the program. The menu bar contains menu titles that, when clicked, drop down to display all the commands associated with that menu name. For example, in Visual Basic's File menu, you can find most of the commands you need to manipulate your program files. In this chapter, you'll discover how to add menus to your own Visual Basic programs.

Introducing Menu Bars

As you know from the previous paragraph (didn't skip the introduction, did you?), a menu bar is an area near the top of a window that contains menu titles. The following figure shows the menu bar on the Windows application Notepad:

The Notepad application has four menus on its menu bar.

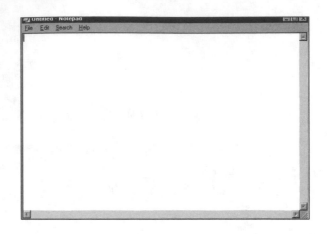

Each of the menu titles represents a group of related commands. For example, the File menu contains commands related to files, including saving files, loading files, and printing files. On the other hand, the Edit menu contains commands related to editing the contents of the currently loaded file. As shown in the following figure, these commands include Undo, Copy, Cut, Paste, Delete, and others:

Each menu title represents a group of related commands.

The point is that when you create your menus, you try to keep related commands grouped together. Moreover, menu bars usually have standard menus, such as File, Edit, and Help that contain a particular set of commands. Your applications should always follow the standards set up by Microsoft for an application's menus. The most important menus are the aforementioned File, Edit, and Help menus, which should contain the following commands:

➤ File Menu—Contains the New, Open, Close, Save, Save As, Print, and Exit commands.

➤ Edit Menu—Contains the Cut, Copy, Delete, and Paste commands.

➤ Help Menu—Contains the About command, which displays a dialog box containing information about the application. Also contains commands for accessing the application's help system.

Of course, nothing about menus is cast in stone. If, for example, your application doesn't enable the user to edit a document, you don't need an Edit menu. Moreover, if your application supports only a Delete command, you don't need to have Cut, Copy, and Paste commands in your Edit menu. However, your Delete command should appear in the Edit menu—nowhere else—because that's where the user expects to find it.

Menus of Your Own Design

You can create menus that are non-standard and specific to your application. For example, an application that displays colored objects might have a Color menu. Just be sure that the standard commands, like Save or Paste, appear in the appropriate standard menus.

Visual Basic's Menu Editor

You'll be pleased to know that creating a menu for your Visual Basic programs requires no programming at all. All you have to do is start Visual Basic's menu editor, and then create your menus visually in much the same way you create the rest of your program's user interface.

To start the menu editor, be sure you have your program's Form window selected, and then press Ctrl+E on your keyboard or select the Menu Editor command from the Tools menu. When you do, the menu editor appears, as shown here:

There's a lot of stuff in the menu editor's window. However, you won't need to mess with most of the settings. To create your own menus, you need only the Caption and Name boxes, as well as the buttons and the large empty area near the bottom of the editor. Of course, the best way to see the editor in action is to start building a menu of your own.

Start a new Visual Basic project (a Standard EXE), and then press Ctrl+E to display the menu editor. In the Caption box, type **File**. The menu title File appears in the menu display at the bottom of the editor. This is the title the user will see on the menu bar.

The menu editor enables you to add menus to your programs.

Now, type **mnuFile** into the Name box. This is the name you will use in your program to refer to the File menu. You could use any legitimate Visual Basic variable name for the menu, but by starting the name with mnu you know the name represents a menu, and by ending the name with File you know the name refers to the File menu. At this point, the menu editor's window should look like this:

Here's the way your new File menu title appears in the menu editor.

Now you have a File menu, but you don't yet have any commands in your File menu. To add a command, click the Next button to create a new line in the menu display at the bottom of the menu editor. Then, type **Open** in the Caption box, and type **mnuFileOpen** in the Name box. Finally, click the right-arrow button in the menu editor's window. This moves the new menu item one position to the right, which makes it part of the File menu. If you left the Open command on the same level as the File menu, you would end up with another menu title, Open, on your menu bar. Now, your menu editor window looks like this:

Here's your File menu with its Open command added.

Now, using the same procedure you used in the previous paragraph (except you won't have to click the right-arrow button), add an Exit command to your File menu. Name the command mnuFileExit, as shown here:

You now have two commands on your File menu. Suppose you want to add a Help menu to the menu bar. Click the Next button to add a new line to the menu display. Then, type **Help** in the Caption box and **mnuHelp** in the Name box. Now, click the left-arrow button to move the menu entry even with the File menu title. Finally, add a About My Awesome Menu App command, named mnuHelpAbout, to the Help menu, as shown here:

You've just created your new menu bar. Close the menu editor by clicking the OK button, and *presto!* Your form appears with its menu bar in place, as shown in the following figure:

Your menus can have multiple commands.

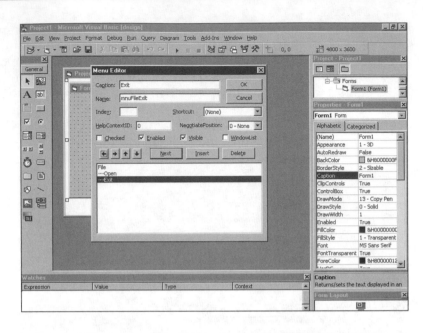

Your finished menu bar has two menu titles containing a total of three commands.

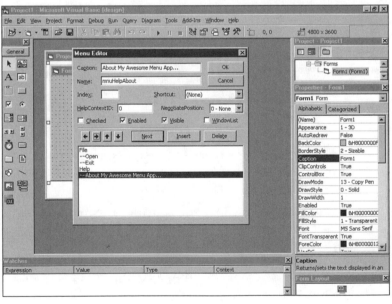

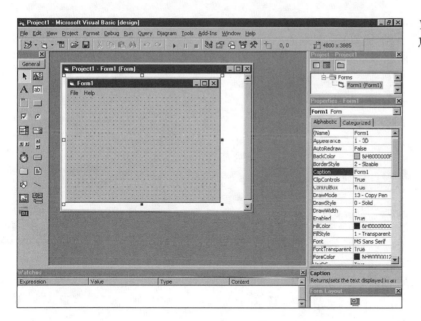

Your menu bar appears on your form.

Menu Separators

One special type of menu item is called a separator. A *separator* is a line that separates one group of menu items from other. For example, if you look at Visual Basic's File menu, you'll see more than a half-dozen lines that separate the menu commands from each other. To add a menu separator to your own menus, just type a hyphen as the menu item's caption when creating the menu item in Visual Basic's menu editor.

Responding to Menu Commands

Just as promised, you've created a menu bar without typing even a single line of source code. For your program to respond to its menu commands, however, requires a little bit of programming—but nothing trickier than responding to a button click. To respond to a menu command, you must write an event procedure for the command.

Try this out now. Put your mouse pointer over the Help menu in your form and click. The About My Awesome Menu App command appears in the menu's drop-down box, as shown here:

You can display your menu's commands by clicking the menu title.

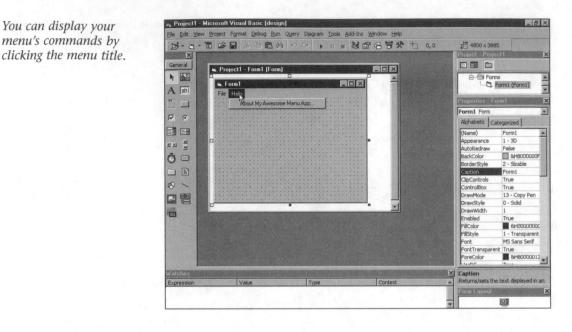

Click the About My Awesome Menu App command, and your project's code window appears with the `mnuHelpAbout_Click` event procedure already started for you. Complete the procedure so that it looks as follows:

```
Private Sub mnuHelpAbout_Click()
    Dim msg As String

    msg = "My Awesome Menu App" & vbCrLf
    msg = msg & "by Me" & vbCrLf & vbCrLf
    msg = msg & "Copyright 1999 by Me"
    MsgBox msg, vbInformation, "About"
End Sub
```

Complete your menu bar by creating event procedures for the remaining commands. Your finished event procedures should look like this:

```
Private Sub mnuFileExit_Click()
    Dim response As Integer

    response = MsgBox("Are you sure you want to quit?", _
        vbQuestion Or vbYesNo, "Exit")
    If response = vbYes Then End
End Sub

Private Sub mnuFileOpen_Click()
    MsgBox "You chose the Open command."
End Sub
```

Now, you're ready to test your menus. Save your work, and run the program. Click the About My Awesome Menu App command on the Help menu, and the application's description appears, as shown here:

Most applications have an About dialog box.

Next, try the Open command. Again, a message box appears, proving that the program responded to your command. Finally, click the Exit command. A message box appears asking you whether you're sure you want to quit. If you are, click the Yes button, and the program ends. If you click the No button, the message box goes away, but your program remains running.

The Least You Need to Know

➤ A menu bar displays the titles for the menus that contain the commands needed to use an application.

➤ There are several standard menus provided by most Windows applications. The most important of these are File, Edit, and Help.

➤ You create your menu bar using Visual Basic's menu editor.

➤ After creating a menu bar, you write `Click` event procedures for the commands in the menus.

Installing Visual Basic

As with any piece of software, before you can start using Visual Basic, you must install it on your computer. This is a fairly simple process if you follow the steps carefully, and pay attention to what you're doing. The steps listed below are an overview of the general Visual Basic installation process for the Visual Basic Learning Edition and the Visual Basic Working Model, which accompanies this book. Your experience might vary slightly depending on the software you currently have on your machine, the edition or version of Visual Basic you're installing, and the installation options you choose.

If you're installing the Visual Basic Learning Edition (or the Professional or Enterprise Edition), follow the steps in the next section. If you're installing the Visual Basic Working Model, skip ahead to the next section.

Installing the Visual Basic Learning Edition

1. Put your Visual Basic CD-ROM in your CD-ROM drive. The Installation Wizard dialog box appears, as shown in the following figure:

The Installation Wizard will guide you through the installation process.

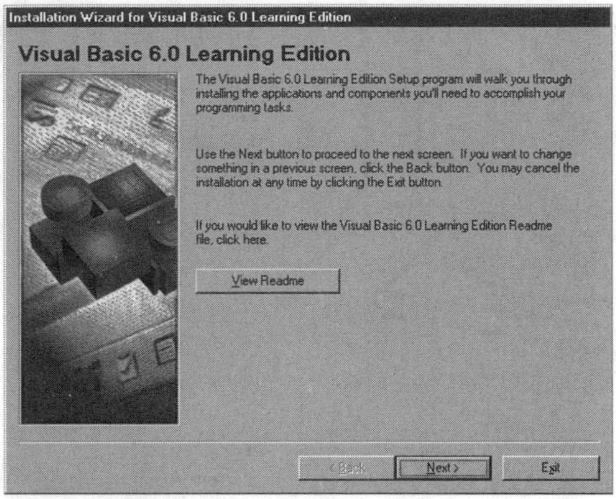

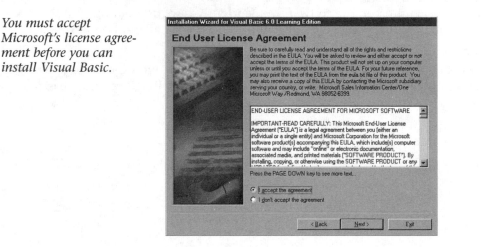

2. Click the Next button. Read the license agreement, and click I Accept the Agreement, as shown here:

You must accept Microsoft's license agreement before you can install Visual Basic.

3. Click the Next button. When the next screen appears, enter the product ID (the CD Key on the back of your CD-ROM's case), your name, and company (if applicable), as shown in the following figure:

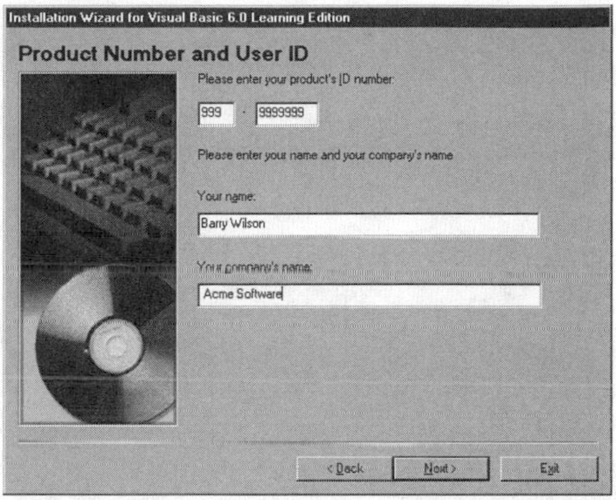

The product ID code must be correct for the installation to proceed.

4. Click Next, and Visual Basic's Setup program starts, as shown here:

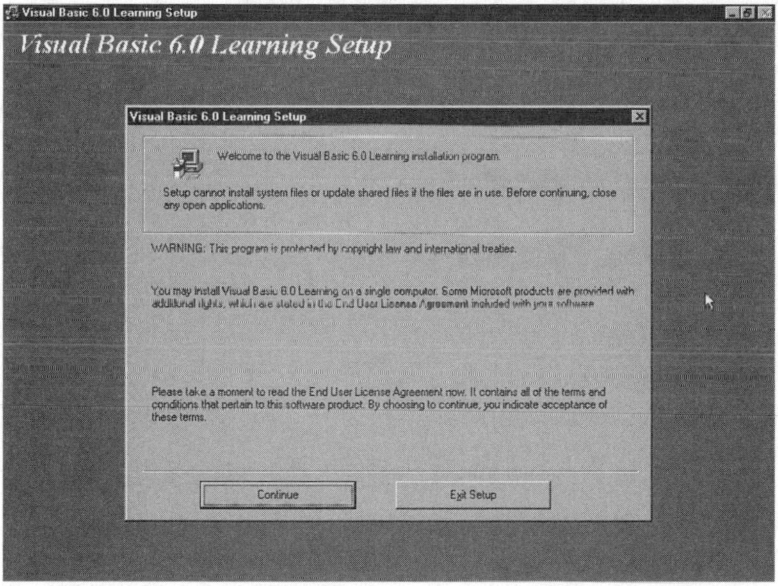

Here, Setup is getting ready to install Visual Basic.

5. Click Continue. When the product ID appears, click the OK button to continue with the setup.

6. Select the Typical setup (change the target folder first, if you want to), by clicking the Typical button:

The Typical installation is a good choice for most people.

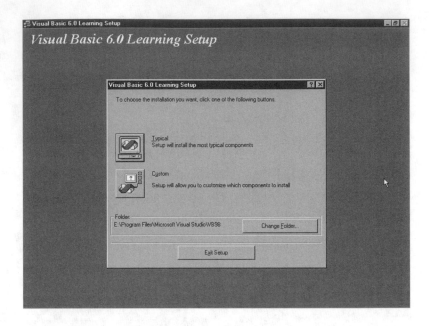

7. Setup starts copying Visual Basic's files to your hard drive, as shown here:

Setup must copy many files, so it might take a few minutes.

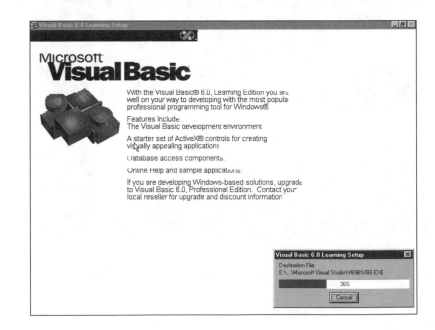

8. When Setup determines that the installation was successful, click the OK button to proceed.

9. Setup asks whether you want to install your MSDN CD-ROM, which contains Visual Basic's online documentation:

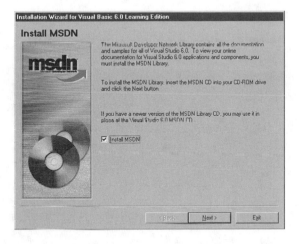

This is the best time to install the online documentation.

10. Place your MSDN CD-ROM into your CD-ROM drive and click the Next button to install the online documentation.

11. Follow the setup procedure for MSDN, which is very similar to Visual Basic's setup.

12. When the Registration screen appears, as shown in the following figure, you can connect to the Internet to register your copy of Visual Basic online, after which the installation will be complete.

Registering online sure beats mailing back those registration cards.

Installing the Visual Basic Working Model

1. Put your Visual Basic Working Model CD-ROM in your CD-ROM drive. The Installation Wizard dialog box appears, as shown in the following figure:

2. Click the Next button. Read the license agreement, and click I Accept the Agreement, as shown here:

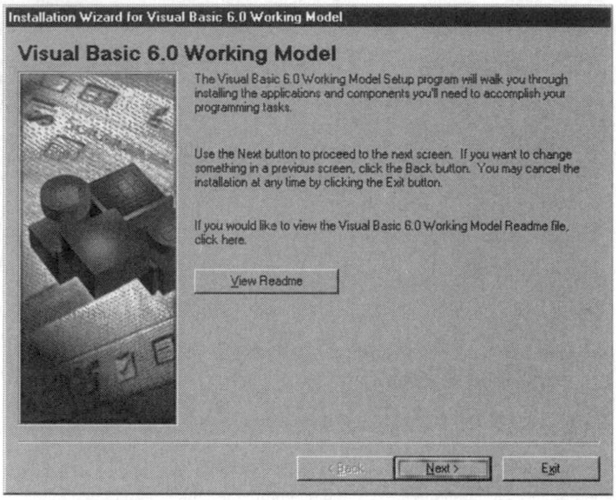

The Installation Wizard will guide you through the installation process.

3. Click the Next button. When the next screen appears, enter your name and company (if applicable), as shown in the following figure:

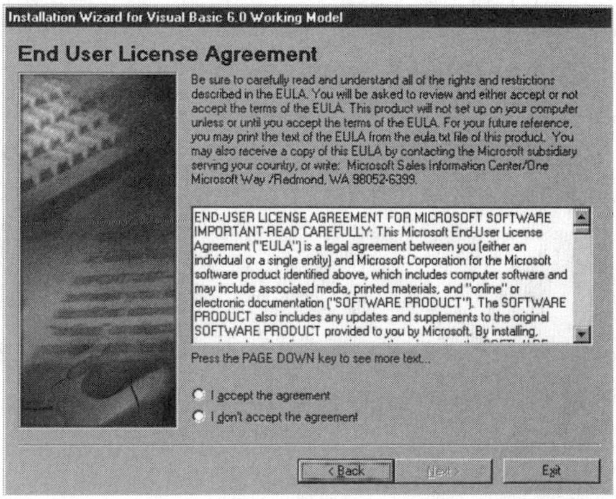

You must accept Microsoft's license agreement before you can install Visual Basic.

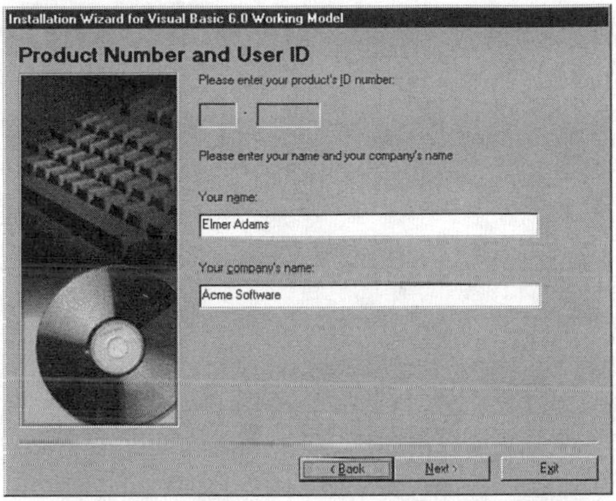

Here, you personalize your copy of Visual Basic.

4. Click Next, and Visual Basic gives you a chance to select the folder to which the files will be installed, as shown in the following figure. If you want to change the installation folder, do so now.

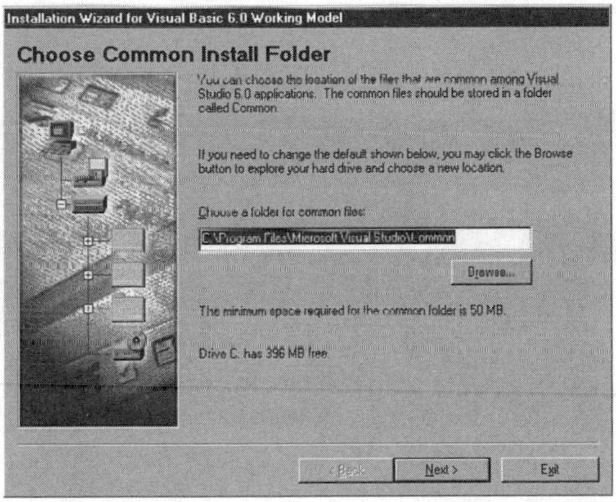

You can select the folder to which Visual Basic is installed.

5. Click Next, and Visual Basic's Setup program starts, as shown here:

*Here, Setup is getting
ready to install Visual
Basic.*

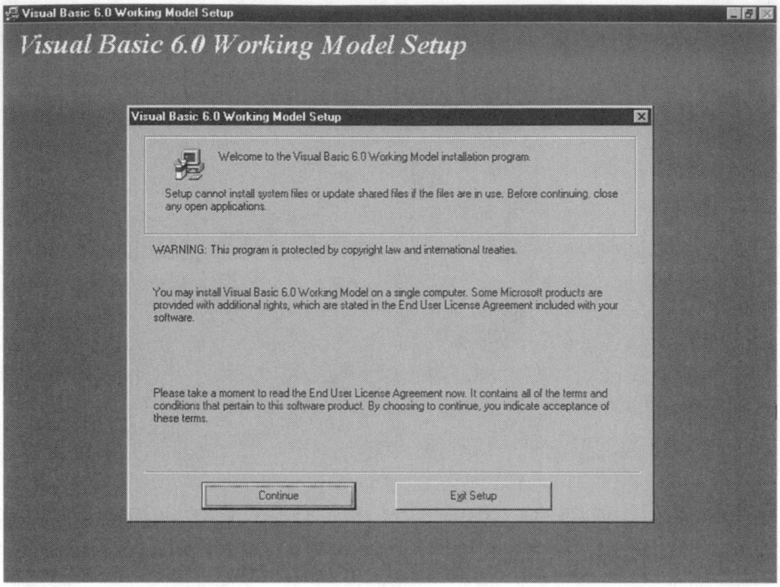

6. Click Continue. When the product ID appears, as shown below, click the OK
   button to continue with the setup.

*This dialog box shows
your product ID.*

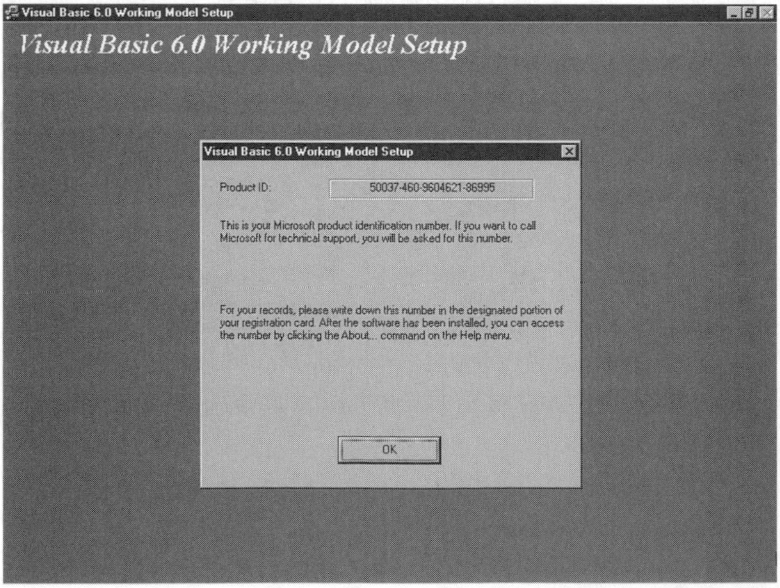

7. Select the Typical setup (change the target folder first, if want to), by clicking the Typical button:

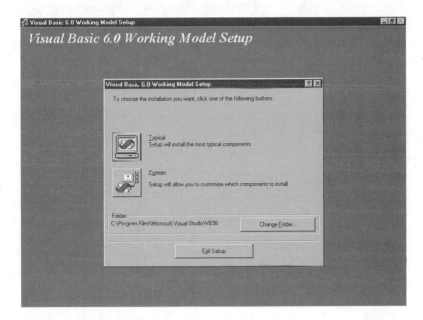

The Typical installation is a good choice for most people.

8. Setup starts copying Visual Basic's files to your hard drive, as shown here:

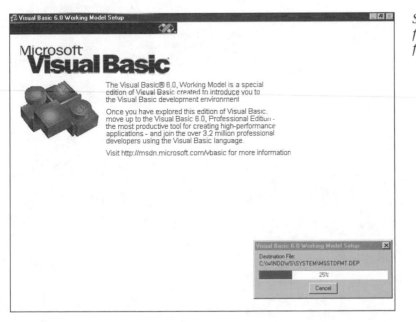

Setup must copy many files, so it might take a few minutes.

311

9. When Setup determines that the installation was successful, click the OK button to proceed.

10. When the Registration screen appears, you can connect to the Internet to register your copy of Visual Basic online, after which the installation will be complete.

Speak Like a Geek: The Complete Archive

Argument   A value that's passed to a procedure or function. Also see Parameter.

Arithmetic Operations   Mathematical operations such as addition, multiplication, subtraction, and division that produce numerical results.

Array   A variable that stores a series of values that can be accessed using a subscript.

BASIC   Beginner's All-Purpose Symbolic Instruction Code, the computer language upon which Visual Basic is based.

Bit   The smallest piece of information a computer can hold. A bit can be only one of two values, 0 or 1.

Boolean   A data type that represents a value of true or false.

Boolean Expression   A combination of terms that evaluates to a value of true or false. For example, (x = 5) And (y = 6).

Branching   When program execution jumps from one point in a program to another, rather than continuing to execute instructions in strict order. Also see Conditional Branch and Unconditional Branch.

Breakpoint   A point in a program at which program execution should be suspended in order to enable the programmer to examine the results up to that point. By setting breakpoints in a program, you can more easily find errors in your programs. Also see Debugging.

Byte   A piece of data made up of eight bits. Also see Bit.

CheckBox   A Visual Basic intrinsic control that enables the user to visually toggle an application option on and off. When the user clicks the control with the mouse pointer, a check mark appears or disappears in the control's box.

Code Window   The Visual Basic window into which you type your program's source code.

ComboBox   A Visual Basic intrinsic control that combines a ListBox with a Textbox, enabling a user to select items from a list or type a selection into the control's text box. Also see ListBox.

Command Button   A Visual Basic intrinsic control that looks like an onscreen pushbutton. The user clicks the button to initiate the command associated with the button.

Compiler   A programming tool that converts a program's source code into an executable file. Visual Basic automatically employs a compiler when you run a program or select the File menu's Make command to convert the program to an executable file. Also see Interpreter.

Concatenate   To join, end to end, two text strings into one text string. For example, the string `"OneTwo"` is a concatenation of the two strings `"One"` and `"Two"`.

Conditional Branch   When program execution branches to another location in the program based on some sort of condition. An example of a conditional branch is an `If/Then` statement, which causes the program to branch to a program line based on a condition such as `If (x=5)`.

Constant   A predefined value that never changes. For example, the constants `vbOK`, `vbNo`, `vbYes`, `vbCancel`, and `vbRetry` represent the return values of the `MsgBox` function.

Container   An object that can hold other controls.

Control   An object such as a Command Button that defines properties and methods, and that responds to events.

Data Type   The various kinds of values that a program can store. These values include `Integer`, `Long`, `String`, `Single`, `Double`, and `Boolean`.

Debugging   The act of finding and eliminating errors in a program.

Decrement   Decreasing the value of a variable, usually by 1. Also see Increment.

Design Time   The period when you're creating a program, either by placing controls on the application's form or writing program source code. Also see Runtime.

Double   The data type that represents the most accurate floating-point value, also known as a double precision floating-point value. Also see Floating Point and Single.

Element   One value in an array. Also see Array.

Empty String   A string that has a length of 0, denoted in a program by two double quotes. For example, the following example sets a variable called str1 to an empty string: str1 = "".

Event   A message that's sent to a program as a result of some interaction between the user and the program.

Event Procedure   A procedure that enables a program to respond to an event. For example, a Command Button control named Command1 might have an event procedure called Command1_Click to which Visual Basic jumps when the user clicks the button.

Executable File   A file, usually an application, that the computer can load and run. Most executable files end with the file extension .EXE.

File   A named set of data on a disk.

Floating Point   A numerical value that has a decimal portion. For example, 12.75 and 235.7584 are floating-point values. Also see Double and Single.

Form   The Visual Basic object that represents an application's window. The form is the container on which you place the controls that make up your program's user interface.

Frame   A Visual Basic intrinsic control that looks like a rectangle with a label. This control is used to associate related controls into a group.

Function   A subprogram that processes data in some way and returns a single value that represents the result of the processing.

Global Variable   A named value that can be accessed from anywhere within a program module.

HScrollBar   A Visual Basic intrinsic control that enables the user to select a value from a range of values. This control looks like the horizontal scrollbars you often see in applications' windows. Also see VScrollBar.

I/O   Input/output, which is the process of transferring data into or out of the computer. An example of input is when the user types something on the keyboard, whereas an example of output is when a program saves data to a disk file.

Image   A Visual Basic intrinsic control that enables a program to display complex images, including photographic-quality images from a disk file. Also see PictureBox.

Increment   Increasing the value of a variable, usually by 1. Also see Decrement.

Infinite Loop   A loop that can't end because its conditional expression can never evaluate to true. An infinite loop ends only when the user terminates the program. Also see Loop and Loop Control Variable.

Initialize   Setting the initial value of a variable.

Input Devices   Devices, such as the keyboard and mouse, that transmit information into the computer.

Integer   A data type that represents whole numbers between –32,768 and 32,767. The values 240, –128, and 2 are examples of integers. Also see Long.

Interpreter   A programming tool that executes source code one line at a time, unlike a compiler, which converts an entire program to an executable file before executing any of the program's commands. Also see Compiler.

Intrinsic Controls   The basic set of controls included with all versions of Visual Basic. Also see Third-Party Controls.

Label   A Visual Basic intrinsic control that represents a line of static text in a window. The user cannot edit static text.

Line   A Visual Basic intrinsic control that represents various types of lines, including thick, dotted, and dashed lines.

ListBox   A Visual Basic intrinsic control that enables the user to use a mouse to select an item from a list. Also see ComboBox.

Literal   A value in a program that is stated literally. That is, the value is not stored in a variable.

Local Variable   A variable that can be accessed only from within the subprogram in which it's declared. Also see Global Variable and Variable Scope.

Logic Error   A programming error that results when a program performs a different task than the programmer thought he programmed it to perform. For example, the program line If x = 5 Then Y = 6 is a logical error if the variable x can never equal 5. Also see Runtime Error.

Logical Operator A symbol that compares two expressions and results in a Boolean value (a value of `true` or `false`). For example, in the line `If X = 5 And Y = 10 Then Z = 1`, And is the logical operator. Also see Relational Operator.

Long A data type that represents integer values from –2,147,483,648 to 2,147,483,647. Also see `Integer`.

Loop A block of source code that executes repeatedly until a certain condition is met.

Loop Control Variable A variable that holds the value that determines whether a loop will continue to execute.

Machine Language The only language a computer truly understands. All program source code must be converted to machine language before the computer can run the program.

Mathematical Expressions A set of terms that use arithmetic operators to produce a numerical value. For example, the terms `(x + 10) / (y + 2)` make up a mathematical expression. Also see Arithmetic Operations.

Message Box A special type of dialog box that can contain a title, a message, and a combination of predefined icons and buttons. A program displays a message box with the `MsgBox` function.

Method A procedure associated with an object or control that represents an ability of the object or control. For example, a Command Button's `Move` method repositions the button on the form.

Modular Programming Breaking a program up into a series of simple tasks.

Numerical Literal A literal value that represents a number, such as 125 or 34.87. Also see Literal and String Literal.

Numerical Value A value that represents a number. This value can be a literal, a variable, or the result of an arithmetic operation.

Object Generally, any piece of data in a program. Specifically in Visual Basic, a set of properties and methods that represent some sort of real-world object or abstract idea. For example, Visual Basic's Printer object enables a program to manipulate the system printer, whereas the Drive object provides properties and methods that enable a program to manipulate a disk drive. The big difference between a Visual Basic object and a Visual Basic control is that objects don't respond to events, whereas controls usually do. Also see Control.

Option Button   An intrinsic Visual Basic control that represents a mutually exclusive option in a set of options. For example, several Option Button controls representing colors might be grouped together, enabling the user to select one and only one color. If the user clicks on a different color, the originally selected color becomes deselected while the new color becomes selected. This type of control is often called a radio button because of how a group of Option Buttons act like buttons on a car radio, which enable the driver to select only a single radio station at a time.

Order of Operations   The order in which Visual Basic resolves arithmetic operations. For example, in the mathematical expression $(x + 5) / (Y + 2)$, Visual Basic will perform the two additions before the division. If the parentheses had been left off, such as in the expression $x + 5 / Y + 2$, Visual Basic would first divide 5 by Y and then perform the remaining addition operations.

Output Devices   Devices, such as the screen or a printer, that accept data coming out from the computer. Also see Input Devices.

Parameter   Often means the same thing as "argument," although some people differentiate argument and parameter, where an argument is the value sent to a procedure or function and a parameter is the variable in the function or procedure that receives the argument. Also see Argument.

PictureBox   A Visual Basic intrinsic control that enables a program to display complex images, including photographic-quality images from a disk file. A PictureBox control can also be used as a container to hold other controls. Also see Image.

Procedure   A subprogram that performs a task in a program, but doesn't return a value. Also see Function.

Program   A list of instructions for a computer.

Programming Language   A set of English-like keywords and symbols that enable a programmer to write a program without using machine language.

Program Flow   The order in which a computer executes program statements.

Project Window   The Visual Basic window that displays the current modules in your Visual Basic project.

Properties Window   The Visual Basic window that displays a control's properties and their settings.

Property   A value that represents an attribute of an object or control. For example, a Command Button control's `Caption` property represents the text that appears inside the button.

Read-Only Property   A property whose value cannot be changed from within a program. However, a program can retrieve (read) a property's value.

Relational Operator   A symbol that determines the relationship between two expressions. For example, in the expression X > 10, the relational operator is >, which means "greater than." Also see Logical Operator.

Return Value   The value that a function sends back to the statement that called the function. Also see Function.

Runtime   The period when a program is running, rather than being designed. Also see Design Time.

Runtime Error   An system error that occurs while a program is running. An example is a divide-by-zero error or a type-mismatch error. Without some sort of error handling, such as that provided by the On Error statement, runtime errors often result in a program crash.

Scope   See Variable Scope.

Shape   An intrinsic Visual Basic control that represents several shapes, including a rectangle, a square, a circle, an oval, a rounded rectangle, and a rounded square.

Single   The data type that represents the least accurate floating-point value, also known as a single-precision floating-point value. Also see Double and Floating Point.

Source Code   The lines of commands that make up a program.

String   A data type that represents one or more text characters. For example, in the assignment statement str1 = "I'm a string.", the variable str1 must be of the String (or Variant) data type.

String Literal   One or more text characters enclosed in double quotes.

Subprogram   A block of source code that performs a specific part of a larger task. In Visual Basic, a subprogram can be either a procedure or a function. Also see Function and Procedure.

Subscript   The portion of an array reference that indicates which element of the array to access. For example, in the line X = array1(10), 10 is the subscript, which is also sometimes called an index. Also see Array.

Substring   A small portion of a larger string. For example, the string "One" is a substring of the larger string "OneTwo". Also see String.

TextBox   An intrinsic Visual Basic control that enables the user to enter and edit text.

Third-Party Controls   Controls that are not part of the original Visual Basic package. These controls can be purchased and added to the Visual Basic toolbox. Some third-party controls can even be freely downloaded from various Web sites.

319

Timer   An intrinsic Visual Basic control that enables a program to determine when a specific period of time has elapsed.

Toolbox   The area of Visual Basic's main window in which you can select the controls to place on a form.

Top-Down Programming   Organizing procedures in a hierarchy, with general-purpose procedures at the top that call specific-purpose procedures lower in the hierarchy.

Unconditional Branch   When program execution branches to another location regardless of any conditions. An example of an unconditional branch is the GoTo statement.

User Interface   The visible representation of an application, usually made up of various types of controls, that enables the user to interact with the application.

Variable   A named value in a program. This value can be assigned and reassigned a value of the appropriate data type.

Variable Scope   The area of a program in which a variable can be accessed. For example, the scope of a global variable is anywhere within the program, whereas the scope of a local variable is limited to the procedure or function that declares the variable. Also see Global Variable and Local Variable.

Variant   A special data type that can represent any type of data. More accurately, Visual Basic manages the data type of a Variant value for you. This data type is very inefficient and should be avoided when possible.

VScrollBar   A Visual Basic intrinsic control that enables the user to select a value from a range of values. This control looks like the vertical scrollbars you often see in application windows. Also see HScrollBar.

Index

A Little Knowledge Goes a Long Way ...

Check Out These Best-Selling COMPLETE IDIOT'S GUIDE

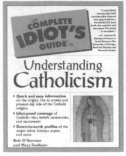

0-02-863639-2
$16.95

0-02-862743-1
$16.95

0-02-862728-8
$16.95

0-02-864339-9
$18.95

0-02-864244-9
$21.95 w/CD-ROM

0-02-862415-7
$18.95

0-02-864316-X
$24.95 w/CD-ROM

0-02-864235-X
$24.95 w/CD-ROM

0-02-864232-5
$19.95

More than *400* titles in *26* different categories
Available at booksellers everywhere

ALPH

What's on the CD

The companion CD-ROM contains the Visual Basic 6.0 Working Model Edition software.

Windows 95 Installation Instructions

1. Insert the CD-ROM disc into your CD-ROM drive.
2. From the Windows 95 desktop, double-click on the My Computer icon.
3. Double-click on the icon representing your CD-ROM drive.
4. Double-click on the icon titled START.EXE to run the CD-ROM interface. You can install the Visual Basic 6.0 Working Model Edition software from the interface.

NOTE

If Windows 95 is installed on your computer, and you have the AutoPlay feature enabled, the START.EXE program starts automatically whenever you insert the disc into your CD-ROM drive.

Windows NT Installation Instructions

1. Insert the CD-ROM disc into your CD-ROM drive.
2. From File Manager or Program Manager, choose Run from the File menu.
3. Type **<drive>\START.EXE** and press Enter, where **<drive>** corresponds to the drive letter of your CD-ROM. For example, if your CD-ROM is drive D:, type **D:\START.EXE** and press Enter. This will run the CD-ROM interface. You can install the Visual Basic 6.0 Working Model Edition software from the interface.